The Magic Power
of
Emotional Appeal

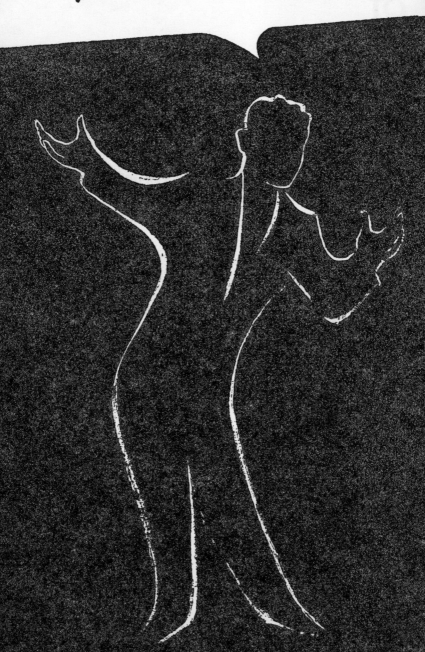

The Magic Power
of
Emotional Appeal

by ROY GARN

PRENTICE-HALL, INC., Englewood Cliffs, N.J.

LIBRARY OF CONGRESS
CATALOG CARD NUMBER: 60-10848

First printing .... April, 1960
Second printing .... July, 1960
Third printing ... November, 1960
Fourth printing .... May, 1961
Fifth printing .... July, 1961

PRINTED IN THE UNITED STATES OF AMERICA

54509—MO

DEDICATION

To Plum and Elsa . . . to the thousands who have studied Emotional Appeal . . . and to the millions who need it.

Preface

This book is the result of more than seventeen years of pioneering in the field of human communication.

During this time, hundreds of people came to me with their "personal problems." In discussion periods, phone calls, mail and consultation that followed radio and TV appearances, public and class lectures and social conversations, thousands more evidenced their individualized attitudes, feelings . . . and *problems.*

These "problems" were problems of person-to-person communication. They indicated a prepotent presence of certain common denominators or "listening factors" that could motivate *any* communication, whether mass *or* person-to-person.

An easy-to-apply, all-embracing communication Technique was developed and intensively tested.

Over 26,000 men and women were taught how to use this ONE Technique for EVERY situation in which it is necessary to use words and actions: at home, in job, marriage, profession or business; in sales, public speaking, advertising, personnel and public relations; in overt, social, intergroup and even the most intimate personal communication.

The Technique is Emotional Appeal Technique.

What is Emotional Appeal? Emotional Appeal is your ability to motivate and make others *want* to listen.

This ability can become your most important personal possession—your key to Personality, Persuasion and Happier Living. Acquiring this ability, however, involves the way you understand and control *yourself* and the emotional reactions of others to *your* words and actions.

As time goes by, these emotional reactions become increasingly vital to your health, disposition, initiative, outlook and success.

THE MAGIC POWER OF EMOTIONAL APPEAL contains hundreds of examples from everyday living that demonstrate the need for Emotional Appeal, and the unfailing efficacy of the Emotional Appeal Technique.

It shows how to:

Make Others Want to Listen.

Making others want to listen can become your prime personal power. This does not involve a talent for speaking *to* people; it does require a capacity to speak *with* them. When you say it with Emotional Appeal, you *succeed* in making others want to listen!

Possess a More Vital Outlook.

Your outlook has much to do with the response to your communication. When there are upsetting reactions or no response at all, frustration and unhappiness will kindle within you. With Emotional Appeal Technique, however, you *uncover* the emotionally "responsive chord" in those with whom you communicate. Thereafter, you can properly direct your words and actions and be more certain of gaining the responses you seek. These responses are emotional indicators *to* you and *for* you. They will contribute to better health and help you possess a more vital outlook.

Understand Yourself.

To understand yourself, you must know what makes you act and react the way you do. With Emotional Appeal Technique, you see yourself in the unretouched mirror of your feelings . . . identify your BIG motivating Emotional Appeal and better understand the *why* for Y-O-U. When you have such understanding, you gain greater control of words, actions and reactions. You become better able to handle fears, worries and upsets and emerge with more refreshing and persuasive personality to others.

Rid Yourself of Money Worries.

What real achievement is realized by the individual who is a financial success at work and a failure in personal and family relationships? "Money success" is rarely followed by "personality success," yet more people worry about money than other echelons of their existence. In Chapter Five, Money is defined and discussed as a powerfully communicative member of Four "Fatal" Emotional Appeals in ourselves and those with whom we inter-

act. We learn *Two Thoughts That Rid You of Money Worries . . .*
why the best way to learn economy is by spending . . . and that,
if you cannot make an emotional success of a money success—
you have no success at all!

Achieve Recognition.

The desire for Recognition is an essential emotional component
in everyone, but few people receive the Recognition they feel
they deserve! Chapter Seven explains why Recognition may be a
dangerous word-or-action explosive as well as a power-packed
drive towards attainment. More important, it demonstrates how
understanding and use of Emotional Appeal Technique in communication *can* achieve Recognition for *you*.

Get a Better Job and Future.

Education for a job or profession is meaningless unless it teaches
you how to *communicate* what you learn. To successfully communicate, you must reach others emotionally! Job relationships
are communication relationships. When communication is better,
your work is more enjoyable and resultful. Chapter Thirteen
shows how Emotional Appeal Technique assures more successful
communication in your job, profession or business. It includes
ideas that will help your future and Five Potent Pointers For A
Job Interview, whether you want to *get* a job or *advance* in your
present one.

Start Romance.

Romance, before and after marriage, is a matter of communication. This is why *any* female—plain or pretty—can get a husband
if she meets the "right" available man and uses the *right* Emotional Appeal in her words and actions. In Chapter Six and
elsewhere, you will notice that Romance is one of the omni-
potently communicative Emotional Appeals whose three prongs
interlock for much more than sex attraction or desire for marriage in woman *or* man. And, "for better or worse," Chapter Six
contains One Sentence With Emotional Appeal That *Always*
Starts Romance!

Secure a More Satisfying Marriage.

The odds against a "happy" marriage are huge. Nearly one-third
of marriages end in divorce and separation and it is almost impossible to estimate how many more are supersaturated with unhappiness. Explanations range from sex to money, upbringing,
beliefs, disposition, in-laws and unique incompatibilities. Why
do marriages really fail? *The main reason why marriages fail is*

*that the husband and wife do not know how to speak to each
other!* Good communication is an essential for better marriage;
without use of reciprocal Emotional Appeal, few marriages can
succeed. Marital mates need more knowledge about one another's *feelings!* Want a more satisfying marriage? Chapter
Twelve is one of the chapters that will help you. It teaches the
importance of your own and your mate's "feelings" and provides
rules you can rely on to promptly add Emotional Appeal to your
marriage and make it far more *mutually* satisfying.

Make People Remember, Respect and Like You.

The person who is remembered, respected and liked is happier,
more persuasive and successful than the one who is not. Why do
people *remember, respect* and *like?* Because of *response* to activating Emotional Appeal in words and actions! Would you like
to gain direction and control of this response? You can! Throughout the Book, and especially in Chapters Seven and Eleven, there
are many illustrations of how to use Emotional Appeal *even when
you listen!* Chapter Eleven lets you "in" on the emotional secret
behind visual effects . . . reveals how to *know in advance* the
"kind" of story that others want to hear, contains four ways to
add Emotional Appeal to *whatever you say,* and emphasizes
Three Thoughts that will unerringly make people remember, respect and like you.

Add Emotional Appeal to Your Voice.

Your voice is a musical instrument. When played, it may give
pleasure, pain or sedation to listeners! Most speaking voices are
not naturally beautiful; usually, they are too high or too low. It's
how you say *what* you say that makes others feel that *you* have
Emotional Appeal! Regardless of your present tonal quality,
Chapter Fourteen lets you prove *to your own satisfaction* that
you can add Emotional Appeal to your voice when you translate three ideas into action. It shows how, in less than five minutes, you can build a "Voice Control Box" that will last a lifetime, offers many suggestions that assure valuable vocal aid for
you and exhibits the permanent personal advantages of blending
the added Emotional Appeal in your voice with attention-getting,
attention-holding "listening factors" in your words and actions.

Successfully Handle Fears, Worries and Upsets.

Fears, worries and upsets grip us in thousands of ways. Distinctively personal, they are blanketed by an emotional individuality
that blends into our personality. Inadvertently, they are reflected
when we communicate! Chapter Eight is entitled: "How Emo-

tional Appeal Technique Rapidly Rids You Of Fears, Worries and Upsets." It explains what happens when you look *forward-to* and *backward-on* such pulsating inner shadows. The Chapter, a powerful portion of the Emotional Appeal communication concept, indicates why "emotional problems" and "emotionally-caused illness" are created by the way so many of our needs are communicatively directed or disturbed. It also presents you with Three Guiding Principles for successfully handling fears, worries and upsets.

Assure More Enjoyable Sex Relations.

Most couples are mismated *emotionally*, not physically! Sex reactions are emotional reactions to communication; satisfying sex relations come only when the Emotional Appeal of one partner's *communication* satisfies the other! Chapter Twelve conveys a way that partners can *remove* their inhibitions, *express* response and satisfaction and *remember* the importance of timing. With Emotional Appeal Technique and the inclusions in this Chapter, *both* can enjoy the benefits of more completely mutual sex relations!

Win Arguments and Disputes.

Too many arguments? Be careful! You may remain so glued to your reactions that you leave yourself wide open for trouble while hammering a nail, talking, eating, walking or driving an automobile. Why allow argument to undermine *your* health and disposition? Chapter Ten lists Eight Argumentative Subjects from which "victory" brings no emotional benefit. It demonstrates a simple, one-two-three method that will *always* help you win an argument, even when personal prejudice is involved! The Chapter shows how Emotional Appeal Technique swiftly identifies "conversational traps," how to handle yourself when you are *with* the person who has upset you and what to do *after* you have left his or her presence. By using recommendations in this Chapter and other portions of the Book, you will have a ready-to-apply method that will win arguments, settle disputes and make you a far more tactful person.

Improve Relationships with Family and Children.

In every kind of communication including that with family and children, we direct our words and actions at Someone. This person is going to react with a smile or a frown . . . with fear, desire, dislike or hatred . . . with disregard, accord or argument. In family relationships, communication is more intimate and feelings are more readily expressed. Such outer expressions are protective camouflage for inner feelings. Once you learn Emotional Appeal Technique, you can identify individual differences in people, pierce these emotional barriers, improve relationships with *your* family and children—or anyone else's!

Relax Emotionally!

Good health, good health habits and good medical care are inseparable; without proper relaxation, though, good health is rarely retained. Why? Because relaxation is an emotional attitude. *To relax, you must successfully communicate with yourself!* Care to feel better and *be* a better parent, friend or lover? Want to fall asleep more easily? Seeking relief from tensions? Need improved personal, family and job relationships? Use the Technique for Relaxation created and developed at the Emotional Appeal Institute in New York City. You'll find it in Chapter Fifteen and discover that it is surprisingly effective. Many benefits will accrue to you when you know how to relax *emotionally*.

Develop Individuality and Personal "Style."

Ninety-nine per cent of people pass unrecognized and unremembered because there is much-too-much sameness and run-of-the-mill in their words, actions, appearance and tastes. What's different about *you?* Do you have an individuality and personal "style" that makes you outstanding? With Emotional Appeal Technique, you *can* add these emotionally uplifting assets to your personality. The latter portion of Chapter Six, "Applying Romance Emotional Appeal To Your Dealings With People," contains many ways to pull yourself out of the rut of routine and melt the mental monotony of others. Other Chapters also point up the ever-present vitality of New Experience Emotional Appeal—why it is emotionally desired, sought-after and hoped-for by everyone and how you can use it to personally profit while you develop individuality and personal "style"!

Command Situations.

Unless your words and actions motivate others to *listen,* you cannot command situations. Questions with Emotional Appeal, properly timed, *instantly* make people *want* to listen. They command and control . . . direct, delay, confuse and identify . . . save time, life and property—even change minds. Chapter Nine, the Question Chapter, describes, exemplifies and labels the nearly innumerable benefits that Questions with Emotional Appeal will give your communication. You read about ways to heighten the listening power of your words and actions, why the obvious is your ally, how Questions build your confidence, and six interlocking rules that command situations and get others to "see things your way."

Handle "Difficult" People.

A "difficult" person is one whose words and actions do not emotionally blend with *your* feelings. With Emotional Appeal Technique, they can more closely be *made* to mesh! As you read on, *The Magic Power of Emotional Appeal* will make you increasingly aware of the objective observation you can use to uncover and identify the BIG response-awakening Emotional Appeal in others. Once identified, you can motivate and "handle" anyone— even the "difficult" person.

Protect Your Person and Possessions.

Few of us will ever be involved in an overt crime of violence, and "criminal activity" has many meanings. The criminal or cheat is undergirded by fears and desires in Four Emotional Appeals that exist for "good" people and "bad" and that are told in the first seven Chapters. He repeatedly communicates this emotional undergirding by words, actions, weapons and guile to "make crime pay." Few criminals are psychopaths; almost all can be communicatively "reached" with the right Emotional Appeal without *danger*—even during the commission of a crime! Throughout the Book, and particularly in the Self-Preservation and Question Chapters, you will learn how Emotional Appeal interlocks with *every* phase of existence and can be effectively used as a weapon to prevent crime and protect your person and possessions if necessary.

Strengthen Intergroup Relations.

There are many problems connected with knitting together individuals and groups of diverse ethnic, geographic, racial, political, cultural and religious backgrounds. Most such problems and tensions are caused by poor communication—our lack of understanding and disregard for feelings. *Problems of intergroup relations demand particular leadership; know-how is needed for words and actions that emotionally interpenetrate group "listening factors" on a person-to-person basis.* Because person-to-person communication is your key to successful mass communication, you can always use Emotional Appeal Technique to strengthen interpersonal and intergroup relations!

Better Your Personality and Persuasion.

Your personality is actually *another* person's reaction to the motivating Emotional Appeal in *your* words and actions. The person who accepts your Emotional Appeal *welcomes* your personality! An improved, more persuasive personality can be acquired and effectively communicated. Chapter Fifteen crystallizes twelve sure-fire ways to do this. It gives directions for making instantaneous emotional contact and may always be used to re-vitalize your Emotional Appeal and better your personality and persuasion.

The Magic Power of Emotional Appeal shows how you can accomplish these objectives and many more by choice, *not* chance.

Today more is known about what makes human communication difficult than what makes it successful. Communication research has not uncovered an art for transmitting feeling and meaning from one mind to another.

There is an urgent need for a specific and practical Technique.

The Emotional Appeal Technique set forth in this volume promises to provide the answer. It teaches you not to generalize, but how to *particularize* your communication.

Among others who have recognized the potential for Emotional Appeal, I wish to thank especially Dr. Mozell C. Hill, Professor of Education, Teachers College, Columbia University, for his enthusiastic encouragement, study of this manuscript and expression that: "Emotional Appeal Technique pinpoints a heretofore obscure problem: the emotions—and how to deal with them effectively."

Whatever your age, marital status or occupation, you *can* better yourself emotionally.

Use Emotional Appeal Technique in your communication. Then prepare to expect the unexpected!

ROY GARN

Table of Contents

The Magic Power
of
Emotional Appeal

Emotional Appeal—the Secret of Successful Human Relationships

A couple of minutes ago, when you opened this book, you were thinking of something else, weren't you?

What are you thinking about NOW? This very SECOND!

Come on. Be honest with yourself. Stop reading, please, and answer the question. Truthfully.

There was certainly something on your mind just before I asked, wasn't there? Of course there was! There's something on everybody's mind, every minute of the day!

I have asked the question, "What are you thinking about?" as my first utterance before lecture audiences, in classrooms, during group discussions and personal conversations. It was amazing to hear how many individually different answers were given, *with none having any relationship to the current subject or situation!*

One evening, in New York City, a tall shapely redhead replied: "I'm thinking about the light that's on in my bedroom." Pressed for further details, she added: "That bedroom light is so on my mind that I can't imagine how I'll really be able to concentrate on your lecture. You see, I came here by subway and, just as the train doors closed, I suddenly remembered that I hadn't turned off the bedroom light. My husband is a very economical man. If he comes home before I do and finds the light left on, I'll never hear the end of it!"

A neat, blue-suited man once said: "My boss wants me to complete a special report for him by four tomorrow afternoon. I wonder how in the world I'll ever be able to have it ready on time!" A plump, fiftyish lady shyly replied: "I bought a green fitted suit yesterday so I can wear it at a dinner tomorrow night. I just hope it's not too tight!"

A thirty-year-old unmarried squirmed obviously while proclaiming her truthfulness. She had been thinking about a phone call from her Aunt that night: "She's trying to arrange for me to meet a young man who's her neighbor."

A soft-spoken, grey-haired gentleman once remarked in a semi-nervous tone: "I'm supposed to see an old friend who has owed me forty dollars for more than a year. I was wondering how I should approach him about it!" On another occasion a square-shouldered, handsome blonde Southerner drawled: "It's kind of stuffy in this office. I was thinkng that I'd rather be out of here having a drink with a girl I met yesterday."

As the years have passed, I have heard many, many more answers to: "*What are you thinking about NOW? Right this minute!*" Isn't it surprising that hardly a reply was ever related to the current subject, situation or lecture topic?

No. It's no surprise at all.

People of all ages are basically and emotionally *Preoccupied* with their personal interests, needs, attitudes and concentrations, their individually different enmeshments of enjoyments, hopes, anticipations, anxieties, fears and memories. All the other times, they are just "blank-minded" or "in a fog" because it's emotionally satisfying.

They'll tell you that they love to listen, but they really hate to.

Ever have someone say, "But I told you to do it. Why didn't you?" And you apologetically reply, "H-honestly, I didn't *hear* you!"

The other person isn't lying, nor are you. Someone spoke: you didn't listen because you were Preoccupied, so you didn't *hear*.

Want to worry about it? *Don't.*

The important thing to do is to learn a communication Technique that can control the reaction to your words and actions and make others want to listen to *you* on any subject, in any situation.

Why?

Because your ability to get others to *want* to listen can become your most vital asset!

It will improve your outlook, personality and power to persuade. Your life, initiative, personal, job and business relationships—even your physical health—can depend upon the extent to which you acquire and use this ability.

Making others *want* to listen will assure greater success in whatever you undertake. It will help you in romance and marriage, set up a more alert look-ahead attitude.

When you have this ability, you can accomplish more rapid advancement, increased sales and income. People will like you more; you will become a much happier individual.

How soon can you begin possessing this Ability?

You can begin immediately!

How do you start?

Remember that Preoccupation is the bugaboo of your existence and that everybody is Preoccupied!

The reason we can't "reach" others 99 times out of every hundred!

Ninety-nine out of every 100 words that people speak to one another are never heard . . . and there's rarely anything wrong with the listener's hearing!

Ninety-nine out of every 100 words that people write to one another are never read, and there's rarely anything wrong with the reader's sight!

When *we* speak, do our listeners really listen?

Usually, their eyes look deeply into ours—but it's almost impossible to know what's on their minds. If they think even *one* thought other than what we're saying, they might just as well be *deaf!*

The ability to break through this Preoccupation barrier and enter the minds of our listeners represents the greatest power that we, as individuals, can possess.

When we know how to enter the Preoccupied minds of others, we can speak more successfully, sell better, prevent suicides, foil robberies, get others to laugh at our jokes, applaud our sing-ing, enjoy our acts—love, hate, reject or welcome.

 The *only* way to break Preoccupation in *any* situation is with words or actions that have Emotional Appeal.

What is Emotional Appeal?

Emotional Appeal is the ability to motivate and make others want to listen.

Communicate with Emotional Appeal and *you* can succeed!

I was one of the first passengers to board a bus during the evening rush hour. Tom, the driver, recognized me.

"This is another night when I wish I had a way of using Emotional Appeal so people would step to the rear of the bus," he sighed. "I've been trying for more than fifteen years without success!"

With a chuckle, I suggested that he sign up for one of the Courses I was giving.

About a week later, I was pleasantly surprised to learn that he had done so.

Tom proved to be a most serious-minded student who not only applied Emotional-Appeal Technique to his day-to-day living, work, and family relationships, but also took special pains to uncover the Emotional Appeal that could be successfully used in difficult situations.

Two months passed. Then, one evening during the rush hour I boarded Tom's bus.

"Want to see them move to the rear of the bus?" he laughed.

I did.

With a warm smile, Tom said "Hello!" to every passenger who came aboard.

When the Preoccupied standees packed the front and middle, he turned around. In a moderate tone, he asked the passengers: "Will you step to the rear of the bus please, *my friends?*"

They moved instantly!

As human beings, we use words and actions to communicate.

The Preoccupation-breaking Emotional Appeal of these words and actions can get a marriage or mend one, start a sale or an argument, even help a bus driver with a problem!

Your paramount personal power.

Betty has sparkling eyes, a Miss America-type figure with face to match, and a wealthy father. She and four others whom she calls "friends" set their sights on a marriage opportunity named Jim. Betty and the four other girls truly put their best moods forward.

But Jim decides to marry Ophelia, the girl with the flattest head, flattest chest, flattest heels and flattest bankroll.

Betty and the others somberly chant the bachelor-girl's wail: "What does *she* have that I don't have—and *better?*"

They little realize that a pretty face and figure may attract a man, but it takes words and actions with the right action-awakening Emotional Appeal to hold him. To become bride and groom, the man and woman must *speak* to each other. What she says to him and he says to her, in combination with the emotional actions and reactions, can be the most important pre-marital contact made.

Ophelia may not have been too pretty, monied or brainy. She didn't have to be.

She used Emotional Appeal; she got into Jim's Preoccupied mind. She didn't only tell him what she wanted to say; <u>she told him what he wanted to hear</u>. By making him want to listen, she made him want to care . . . for *her*. He even wound up claiming: "Ophelia's so *different* from other girls, Mother!"

Betty, Ophelia and the other girls were competing of course, but <u>all</u> competition—even the competition to get a husband—<u>is a competition to enter the mind!</u>

People, products and services are essentially the same. To succeed in the competition, you need your paramount personal power—your Emotional Appeal—to pierce Preoccupation and set up a competitive advantage.

That's how you get people, including millions of Jims, to say, "I do!"

Sometimes a person is so intensively Preoccupied that it *seems* impossible to break through. It *never is* when you <u>use the *right*</u> <u>Emotional Appeal</u>.

A fashionably dressed woman of 45 precariously perched high up on a river bridge, intent upon suicide. In a short time, over a hundred people and a policeman gathered. For twenty tense minutes, the officer and the crowd tried to get one idea across: "Don't jump!"

But the woman cried out that her husband had left her and her children had lost their respect. Nothing was left.

She removed her jacket and was about to jump when the policeman hushed the others, cupped hands to his mouth and called out: "Lady, if you're going to jump, go ahead. But you'll jump into some awfully *filthy water* down there!"

Instantly, the woman pulled back, came down off the bridge into the waiting policeman's arms. The words "filthy water" had done the job.

Now, what did *these* words have that thousands of words used by the policeman and more than a hundred people did not have? These words had Emotional Appeal for this woman. They made her listen. Because she listened, it was possible to *enter* her Preoccupied mind and change it!

Would "filthy water" be the right words to use on another man or woman in a similar situation? "Yes" or "No," depending upon the emotional makeup of the individual involved.

Individuals differ in the strength of their emotional makeup. As a group, however, they react with almost mathematical certainty to the power of the *right* Emotional Appeals. Since an attention-getting, mind-changing Emotional Appeal can be uncovered for any service, product or situation, some reaction will be immediate.

Sometimes this immediacy can be a life-saver.

One cold winter night, a young married couple became embroiled in their first violent argument. The husband refused to help with the dishes; the wife insisted. One word led to another; they screamed, shouted and threatened, even banged on furniture. The noise not only awakened their eight-months-old baby asleep in the next room, but so disturbed their neighbors in the apartment house that someone telephoned the police. The wife answered the doorbell and allowed a police officer to come in.

The neighbors pushed their way in, too.

When the husband saw the policeman and the surging crowd he became panicky. He rushed into the bedroom and picked up the baby with one hand. Slowly, he moved back before the crowd and raised the window with his other hand.

As the wintry wind blew in, he warned, "You move another step closer and I'll throw this baby right out of the window!"

The policeman and crowd knew he meant it. They halted.

The fearful wife's eyes almost popped out of her head.

Then, a 12-year-old boy who had just entered the apartment said, "It's bad enough that you want to kill your own baby, Mister. Why have her *catch a cold* too?"

The husband blinked his eyes, stared at the baby, closed the window and handed the baby to his wife. He lowered his head and murmured an apology. The suggestion that he was trying to force his baby to catch cold had caused an immediate emotional reaction.

By doing so, a tragedy was averted!

Were the young husband and the woman on the bridge "mental cases?" Hardly. They were emotionally upset. How? Because, to begin with, they emotionally reacted to the stimulus of other people's words and actions.

We could get that way too—if we allow our "upset" to go that far!

Remember, please. Emotional reactions to words and actions go on in everybody almost every hour of the day. Some of us never reveal the extent of our fights, arguments or ways we "got even" with those who provoked us.

About 97 per cent of all people go through fairly "normal" lives without getting their emotional stresses written up in the papers. When some "average" person goes off to an eventual suicide, criminal activity, or types of anti-social behavior, you can usually bet that coincidence, fate or time helped set up the original emotional stimulus.

How often, for example, will people see each other at regular intervals, at work, socially, in school or as bus acquaintances, without really "jelling." Then, of a moment, an unanticipated situation causes a remark; someone smiles, agrees, criticizes or frowns. Even *such* emotional reactions can kindle love, friendship or hatred!

Usually the man and woman who know each other for years don't dream of marrying. Then, in an unexpected circumstance, one makes a comment that the other appreciates. *Ping!* For the first time they've *reached* one another and *click*—Love walks in.

Who are these people?

They're the "normal" ones . . . and they're always creatures of their emotions and instincts. If provoked too far emotionally . . . they could quickly, or slowly and eventually, react to words and actions with an attempt at suicide or a threat to throw a beloved baby out of a window.

So could you.

This is why the ability to better control and understand your own motivations and emotional reactions is so necessary. This is repeatedly the reason why the power to control and understand the reactions of others is so important to your success and happiness. This is why it becomes more urgent to use the technique of Emotional Appeal.

Whether between a husband and wife, salesman and customer, doctor and patient, mother and child, situations with Emotional Appeal are everywhere everyday.

The mother of five-year-old Sue is exasperated. The child had just broken an expensive green vase. "It will be months before we can afford to get another one half as good," announces the mother. "I warned you not to go near that vase." In a foreboding manner, she places her hands on her hips. "You go into the tool closet and get your father's spanking belt, Sue. I'm going to give you a licking that you'll never forget," she screams. "I'll make your backside so red that you'll listen to me the next time and you'll stop breaking things. Go on. Get that belt!"

The little girl walks away.

A few moments later, she returns with a hammer.

"Here, Mommie," she says. "Why don't you hit me with *this?*"

The mother stares at the hammer, looks into the child's eyes and turns away. Almost inaudibly, she says: "Go to your room, Sue, and don't let it happen again!"

Had the emotional reaction to the hammer negated feelings about using the belt? Yes.

It had also changed a mother's mood!

<u>Selling situations are communication situations too.</u> If there is no emotional reaction to the seller's offer, there is no sale.

Four lingerie shops on the same block displayed similar nightgowns. One store had two nightgowns ticketed, "$3.95 each, formerly $5." Although the nightgowns had the most prominent display area for more than three weeks, hardly a customer made an inquiry. Then, upon a suggestion, a plain $3.95 price ticket was placed on each. Upon the one nightgown was placed a sign, "For Saints," and upon the other, "For Sinners."

In three days, the store sold out its stock of the nightgowns and started reordering. Nearly every customer bought one of each type—or two at a time—because she wanted to be certain that the salesgirls could not identify her as a "Saint" or a "Sinner!"

<u>Since people love to buy, but hate to be sold, there will always be almost unlimited opportunities to set Emotional Appeal to work towards creating a competitive advantage.</u> Sometimes your own name may be your best Emotional Appeal!

A housewife wanted her living room furniture reupholstered. She consulted ads and the classified telephone directory. More than ten salesmen called. Their prices, fabrics and delivery promises were similar. Each left his business card. One, however, remarked: "My card will help you remember me—and it will give your husband a laugh! You see, my name is 'Wolf.' Wolf by name, but not by nature!" They both grinned.

Some days later, when the woman wondered about which firm to call, she immediately recalled "Wolf." He, alone, had broken her Preoccupation, captured her attention and individualized himself in her memory.

He made the sale . . . and even her husband voted for him!

<u>Words are emotional pranksters.</u> After they leave our mouths, they step aside to see what happens. And what happens always happens to somebody. That somebody is our Listener. He either remains Preoccupied because our words lack a stimulating Emo-

tional Appeal, or the Emotional Appeal is so powerful that the Listener changes his mind even though he hadn't wanted to!

A Philadelphian flew to the West Coast on business. Half a day ahead of schedule, he decided to visit Las Vegas, Nevada, for a few hours, just to tell his Eastern friends that he had done some gambling there. Since his funds were running low, he resolved to limit his gambling to ten dollars in all.

At a Las Vegas gambling casino, he changed a five dollar bill into five silver dollars. He promptly lost these in a slot machine. Now he determined to be extremely careful.

He changed a twenty-dollar bill, placed five silver dollars in his right hand—and fifteen silver dollars in his left. He moved towards a dice table, telling himself that he'd bet no more than the five dollars "come Hell or high water!" To be doubly sure he'd resist temptation, he dropped the fifteen dollars into his coat pocket.

At the dice table, a middle-aged woman supervised six or seven players. She looked up, saw the Philadelphian approach and said: "Move over and make room, Folks. Here comes a *real* player!" The Philadelphian reached back into his pocket, his two hands hit the table at the same time. And he bet the entire 20 dollars!

He also lost it.

But the Emotional Appeal of the woman's words in the presence of others was more powerful than the emotional reason why he had decided *not* to bet the Twenty!

There is little doubt about it.

Every minute, every day, in every situation, people are Preoccupied. Even though they are hungry or thirsty, happy or sad, passionate or panicky, you must get them to *hear* you when they *seem* to be listening.

Even your best friend may stare into your eyes when you speak, but have his mind on a subject or situation one hundred miles away.

If he tells you, "Shut up!" why become angry? Perhaps you should thank him. It can be good advice!

When you are speaking and your listener is *not* listening, might it not be better to "shut up"?

But you *can* make people want to listen, quickly and easily, by learning how to more effectively project your Emotional Appeal.

Whether you speak, sell, perform or write, keep constantly alert to the fact that people are Preoccupied. To reach them, you must break their Preoccupation with a well-directed Emotional Appeal.

Whoever you are, whatever you do, wherever you live, the "listening power" in your communication is your initial step towards a better outlook, personality and persuasive skill.

People must communicate. To do so, they use words and actions.

For good or bad, the motivating effect of these words or actions can make friends or enemies, lovers or leavers, a sale or a heartbreak. This is why the *way* we break Preoccupation and enter the minds of others must be our first move along the pathway towards impressing, hypnotizing, teaching, memorizing, influencing, directing, persuading and affecting others.

It is also the way others can impress, hypnotize, teach, remember, influence, direct, persuade and affect *us!*

Eve said it with Emotional Appeal and Adam couldn't resist. Today there are more Eves, more apples and more Adams. But Emotional Appeal is still the reason why people *want* to listen, whether we're speaking about apples, religion, baseball or pimento pushers.

If you really want to "hurt" somebody, you don't need to use a lead pipe. A few words with the wrong Emotional Appeal will break Preoccupation, get into the mind and stay there, and there'll be no bandage big enough to cover the emotional injury.

On the other side, it is *absolutely impossible* to win friends, influence people or make a sale without *first* breaking Preoccupation with an Emotional Appeal!

When you communicate with Emotional Appeal, you succeed! Even in the Smith household.

Mrs. Smith says to her husband: "Honey, when you go to the store, buy a pound of butter." Mr. Smith buys cigarettes and returns without the butter. Mrs. Smith is angry. "You never listen to me," complains she.

"I didn't hear you," says he.

There is an argument. The Smith children have to listen to it all through dinner. Meal enjoyment is ruined. So is the evening.

Often, what is said at a table is the beginning of an unhappy family relationship. Most marriage counselors agree that a huge number of separations and divorces are caused by trivial things.

These "trivialities" are often indications of something much bigger, the failure to use the right Emotional Appeal by people whose communication interaction is undergirded by their emotions at all times!

Was there anything wrong with Mr. Smith's ears? No.

Anything the matter with Mrs. Smith's voice? No.

Why, then, did her communication fail?

He was Preoccupied. She was speaking, but he wasn't listening. His wife did not know how to break his Preoccupation.

Amazing, isn't it? She has been married to the man for 12 years; they were "keeping company" for four years. Sixteen years of girl and woman in intimate relationship—and what does she truly know about him?

Not even enough to motivate him with an Emotional Appeal that will get him to remember to bring back a pound of butter from the same supermarket where he buys his cigarettes.

And *Mr.* Smith?

He probably knows *less* about the communicative art of Emotional Appeal than she does.

As almost everybody, he has eyes that see not, ears that hear little.

He's Preoccupied.

So are you.

Words are emotional.

Words are emotional.
They are used on people who are emotional and react in terms of themselves.

When a neighbor says: "Your daughter is a nice kid—but not very bright," it breaks your Preoccupation instantly. You resent the statement. You feel the hurt *even if you agree with the speaker!*

If someone observes one of your actions and remarks that you're a "cheap skate," you seethe with displeasure whether you deserve the comment or not.

By the same general emotional reaction patterns, you'll react instantly if somebody says something *nice* about you, that you're a "good sport," that you look or dress well, or "haven't aged a day in the last ten years!"

These are emotional reactions from an emotional make-up that's as identical as if you walk across the street and a truck bears down upon you. You are in danger—so you jump out of the way. If the truck is far off and you feel safe, you may chance the crossing.

Again, the emotional reaction road runs two-ways, yours *and* the truck driver's! So too, are the emotional motivations for and reactions to communication.

Recall what happens when a doctor seats you, crosses your legs and hits you below the knee with a rubber hammer? When he hits in the right place, you kick-reflex. Wrong place? No reaction, or it hurts.

Words and actions can work in a similar manner. Certain ones may affect others, but have no affect upon you because of your emotional individualities. When words or actions affect you in a place that counts, you reflex, for good or for evil!

And *your* words and actions can do the same to your listeners.

In a lecture to nearly five hundred men and women, after the first ten minutes the lecturer basked in the glow of an enthusiastic, attentive audience that welcomed whatever he said.

A handsome, dark-complexioned man in the seventh row was particularly interested. From time to time, he would nod in agreement.

Then the lecturer raised his voice for emphasis and said: "Never, never forget this fact—or you may just as well bury your heads like the Arabs and steal silently into the night . . ."

"No!" suddenly shouted the man in the seventh row. A bitter scowl splashed across his face. "I don't like that remark. *I am an Arab!*"

The lecturer's words had not upset anyone else in his audience, but they *had* bothered this man. Attention was focussed away from the speaker and some five hundred people had an unexpected and unforgettable demonstration that words are emotional.

So did a certain lecturer!

And you can project the idea to the *simplest* situations.

You walk down the street. Coming towards you is Martha. You call out: "Hello, Martha!" Martha returns the greeting, says: "Hello, Gerry," and goes on her way. You keep going too and that's all there is to it. You have received the emotional reaction you sought.

But, suppose you say: "Hello, Martha!" and Martha, Preoccupied, shows no sign of recognition and continues on her way. You stop, look after her and mutter half-aloud: "Why, that Martha! She walked right past me, and I've known her for more than ten years! Ever since her husband won that money at the race track and bought those two parking lots and the Cadillac, she's become plenty snooty. Wait till I tell Helen about this!"

Now, you see, there's a husband and money, a race track, two parking lots and a Cadillac in it—all because Martha didn't say, "Hello!" Words, or the lack of them, are emotional. So are the people who use them, even if they have never met each other before.

A jaunty fellow may look at us, grin and add: "Hello there!" Before we even stop to wonder why we're doing it, we return the smile and greeting. Seconds later, we raise our eyebrows and feel: "He seems to know *me*, but who the heck is *he?*"

Or, just smile and extend your hand to a perfect stranger. She won't know why, she may peer at you peculiarly, but she'll shake your hand. So will *he!*

When we go precisely into the portions of the Emotional Appeal Technique, we'll learn that we're emotionally reacting to an action that seemed to say: "How do you do?" And, for reasons of our own Recognition, it may be important to look good and proper; even in the eyes of a stranger!

Some years ago, a client made thousands of dollars in extra

sales by using the powerful response-stimulation of a smile and a handshake.

For a retailer of TV and home appliances, there was created a slogan "The Store Where You Buy A Handshake." Since retail TV and appliance selling is one of the most competitive, price-cutting businesses, the personality and friendship factors were paramount in establishing a competitive advantage.

The "Handshake" idea was promoted in all advertising and window displays. There was a "Handshake Credit Plan" and "A Handshake Does It" for the purchase of anything from a toaster to a washing machine. But it's one thing to make people remember a store—and another thing to make a sale. Once attention is attracted and Preoccupation broken, in successful selling you need the words and actions of a personable and persuasive salesman.

Every sales person in the store, as well as the owner, was trained to follow through. As soon as a customer entered, and sometimes *before* he stepped thru the doorway, the salesman would walk towards him, smile and extend his right hand. The potential customer, usually a stranger who was "just looking" or "pricing" would automatically shake the salesman's hand. Before the customer could become embarrassed, the salesman would smile again, point to a sign and courteously remark: "This is the store where you buy with a handshake."

Preoccupation had been broken, emotional contact had been made, the feeling of friendliness and *buying* there had been planted.

This Emotional Appeal not only pushed up the store's sales but caused the owner to receive employment applications from salesmen who worked for competitors. The controlled emotional reaction to a smile and an extended hand was helping to make sales almost as easy as saying, "Hello!"

That word "Emotional!"

"Emotional" is one of the most incorrectly used words. As it is commonly and sometimes professionally spoken or written, there is often an inference that certain people are "emotional" and others are not; that an "emotional person" is someone who is quick tempered, moody, giddy, changeable, one who can readily "fly off the handle" or plunge into prolonged periods of silence. Actually, every human being is "emotional" and possesses feelings that can be motivated, disturbed, or agitated.

We are liable to have any one of these individual "feelings" as we meet our daily need to communicate with our fellow human beings. Certain subjects, words or actions may make us laugh, cry, harbor a grudge, hate the speaker, lend money, "love" another, stimulate jealousy or curiosity, or provoke an argument.

These "feelings" originate from a past experience or series of experiences that have caused an active or passive reaction, but a reaction, nevertheless! Or, if the past has not set up the origin of our emotional reaction, it is often a hope or fear concerning the future that is stored up in our attitudes, needs or activations, that blends into our preoccupation.

The same thing happens to our listeners, customers, patients, and clients.

There isn't anyone who will not emotionally react to words, actions or situations that affect his or her own emotional makeup or experience. In understanding, or being understood, communication reveals our particular emotional makeup. When we react, it means that our preoccupation has been broken whether we're spoken or written to as individuals or as a member of an audience of millions. Actually, the more important social effects of mass communication are reactions individually expressed.

We may respond suddenly, softly, fearfully, reassuringly, laughingly or argumentatively.

It will always happen this way whether you're in a run-of-the-mill job, social or family situation, or at home in an intimate situation with your mate as your enjoyment of each other is growing. "I love you," you sigh. "And I love *you*," comes the reply, "but I wish your mother weren't such a *numbskull!*"

"What?" You raise your voice, completely forgetting that it's past midnight. "My Mother a *numbskull?* Why—why, there isn't a single one in your family that's half as good-natured as she!"

"Good-natured? GOOD-NATURED! She's so stingy that—."

On and on goes the argument. You sleep back-to-back and hardly speak a word to one another for days!

A few words awakening the wrong emotional response are powerful enough to change a person's mental direction. In all our communication, we find that the correct Emotional Appeal can break Preoccupation and cause an affirmative reaction. When no Emotional Appeal or the wrong Emotional Appeal is used, other people will either remain preoccupied or react negatively!

Many wives use the wrong Emotional Appeal without meaning to. So do husbands, employers, friends, social, political and professional people.

Doctors in general practise admit that more patients come to them with ailments that the right *words,* rather than the right treatments will cure. Yet, how many doctors have actually been trained in a Technique to uncover and control the emotional reactions to their words and actions?

With correct Emotional Appeals you will have the ability to motivate and make people want to listen. To do so, you must pierce your listener's Preoccupation. Before you can do this, however, the "listening factors" in your communication must be identified and particularly directed to the people or person you want to "reach." One must always take into account the emotional undergirding of the idea communicated!

You may have a pretty face and figure that attract men, but you need the *right* Emotional Appeal in your words and actions when you want a man to marry you and stay happy while married. One way to capture one kind of man's heart may be through his stomach, but you must first use the individually motivating Emotional Appeal that helps persuade him to join you at the table! And not every man will be "captured" in this way.

There are differences in subjects and juries too. Even "12 good men and true" must be given an emotionally appealing reason why they should listen, or they will remain preoccupied and refuse to be persuaded.

This is particularly so in libel actions, which many attorneys claim are difficult to win. In Ohio, however, a country lawyer once welcomed the opportunity to sue a newspaper editor for libel. Throughout the trial, the attorney was said to have pronounced the word: "libelous" as "liBEELEOUS." He repeatedly referred to the "liBEELEOUS" actions of the defendant. Not even during his remarks to the jury did he pronounce the word properly!

He won the case.

Afterwards, when an attorney on his staff asked why he insisted on mispronouncing the word, he chuckled: "The word 'libelous' lacks color. It's just another dry-sounding word that passes over people's heads. As 'li-BEELEOUS' it sounds evil and wicked, doesn't it?"

Knowing that his client had an excellent case and that certain men on the jury were devout individuals, he felt that they would be aroused by that which *sounded* as well as *was* evil!

The jury's Preoccupation was pierced, their minds were entered and it became easier to present the facts.

In breaking Preoccupation, in using Emotional Appeal, you must first *emotionally* fit your subject to your listener. When you cannot find an emotionally-appealing relationship between your subject and audience you have no reason why anyone will listen.

If people won't listen, you cannot persuade them to do anything.

What makes people want to listen? Their *personalized* emotional reactions to what they *want* to hear or what they *fear* to hear.

Can these "listening factors," the factors in a person to which that person responds positively, be uncovered to fit *any* person, product or situation? They can be when you use Emotional Appeal Technique.

Emotional Appeal Technique:
Common Denominator for All People

Emotional Appeal is a communication Technique that offers you the opportunity to understand yourself better and to control more successfully the emotional responses of others to your words and actions.

The Technique is the result of more than seventeen years of research and word-and-action reaction tests on many thousands of people of all ages and occupations, both individually and in groups. By combining a realization of the Preoccupation factor in everyone with objective observation of the Four Preoccupation-breaking, Preoccupation-holding Emotional Appeals, hereafter explained, you can effectively apply Emotional Appeal Technique to *any* communication situation in which the *right* words and actions are needed.

With the Technique, you can use Emotional Appeal by intention, not by accident; by choice, not by chance.

The people with whom you live, work and interact rarely want to think; they emotionally enmesh with what they *feel!* These individualized *feelings* are emotional *activators* as well as *barriers* for communication.

Pierce these feelings with the *right* Emotional Appeal in your words and actions and you capture the ability to make others want to listen. This is the interlocking common denominator for better human relations, *your* key to happier, more successful living!

19

Emotional Appeal Technique has three facets:

1. Everyone is PREOCCUPIED.
2. SUBJECT will "reach" AUDIENCE when the *right* Preoccupation-breaking Emotional Appeal is used.
3. To uncover the *right* Emotional Appeal, you search out the *"Fatal Four"* Emotional Appeals of:

> Self-Preservation
> Money
> Romance
> Recognition

The expression "Fatal Four" Emotional Appeals has been used for many years and has proved to be easily remembered. The Emotional Appeal Technique emphasizes that the "success or failure" and "life and death" of communication are inextricably embodied in the emotionally prepotent Four parts of Self-Preservation, Money, Romance and Recognition.

Unless you can uncover at least one of the Fatal Four that emotionally ties *what* you are communicating into the *feelings* of those with whom you communicate, you have no *big* reason why your listener will listen. When your listener does not listen, he remains preoccupied, listening to himself, not to you!

All Four Emotional Appeals are in every one of us, in every subject and every listener, whether one or one million. They are inbred; people *cannot* fight them.

One of these undergirding Emotional Appeals is the *big* reason why our listener *wants* to listen or fears to! Sometimes this *big* Emotional Appeal interlocks somewhat with a second Emotional Appeal of the Four, but you will rarely find more than two that represent the "responsive chord" that empathically knits subject to audience, writer to reader, speaker to listener.

Directly related to the ability to get *others* to listen must be your *own* talent for listening. Since there are preoccupations in every subject, the person who would persuade others must be a good listener himself in order to uncover and identify these preoccupations.

With awareness and observation in your own communication with others, you will notice the omnipresent vitality of the Fatal

Four Emotional Appeals that so affect your life. As time moves along, use of Emotional Appeal Technique in your daily living will quickly improve your personality, persuasion, health and outlook. Important powers of creative imagination will be unleashed, your initiative will be sparked, and you will become more the person you *want* to be!

The three links in the Emotional Appeal Technique

Now, let us indelibly imprint the three links in the Emotional Appeal Technique with this chart:

When we apply the Technique, we shall find again and again that <u>the difference between *trying* to communicate and *successfully* communicating lies in our choice of the *right* Emotional Appeal</u>. This is always so, even if you try to protect your life or property!

After appearing on a TV show in New York City, Mr. R. took a subway downtown to where his car was parked. He then drove uptown along the Bowery.

It was 9 P.M. and the Bowery was deserted.

As R. approached a traffic light, he noticed a tall, hulking figure moving towards him from out of the darkness ahead to his left. At just that moment, the traffic light turned *red*. R. stepped on the brake.

A pair of big hands clutched the door ledge next to the steering wheel and R. heard a sneering voice near his left ear say:

"How about a couple of bucks for a meal, Buddy? I didn't eat tonight."

The tone was ominous; the setting was perfect for a mugging or a robbery. If he reached for his wallet, the man would know where his money was. Instead, R. reached for his most powerful personal weapon, the Emotional Appeal in his words and actions!

Without removing his eyes from the road ahead, he growled: "Mister, I can't take my eyes off that car up ahead. *I'm on duty so beat it!*"

The man did and fast!

The words: *"I'm on duty"* probably scared him more than he had scared R.

He *heard* those words. They *entered* his mind and *changed* it!

Like most people intent upon a criminal act, he was as fearful of tangling with the police and getting caught as he was courageous enough to dare to commit the crime. R.'s inference that he was a police officer had such an emotional effect that the would-be criminal even mumbled an apology as he scurried off into the Bowery darkness!

We shall soon understand why use of the Preoccupation-breaking Self-Preservation Appeal instantly made the man listen in this situation. His attempt may have been motivated by a Money desire, but his fear of getting caught and jailed had been made more important emotionally than completing the crime.

Deep down in this event and every other, there can be uncovered the *big* emotional listening factor. It's there, but can *you* find it in time?

You can with the Emotional Appeal Technique.

For many years, one of my students was Head Counselor of children's summer camps. Counselors were referred to as "Uncles" and "Aunts" and were often chosen because of educational experience or personal experience with certain phases of camp activities.

One summer, the Head Counselor told me his baseball counselor was an "Uncle Charlie." Charlie had been listed on an number of all-American selections as one of the best college ball players. The boys at camp loved his baseball instruction and often discussed his prowess and fame. All, except thirteen-year-old Ronnie.

Ronnie, a fine athlete, showed interest and excellence in just about every camp activity except baseball. After patiently doing his best, Uncle Charlie was ready to give up. "I just can't get through to him," he complained to the Head Counselor. "Ronnie refuses to listen. He's forever looking off, making faces and inciting the other boys. I'd like permission to drop him from the baseball classes because he's spoiling them for the others."

That afternoon, after lunch, the Head Counselor summoned Ronnie to his cabin.

"What's wrong?" he asked. "You get along with the other counselors, but not with Uncle Charlie. You know that he's one of the top college baseball stars. Don't you think you might learn a lot from him?"

"Oh, no!" he replied. "I can't learn *anything!*"

"Why?"

The thirteen-year-old put his hands on his hips and, with complete assurance, remarked: *"Since when can a Giant fan teach a Dodger fan how to play baseball?"*

The Head Counselor and Uncle Charlie had another session.

Next morning, at baseball instruction, Uncle Charlie said to Ronnie's group: "You all know that I'm a Giant fan and that the Giants and the Dodgers represent one of the most bitter rivalries in big league baseball. Well, even as a Giant fan, I must admit that the Dodgers are much better than the Giants in certain portions of the game. Take their pitching and double-play averages, for example. . . ."

Ronnie perked up. For the first time, he wanted to hear Uncle Charlie say more. He and Uncle Charlie wound up the summer season as warm friends, and Ronnie became a much-improved baseball player.

There had been an emotional, preoccupation-holding reason why he had not wanted to listen. When this communication barrier was pierced by words of Recognition, the *right* Emotional Appeal for him, he listened.

The Head Counselor told me that continued objective observation of Ronnie's words, actions and reactions revealed over and over again that Ronnie's *big* motivation for *doing things* and for *listening to others* was in the Recognition Emotional Appeal!

One fall, during the football season, Yankee Stadium's grandstand was jam-packed. The game was so exciting at times that many of the spectators half stood up in their seats or spilled over onto the steps and passageways to see better. Just before a tense moment, a young hawker wearing a white jacket tried to push his way through the crowd so he could more easily reach a stairway and sell his wares on the next aisle.

The spectators wouldn't budge.

Gripping his basket tightly, he yelled: "Coming through, please." No one moved, so he tried again. "Hot stuff, folks. Move over. I've gotta get through!" They continued to block his way. After a few more tries, he gave up and started to go far out of his direct path in order to reach the other side of the stairway.

A spectator sitting higher up saw what had happened. He called the young hawker and whispered a few words. Shrugging his shoulders, the hawker returned to the fringe of the crowd. This time, he moved forward, clutched his basket and shouted: "Coming through. WATCH OUT FOR THE MUSTARD!"

The men and women spectators immediately whirled around, jumped aside, grabbed their coats, and cleared a path!

Just about every person within his hearing had been emotionally tapped in the right place at the right time. Here, despite the preoccupation-holding Self-preservation factor of enjoyment, the spectators were treated as creatures of their emotions. "Hot stuff," the suggestion of being burned, also represented Self-preservation, but it was the wrong appeal to the Audience at this time and place.

The place was the Yankee Stadium, where hot dogs are a common sight. The word "Mustard" meant damage to clothes, cleaning bills, sloppy or embarrassing appearance. The audience viewpoint was clear. Recognition was the *big* Emotional Appeal, with a fine assist from Money. The Emotional Appeal pierced Preoccupation, hit way down into the emotions of hundreds of people!

Words are spoken.

People react, or they don't!

Little words can create a huge, unexpected new world of meaning. What an emotional powder keg they can explode!

Beautiful words can join voice tones and actions that set the heart romantically beating faster. Despairing words can create sorrow, instill disbelief. Emotionally appealing words can stir confidence, bravery, loyalty, kindness. Caressing words may inspire love. Sarcastic words often spill the passionate cup of defiance and anger. Words of thoughtlessness help conjure up permanent hate and suspicion.

How are *your* words today?

Did they make your listeners glad to have you near, laugh, cry, hope, worry, fear, suspect, despise you, shy away, or not listen at all?

Think!

Did you really make your words and actions do your bidding today? Did you awaken the response you were seeking by putting your emotional taps in the *right* places?

You *can*, and your success will not depend upon knowing the "right people." At this moment, it's much more important to realize that *every* person, and *every group of individuals*, will listen when you use Emotional Appeal. You can find the right Emotional Appeal for any situation.

Whoever you are, nothing real ever happened to you without having something happen to someone else. That something was an emotional reaction to your words and actions once or many times tied in with one or more of the Fatal Four Emotional Appeals. Not only on one person, but on many in your up to this minute lifetime.

The person who really "gets somewhere" gets there on the wings of words and actions that take him where he wants to go! They attain his objectives with Preoccupation-breaking Emotional Appeals that strike responsive chords in people.

This is true even in the discussion, "She was a nobody, and look at the man she married!" And, "He didn't have a dime, didn't know any influential people. Now he's running a big business!" Or, "She couldn't even win an amateur contest when we were kids. Now she's a big name on TV!"

A former student started from the proverbial nothing. Poor

family, wrong neighborhood, no friend who "amounted to anything," little formal education, with an obvious lisp. But he developed a knack based on an emotional appeal for being invited to interesting places by people he met for the first time.

Before parting company with the person and wherever he felt it deserving, he would say, "I'm glad we said 'Hello.' Although I've known you only a short while, I certainly think that you're an interesting person."

The other, emotionally tapped, usually wanted to see him again.

Gradually, his circle of friends widened; so did his career opportunities.

When a friend accompanied him to a Sunday concert and remarked that he wasn't enjoying it, my former student remembered this indication of viewpoint. Just before parting, he'd say: "I guess the concert wasn't so good, but those adventures of yours in Canada will have me chuckling for months. You made this one of the best Sunday afternoons in a long while!"

Although this was his way of saying, "Thank you for your company," he had also used a fine Emotional Appeal to his listener, because Recognition desires are in everyone's makeup.

In general, the words "Thank You" usually prove an excellent emotional tap in all buying, selling and incidental conversation. People enjoy being thanked for even the tiniest favor.

In Chicago, two newsstands stood within fifteen yards of each other and offered the same wares. One newsdealer, even during "rush hours," found time and the patience to say, "Thank You" to everyone who bought a newspaper. His competitor just said: "Next?" or "What do you read?"

In less than one year, the newsdealer who said "Thank You" began to sell nearly four times more newspapers per day than his competitor who had the same number of potential customers. People were willing to walk an extra fifteen yards, even when they were in a hurry, just to be thanked!

In New York City, many subway newsstands use a different Emotional Appeal to "up" their newspaper sales. Instead of giving coins as change for a newspaper purchase, they include the equivalent in a subway token. This saves their customers the time and trouble of standing on line to buy tokens at the subway change booth. It helps the subway change-makers too, and is a great Self-Preservation appeal!

Yes, if the emotional tap is right it will always prevail even if it *seems* almost the same as the wrong one.

A minister once told an anecdote about two clergymen who were close friends and heavy smokers. Each wrote to his superior. One asked: "May I smoke while praying?" Permission was denied. The other wrote: May I *pray* while smoking?" Permission was granted!

Emotions are so lavishly apportioned to our beings that we would more often say, see, hear or do things that give us pleasure than stop and wonder *why* we are thus saying, seeing, hearing or doing.

If a jacket or dress makes us "feel" like a million dollars, we're apt to love the item while forgetting cost or quality. If a cheaper suit or dress is better value, but doesn't make us appear better *looking*, we'll rarely buy.

"I think I have no color prejudices, nor caste prejudices, nor creed prejudices," said Mark Twain. "All that I care to know is that a man is a human being. That is enough for me; he can't be any worse!"

Mark Twain was right.

People want to see or listen to things that concern themselves *emotionally*.

This holds true whether we try to tap emotionally one, three or thirty thousand people; or thirty million.

The New York Police Department's Redmond O'Hanlon proved it. As one of the earliest contestants on a TV program called "The $64,000 Question," his ability to answer questions about William Shakespeare had won him $16,000. The next week, he was to return to the studio to tell the quizmaster and coast-to-coast audience whether or not he wanted to take a chance at being able to answer the next question worth $32,000.

Newspapers and other publicity media all over America ran pictures and stories about Patrolman O'Hanlon. People everywhere discussed this-father-of-five-children man who, living on a policeman's salary, would lose almost all he had gained if he failed to correctly answer the $32,000 Question. Should he "play it safe" and keep his winnings or try for the $32,000?

The situation had emotionally tapped more than 30,000,000 people. Despite individual differences among them, here was the entertainment portion of Self-Preservation to some, the Money Appeal to many, the new experience Romance portion, and recognition too. These reactions helped launch the then-new show on to command a larger viewing audience than any other TV show in America.

Knowing that some of the millions wanted him to quit and that others wanted him to take the next question, Patrolman O'Hanlon wisely chose to say, in effect: "On one hand, I see myself as a researcher and student of Shakespeare. As such, I would like to receive the recognition that winning more money would mean. That might make me want to take the next question. On the other hand, I see myself as a policeman with five children, a wonderful wife, a mortgaged home and a policeman's salary. This is why I am going to stop now and take the $16,000."

Just about every one of the televiewers felt that Patrolman O'Hanlon had done the right thing. Even those who wanted him to take the next question!

Some years later, when certain TV quiz programs suffered disrepute after individuals had won more than $100,000, the sincerity of O'Hanlon's words retained respect in the memory of millions!

Everyone is an individual. Each of us has a personal axe to grind. We have differences of taste in tobacco, men, women, clothes, hats, sex, automobiles, TV shows, religion, friendships, ties and washing machines.

Yet, we're all human beings. That's the prime basis for mutual accord and the source of the Fatal Four in every one of us. The Self-Preservation, Romance, Money or Recognition drives are often so deep down that we act before our brains stop and figure things out. When our words or actions, written or spoken, tap these emotions in others, we have an excellent chance of persuading them and even of presenting them with the facts of a case.

Owen D. Young once advised: "The person who can put

himself into the place of others, who can understand the workings of their minds, need never worry about the future or what it has in store for him."

The application of this advice to modern women, who have taken a wider range of responsibility in the social and business worlds, is apparent.

In a residential community in Ohio, a stationery store changed hands seven times in four years. Each owner had tried to lure and hold customers with price appeals, bargains, prizes, window and counter displays, but had failed. Customers preferred to patronize a large chain and variety store about a quarter of a mile away.

A young couple became the eighth owner. The husband, an injured war veteran, had a speech difficulty. Mrs. Veteran possessed a ready smile, and determined to learn the names of all customers, big and small. She had few to start with, but her greeting wasn't a mere: "Good morning." It soon became "Good morning, Mr. Brown" or "Hello, Julie." She truly personalized her relationship with every customer and so did her husband. Customers felt welcome and important, even if they made a trivial purchase or used the phone booth. The word got around.

Recognition and the convenience factor in Self-Preservation are usually more important than price appeal in fitting a small store's service to its customers' emotional needs. Customers are people. Give them a needed Emotional Appeal and they'll return for it over and over again!

Today, people, products and services are essentially the same. The competition is the competition to enter the mind of the listener, customer, client, patient or viewer. And no one can enter this Preoccupied mind without an emotional tap in the right direction.

Sometimes you use spoken words or actions; sometimes one *written* word can cause the intermagnetic sympathetic reception of the right Preoccupation-breaking Emotional Appeal!

At 8 o'clock on a Monday morning, while impatiently awaiting a bus, a former student of mine offered me a lift to the subway in his car.

"I'm mighty glad to see you," I said. "The bus is late and so am I."

"Don't worry," he replied. "I'll get you to the subway in jig time."

"With all this traffic?"

"You just watch," he grinned. "You always told us that the right Emotional Appeal can accomplish just about anything!"

The highway was thick with trucks and automobiles. Yet, when he made a hand signal before leaving the curb *the other drivers slowed down or stopped and gave us the right of way!* When we entered the heavy traffic on a parkway, the same thing happened. During the entire twenty-minute trip, the amazing phenomenon continued. My jovial former student had somehow become "King of the Road!"

When he was about to let me out, he blithely signalled with his left hand and *every car beside or behind us slowed down or stopped!* Not even a tough-looking truck driver dared to pass.

When he pulled away from the curb, I saw the reason. Under his back window, in red luminescent letters about seven inches tall, my former student, a licensed driver for more than 15 years, had printed one word, a word with such terrific Emotional Appeal that it made every other driver take notice.

The word? L-E-A-R-N-E-R!

No matter how steeped in their own Preoccupation the other drivers may have been, the Self-Preservation injury or accident Appeal and the possible Money-cost Appeal alerted them *instantly!*

Wouldn't it alert you too?

There was a special reason why the word had been put on the car. About a year before, my ex-student's wife had wanted to learn how to drive. A friend gave her a book on driving that contained the reference that ". . . the gas is your enemy; the brake is your best friend. . . ." With a learner's permit and my ex-student beside her in their car, she slammed on the brake so often that her husband feared a serious accident almost more than cracking his own skull on the windshield. To protect themselves as well as others on the road, he put Emotional Appeal

to work in the situation and conceived the idea of placing
L-E-A-R-N-E-R on the car.

After proving the power of Emotional Appeal in solving *such*
a difficult problem, my former student told me that he removed
the word L-E-A-R-N-E-R. He felt that its continued use might
raise too many questions about his *real* reason for using it!

Even if you're in the Romance department and want to get
married, you'll have to say it with Emotional Appeal!

Many women will tell how they met their husbands. Coyly,
they add: "He looked at me and I looked at him and it was
'Love At First Sight!' "

Don't believe it.

"First Sight" may be pleasurable to both parties, but neither
truly falls in love unless the other says and does something that
sustains interest. Real love is deeper and takes time to develop.
Whether it does or doesn't depends almost entirely upon the
words and actions used by the parties in their attempts to persuade one another. And this communication must activate the
right emotional response!

The male, we'll say, is lonely. He'd like to be independent.

He's a grocery clerk who someday hopes to own his own
store. To achieve this objective, he saves regularly. Mr. Male
wants the prestige and community standing of a man who owns
his own business. He's serious minded, but has had a life-long
hobby of collecting and building cuckoo clocks. He lives with
his parents and three younger sisters and most of his friends
assure themselves that he's almost as cuckoo as the clocks he
keeps.

At any rate, the five room apartment that he calls "home" is
overcrowded even without his large collection of clocks. Mr.
Male hasn't given much thought to marriage. He's known many
girls, had a few flirtations and small "affairs."

One evening, while sitting on the sidelines at a club dance,
he meets Miss Female.

She's not really pretty, wears glasses, dresses on the plain side
and possesses only a fair figure.

Mr. Male certainly would not fall in "love at first sight" with

Miss Female. But, when they're introduced, she says: "I'm very glad to meet you Mr. Male. My friend Madge told me about your unusual hobby."

"She did?" blurts Mr. Male, wondering what's coming next.

"Yes," replies Miss Female, "and I think that collecting cuckoo clocks is one of the most original hobbies I ever heard of!"

"You *do?* Gosh," splutters Mr. Male, "most of my friends think I'm kind of nutty. And my three sisters . . ."

"They're nice girls, I hear. Perhaps they and your friends are just a wee bit jealous underneath because their minds aren't as mature as yours. Now, won't you tell me more about your cuckoo clocks, Mr. Male?"

"More?" He touches her elbow and leads her towards two chairs. "Say, why don't you call me George?"

"Gladly, George. And you call me Dorothy. Now, about those cuckoo clocks. Was there a reason why you chose that hobby?"

You can follow the pattern thereafter. Miss Female started with a small knowledge of Mr. Male's emotional viewpoint, his desire for Recognition. Her desire was for Romance and marriage. She quickly broke George Male's Preoccupation with a Recognition appeal. This emotional contact established cordiality and interest between them. Soon she will learn more about Mr. Male and his job, his hopes to own his own grocery store, and his wish to have more room to indulge his cuckoo clock hobby without being heckled.

She continues to tell him not so much what she wants to tell him, but more of what he wants to hear emotionally.

Soon George Male decides that Dorothy Female is just the person he wants to marry. She understands him. He can't enjoy being away from her. She's so "different" from other girls. This way they'll have their own apartment, "with plenty of room for my hobby."

So they get married.

Love at first sight? More like "Love at first communication," thanks to the right Emotional Appeal.

Now, let's say that Dorothy Female is not interested in Romance. Suppose she's happily married, has three lovely children and is forty-five years old. She's at the club dance to chaperone her sister's daughter, who is George Male's age, but engaged to someone else. When she is introduced to George Male, she says: "I'm very glad to meet you, Mr. Male. My friend told me about your unusual hobby."

Do you believe that George will be receptive? He *will* because Recognition is his *big* appeal. His Preoccupation will be broken immediately. Perhaps Mrs. Female merely wants to make a good impression because she would like extra personal service on the morrow, when she'll buy groceries in the busy store where George Male works!

Or, maybe Dorothy Female is a travelling saleslady who sells books that show people how to operate their own businesses. Actually, she has no real interest in Mr. Male's cuckoo clocks, marriage or a favor. She uses the words, "I'm very glad to meet you, Mr. Male. I've heard about your unusual hobby," as an attention getter and an opening wedge that will give her a favorable interview for the books that she wants to sell.

George Male is an emotional individual, whose Preoccupation is filled by the Fatal Four Emotional Appeals of Self-Preservation, Money, Romance, and Recognition, but *one* of these four is his *big* motivating and listening factor. Once you identify it, you can break his Preoccupation and get him to listen intently to anything from marriage to buying to doing a favor in a grocery store!

For emotional reasons, each person sees what he *wants* to see and hears what he *wants* to hear. He also fails to respond to what does not emotionally interest him! The motivating communication stimulus for every individual lies within the realm of the Fatal Four Preoccupation-breaking, Preoccupation-holding Emotional Appeals, which are basic to the Emotional Appeal Technique.

In the pages that follow, hundreds of examples of Emotional Appeal within the Fatal Four will be defined, illustrated and interlocked.

Once you apply the Technique to make your daily living happier and more successful, you will repeatedly recall the story of the factory owner who was suffering heavy damage because of faulty plumbing. He called many plumbers, but they could not find the trouble. Then he called one who worked alone and carried a small bag of tools. The plumber went to the third floor of the factory, removed a small hammer from his bag and knocked on a pipe. This solved the problem.

When the factory owner received a bill for $100, he was irate. He phoned the plumber. "You were here less than ten minutes. All you did was knock on a pipe. Then you bill me one hundred dollars. If you want to get paid, you'll have to *itemize* your bill so I know what I'm paying for!"

The plumber complied and sent his bill, itemized as follows: "For knocking on pipe—$1. For knowing *where* to knock—$99. Total—$100."

The plant owner paid the bill and became a regular customer of the plumber!

With every person, whether in speaking, selling or advertising, you must know *where* to knock, where to tap the emotions to communicate.

You will learn that response-awakening Emotional Appeal is a force for Good as well as for Evil. The crook, the murderer, the confidence man, or the quack, may try to use it. Certainly. But it must also be effectively used by the Priests, Rabbis, Ministers, Educators, Philosophers and "good" people everywhere.

A person cannot be known as "a good person" unless his or her words have been emotionally appealing to the people expressing the opinion!

We believe as we do for emotional reasons. Even law enforcement organizations seem to realize this.

The FBI once sought a criminal wanted for jailbreak and robbery. Aside from the man's physical description, he was known to be quite vain. The search narrowed to the Cincinnati vicinity and "Wanted" posters were distributed and hung. The FBI agents captured the man right in the Federal Building while he was standing, admiring his own picture!

Everyone has a viewpoint. It is *individually* emotional. By sharpening our observation of people's words and actions and making some mental notes, we can become truly adept at applying Emotional Appeal, a Technique for uncovering and identifying the *big* motivating factors in listeners so that communication with them can be more mutually rewarding.

As time goes by, we shall find that the way others *listen* to us can be our best approach to happier, healthier, more successful living. Whether we are handsome or homely, whether we have a physical disability, two heads or a very thick accent, whether we stutter, stammer, or have a nose like a banana, it makes no difference.

When we know how to use Emotional Appeal Technique for communication, we can succeed in developing more initiative and creative imagination, better Outlook, and better powers of Personality and Persuasion.

And now, let's find out how our knowledge of the Fatal Four Emotional Appeals in everyone can *always* motivate and make people want to listen—to *us!*

The "Fatal Four Emotional Appeals" That Make People Want to Listen

"You *certainly look lovely in that dress*," says Mr. Jackson to his wife.

In her own little world of friends, relatives and neighbors, Mrs. Jackson may be regarded as a wonderful wife, good mother, excellent hostess, nice person, or marvelous housekeeper.

When she communicates with others and when others communicate with her, however, she is *always* an individual!

Her reaction will be based upon many circumstances that have blended into her *inner* makeup.

As a result, she may reply: "Thanks, Sweetie. Now I know that I'll really enjoy wearing it!"

She may acidly retort: "Not as lovely as your friend Lottie looks, I suppose?"

Or, her answer may be: "You're only saying that because this is a cheap dress and you know it. If I had paid what I ought to spend for a dress, you would scream a-plenty!"

Perhaps she merely puckers, links her hand in his, kisses his left ear lobe and whispers: "That's blarney and I know it, but I love to hear it from you!"

Each answer helps reflect a viewpoint, the viewpoint of the *real* Mrs. Jackson. And the reply that so quickly exhibits it didn't just happen then and there.

It required plenty of time to arrive!

From infancy, each of us experiences billions of words, actions and situations. To infancy, we bring certain hereditary emotional factors simply by being born.

As the years pass, our communicative actions and reactions indicate more and more emotional identifications specifically related to one or more of the "Fatal Four" Emotional Appeals of Self-Preservation, Money, Romance and Recognition.

Despite entangled fears, hopes, attitudes, and desires within *all* Four, time reveals to us and to others that *one* or *two* of the Four are the over-all major reasons why we tend to act, react and feel the way we do. Then *one* becomes the *big* Emotional Appeal that most quickly awakens response, stimulates us, makes us listen, keeps us Preoccupied, gets us angry, happy, upset or opinionated.

How vividly this was illustrated in a discussion period that followed a lecture!

A doctor rose, introduced himself and told us about a very fat young man who had come to him for treatment. The need for a reducing diet was definitely indicated. After prescribing the diet, he had given his patient, an expensively and meticulously dressed fellow, this warning: "Stick to the diet and don't let temptation get the better of you!"

The patient, whom he referred to as "Mr. X," promised to heed the advice.

Some weeks later, Mr. X returned. His health was worse. There was little doubt about it. He had not followed the diet.

Once more, the doctor cautioned him but to no avail.

During the next four months, Mr. X shuttled to and from the doctor's office. "Mr. X," admonished the doctor, "if you don't lose weight and stick to the diet, you may shorten your life!"

"Maybe so," replied Mr. X, "but I have a 'here today gone tomorrow' philosophy. I think better than most people and I can't help thinking that I ought to enjoy myself. Eating rich foods happens to be one of my great enjoyments, but I'll try my best to stay on the diet."

For nearly a year, the doctor silently confessed his despair after each visit. He knew how important it was for the patient to diet, but he deplored his inability to get a powerful enough reason to make Mr. X listen.

Mr. X returned one evening, very ill.

After examination, the doctor asked Mr. X to dress. He phoned a nearby pharmacy and asked for a prescription to be ready for pickup.

"It's for Mr. X," he told the pharmacist. "You'll recognize him because he'll have my prescription and *he looks like an elephant,* he's so fat. But he's the best dressed elephant I ever saw!"

Fat Mr. X stopped dressing and hastened to the doctor's desk. "Wait a minute, Doctor," he pleaded. "Don't think of me as an elephant. This time I'm going to stay on the diet!"

And he *did!*

Why?

The doctor had been trying to get his patient to adhere to the diet by using variations of the Self-Preservation Appeal. "If you don't lose weight, you may shorten your life . . ." was not the *big* Emotional Appeal for Mr. X. His repeated refusal to follow the diet should have indicated this. The answer to the doctor's dilemma was not mainly evidenced in the Money or Romance Appeals either. By elimination, the answer had to be within Recognition.

Actually, Mr. X communicated much of this on first glance. He was a "meticulous dresser" who wore "obviously expensive" clothes. During the visits, there were other Recognition clues including the fact that Mr. X had often boasted about his abilities and achievements. "I think better than most people," he had once said.

Recognition was written all over Mr. X.

When the right Emotional Appeal was used, when the word "Elephant" was set up for comparison, particularly the expression "best-dressed elephant I ever saw," Mr. X's Preoccupation was truly pierced. His mind had been entered. For the first time, he became *emotionally* receptive to the doctor's efforts to have him stay on the diet.

Mr. X had begun to interpret the doctor's advice *in terms of his own emotional needs!*

People do not change their spots emotionally.

People, like leopards, never change their spots emotionally.

From childhood on, each person retains certain emotional identifications related to the Fatal Four Emotional Appeals. These are the common denominators for successful mass communication and person-to-person communication because they can awaken response in any individual. It is always important, however, to seek out the *right* ones that fit Subject to Listener, even in parent-child relationships.

Little "Freddie" won't eat his cereal. His mother's impatience mounts. She has other things to do. "Freddie, please! This farina is good for you. You've been sitting there for nearly an hour. Come on. Open your mouth and swallow this spoonful!"

Freddie continues to dawdle and trace the tablecloth design with his right index finger.

"Look, Freddie," insists his mother. "You eat your cereal or you'll get a spanking. You're a big boy now, but I'm going to put you over my knee and make your behind really hurt. This is your last chance. Open your mouth and eat this farina, or I'll hit you and you'll cry!"

The Self-Preservation "Freddie" reacts instantly to the threat. He says or feels, "Don't spank me! Don't spank me!" and starts doing what his mother wants. Emotionally, he does not relish the pain and he fears the spanking. So he listens.

As he grows older, his words and actions will evidence to a larger and larger extent that his *big* Emotional Appeal is Self-Preservation. He'll show this by his special concern for personal enjoyments, doing thing an easier way, fear of illness, death and injury, avoidance and dislike of possible pain, impatience when inconvenienced and other attitudes in the Self-Preservation Appeal. He'll usually have strong feelings about religion and demonstrate his belief that blood is thicker than water.

This "Freddie" will become a "Self-Preservation Cow!"

Another kind of Freddie won't give a hoot about the threat of being spanked if he doesn't listen to his mother! He's been spanked before, of course. Maybe he didn't like it, but it didn't mean much either. He recalls that most of the time his mother or father only threaten him and don't follow through. It's fun to see if he can outsmart his mother and maybe get some kind of a present just for eating the cereal! He's a child and he's going to act like one, just as he has heard his father tell his mother so often.

He starts to retrace the tablecloth design, but first makes certain that there's more farina splashed on the spoon.

Then his mother says: "Freddie, listen! If you eat all of that cereal, I'll let you stay up an extra half hour tonight to watch TV. I may even buy you a nice play toy when we go to the store."

"You *will?*" This "Freddie" perks up and eats the farina!

Getting a reward has a *big* Appeal for him. Emotionally, he likes to be "paid" for what he does. With little doubt, he's the kind of a "Freddie" who will follow this emotional pattern through the years. Money: getting it, earning it, saving it, fear of losing it, factors of economy, waste and related elements, can mushroom into his *big* Emotional Appeal. Whoever learns this can "reach" him, because Money Appeal is the main Emotional Appeal that makes him want to listen!

But suppose that threat of punishment and offer of reward approaches have *failed* to start Freddie doing as his mother wishes? Is the situation hopeless?

Certainly not.

There are millions of "Freddies" whose *big* Emotional Appeal lies in the realm of Romance!

Perhaps the Sex and Future Promise portions of the Romance Emotional Appeal have not developed in Freddie as yet because he's too young. Yet, the desire for satisfaction of curiosity or the wish for New Experiences may be exactly the responsive chord within our third type of "Freddie." Maybe Freddie has lost interest in eating the cereal because there's too much sameness, monotony and routine connected with it! Right this moment we notice that he is intertwining a fork onto the farina—splattered spoon and is beginning to retrace the tablecloth design in a way he has not previously tried!

"Freddie, remember the airport where we saw those planes take off and come down?" asks his mother.

"Uh-huh," mumbles Freddie. "I sure wish we could go again. There were lots of different kinds of planes there."

"Let me have the spoon and we'll make believe that we're there right now." She dips the spoon into the cereal and holds it high above the table. "The spoon is a silver-colored plane and it is loaded with cereal. Open your mouth wide and see how the plane zooms down and delivers the farina ready for you to swallow."

His eyes light up and he complies.

Offshoots of this theme at mealtime help this "Freddie" eat and try foods that aren't his favorites. In other situations, he especially responds to novelty and originality. As he grows older, he develops stronger desires to give or get new experiences. He is powerfully attracted to the opposite sex; he demonstrates higher than average Romance motivations. He perennially strives for individuality in his actions, has a fine sense of showmanship and develops a "personal style" that "trademarks" him to others.

Does he possess *all* of the Fatal Four Emotional Appeals?

Surely. They'll interlock to a larger or lesser degree within him, depending upon the situation at hand and its emotional relationship to Freddie. But Romance Emotional Appeal is the BIG Emotional Appeal for him. The one who can say it with ROMANCE Emotional Appeal can succeed with *this* "Freddie" because *this* "Freddie" is a "Romance Cow!"

Now, if "Freddie" has not responded to carefully applied Romance, Self-Preservation or Money Emotional Appeal attempts to motivate or make him listen, there *must* be a reason: He is either physically ill, too immature to emotionally respond to communication, he has not found the language clear and comprehensible, or the *right* Emotional Appeal has not as yet been used.

All other considerations aside, the answer will be found in the area of Recognition.

When this fourth type of "Freddie" is just about to show his mother how nicely he has piled the farina into five equal piles, she says: "See the kitchen clock, Freddie? If you finish all the cereal before the big hand goes across the six, I'll tell your grandmother what a good boy you are. I'll tell Aunt Betty and I'll tell your father too, the minute he comes home. If you can do this, we'll all be proud of you and be able to say: 'Freddie was able to eat all the farina before the big hand on the clock crossed the six!' Are you ready? Set? Go!"

Freddie, almost entirely unresponsive to other Emotional Appeals, tries to beat the clock!

Recognition happens to be his *big* Emotional Appeal. Throughout youth, adolescence and adult years, gathering experiences make this very evident. He has an innate pride and does not care to have it upset. He obviously communicates his desire for popularity, reassurance, and appreciation. He does not like to be criticized but often likes to criticize others even in jest. Those who offend his ego must expect him to go to great lengths to "get even." He is careful about his appearance and choice of friends. He exaggerates at times and is responsive to "name-dropping." He vibrantly enjoys a sincere compliment, especially in the presence of others. His sense of humor is quite good, he relishes gossip, and he glows when asked his opinion.

Emotionally, he is mainly a Recognition Cow. Like all of us, however, he can be a "very nice person," and he is part Self-Preservation Cow, Money Cow and Romance Cow.

Did we say "Cow?"

Yes.

Why a cow is always a cow.

If you take a walk in the country and see an animal that has udders, says "Moo!" and gives milk, you would call that animal a cow—not a horse, elephant, snake or rabbit.

The animal has the *identifying characteristics* of a cow. It *has udders, gives milk,* and says *"Moo-o-o!"*

Remember these characteristics, please. They will help remind us that people, subjects and situations have identifying characteristics too, usually written all over them emotionally.

But are we alert enough to read the writing in terms of the Fatal Four response-awakening Emotional Appeals?

A student worked for an advertising agency. He helped prepare an advertising and promotional campaign that the agency wanted to sell to the head of a mail order house. The presentation represented a large investment of money, time, copy and artwork. After two visits, my student, Ralph, and his employer had been unable to get past the cold exterior of the mail order executive, Mr. P.

Ralph's employer was disheartened. Ralph was not.

With the costly presentation under his arm, he went to see "one-and-one-makes-two" Mr. P. Right after a perfunctory handshake, he said: "Mr. P. may I ask you a question?"

"What's the question?" snapped the mail order executive with obvious impatience.

Raising his eyebrows and looking directly at Mr. P., he replied: *"How would you like to become the biggest man in the mail order business?"*

Mr. P.'s cold eyes bathed twinklingly and he grinned.

The answer did not have to be spoken.

Cordiality was established and it was not too difficult to gain and hold his attention. Some time later, the agency secured the account and Ralph was rewarded.

How did this happen?

It happened because tough Mr. P.'s hard exterior had been emotionally softened within the first few seconds of his interview with Ralph. Deep, deep down, this Preoccupied and capable executive, "a sharp businessman who watches his pennies" had a *big* desire to increase his business. Since he was a man who owned his own business, Money tended to be his *big* Emotional Appeal as it is with so many businessmen.

Once Ralph's words hit him emotionally, he changed his outward attitude and became more receptive. Now he was interested in a tangible *plan* that might eventually make him a *bigger* man in the mail order business!

The plan, in the form of a campaign, was then shown.

As he studied the presentation and listened to Ralph's accompanying explanations, he felt it in terms of becoming the *"biggest man in the mail order business."*

Emotionally, he had been told what he wanted to hear, and it made him much more interested in learning the facts!

Yes!

The smarter they are, the harder they listen when you uncover the right Emotional Appeal that fits your Subject to your Audience.

But *you* must do some listening and observing too.

If you don't, you'll remember that a Cow is always a Cow and forget that a Person is always a Person emotionally.

A Person does not change strong and weak emotionally established characteristics any more than a Cow does. Tapped at the right time and place in the right way, a Cow gives milk. Tapped at the right time and place with the right Emotional Appeal, a person, even a huge group of people, will be responsive to *you!*

The weak spots in everyone.

No matter what the subject, each person has an emotional "weak spot" related to it. Certain desires, attitudes, wishes or fears can bring us out into the open.

When we do this, we *can* be persuaded even if we try to "cover up."

In response to a newspaper ad, William, a former student, applied for a job as assistant to the president of a fair-sized corporation. Competition was keen and the situation was complicated by the fact that the president wasn't entirely certain that he needed an assistant.

At the first interview, he told William: "I really don't need an assistant. I'm in good health. I built this company, and only my wife thinks that I shouldn't handle things myself. Matter of fact," he emphasized, "I don't care if I have to work seventeen hours a day every day!"

For the first time, William felt that he had uncovered the president's viewpoint and "weak spot."

"I hope you'll pardon me for saying this, but you remind me of a remark that my doctor made last year when I had my annual physical checkup."

"What was the remark?"

"He said," answered William respectfully, " 'Do you know that *over 60% of the wealth in the United States is in the hands of widows?* ' "

The corporation president immediately reacted. For a half minute, he remained so silent that William felt he could hear the seconds tick past. Then the man who claimed he could "work seventeen hours a day every day" grinned.

"You're very convincing," he said, "and I like you."

An appointment was set for the following Wednesday. Two weeks later, William's title became "Assistant to the President."

His words about "60% of the wealth in the hands of widows" had smacked right into Self-Preservation and Money, the *right* Emotional Appeals for the corporation president! He had instantly made the man think: "Who am I working for, my *widow?* Maybe I'd better start getting more time to have more enjoyment while I'm *alive.* Maybe I *do* need an Assistant!"

The *right* Emotional Appeals are so important—even to a lady who shops for a tie.

Shortly before "Father's Day," Mrs. S. sets out to buy a tie for her hubby. She sees hundreds, but can't decide, despite words like: "Good looking . . ." "Wonderful value . . ." "Imported . . ." "Remember, this is pure silk."

She enters a fourth store. A salesman hears her say: "My husband is difficult to please. He usually criticizes what I select!"

This salesman shows her a group of ties, watches her gaze hover over two or three and points. "Madam," he assuringly remarks, "your husband will compliment you upon your good taste when you give him *this* tie!"

She thanks him for the suggestion and buys!

Another woman, Mrs. J., walks in and out of three stores seeking a tie for her father. In each store she mentions that "My father wears very expensive ties, but I have only about two dollars left to spend."

These words go unheeded until one clerk, taking the cue, tells her, "That's nothing to worry about, Madam. I'll show you some two dollar ties that look, feel and knot like they cost as much as three times more."

A few minutes later, she makes a purchase.

Each of the women had an emotional motivation for buying. It was revealed by their words as their emotional "weak spot."

Mrs. S. had Recognition; Mrs. J.'s needed response was in Money. These motivations were more important to them than "If I don't buy him something for Father's Day, he'll forget me next Mother's Day."

Emotionally, each received words of assurance that she alone sought.

In all relationships we try to communicate to others and to ourselves.

There's an *individualized* viewpoint that stimulates our actions and our thinking, whether we are out to buy, or inquire about a bank account.

A middle-aged, auburn-haired woman shyly took a seat at the desk of an officer in a savings institution. "May I, please, find out the balance on my account if I take the interest to date?" She reached into her purse for her passbook.

The white-haired bank officer nodded, glanced at the first page in the passbook and picked up his phone. "May I have the balance on Mrs. L.'s account if interest is added to date, please? That's Mrs. L., Passbook 'Number LL 198,532.'"

In a few minutes, he gave Mrs. L. the requested information.

Mrs. L. thanked him. "You just did something that makes me very happy to do business with you," she said. "When you asked for information about my account, you referred to me by name not by number. That's the way I want to be referred to." She stood. "I have two accounts in another bank next block. Whenever I ask them for information about the accounts, they always refer to me *by number not by name.* You're much more thoughtful. In a few days I am going to transfer those accounts here."

Three days later, she transferred two accounts totalling more than $22,000 to the bank whose officer had referred to her *by name* not by number!

Nearly a month later, I was greeted by the bank officer.

"Remember that nice lady whom I referred to by name, not by number?"

I certainly did.

*"She told me that her first husband, from whom she was di-
vorced, was a convict!"*

When the woman entered the bank, she did so for a personal
reason. When the bank officer referred to her by name, not by
number, he broke her Preoccupation and captured her attention
emotionally though not intentionally.

She listened and reacted in her *own* way because of emotional
experiences specifically associated with her former husband.

Could the fact that the motivating Emotional Appeal of a few
words became worth $22,000 in extra deposits possibly provide
a lesson for our own lives? Certainly.

Each of us has a personal history that consists of a vast number of experiences with people *and* our spouses. We have had
good and bad emotional reactions from words and actions and
we are filled with resultant Preoccupations.

So are the people who work *with* us, *against* us and *for* us.

In Phoenix, Arizona, for instance, a woman engaged a roofer
to put a new roof on her house. The roofer completed the job
and she paid him. Some time later, she started a fire in the stove.
In less than twenty minutes, the house became filled with smoke
and the Fire Department was called. Investigation revealed that
the roofer had forgotten to put back the chimney!

Yes. Whether we are roofers or women walking into a bank,
we are Preoccupied. No one can break this Preoccupation and
make us want to listen, unless this person's words or actions
relate to one or more of the Fatal Four Emotional Appeals
within us.

We are *emotional* human beings.

We prefer to be referred to by *name,* not by number, even
though our first husband was *not* a convict!

Uncovering individual differences.

In everything from etiquette to buying, from love to marriage,
in every relationship, the importance of Emotional Appeal is
more and more apparent. Properly directed Emotional Appeal
can break Preoccupation, "reach" your listener and stimulate a
sought-for result.

But the tap must be made at the right time, in the right *emotional* place.

I was in one of Boston's ladies apparel stores one Autumn day when a pretty customer walked over to a ho-hum saleslady. The customer, who looked like a teen-ager, asked for a suit that had been advertised in one of the morning newspapers.

Apologetically, the girl said, "I may look younger, Miss, but I'm really twenty-one years old!"

The saleslady shrugged and wandered off towards the suit racks, mumbling, "Okay. I'll find you something nice. We got some new suits in for the sale."

The youthful-appearing customer tried on more than seven suits during the next twenty-odd minutes.

Meanwhile, one of the store's advertising men, for whom I was waiting, came over to me and noticed my interest.

I smiled and told him that I would appreciate it if he would watch what was going on.

The first saleslady became impatient with the young lady customer and called another salesperson in an attempt to swing the sale. The second one, after bringing out four more suits, summoned the section manager.

All three now tried to convince the customer to buy a grey plaid suit she had just tried on. Suits were scattered helter-skelter over five chairs and a table. The three salespeople were exasperated. The attractive young lady refused to make up her mind.

My friend, the advertising man, leaned over and assured me: "Just the kind who shops around. She's a time waster; really not out to buy!"

I shook my head. "Maybe it's that way with some customers," I emphasized, "but that girl will be glad to buy if your sales-people will use some words that she wants to *hear!*"

"What does she want to hear?" derisively asked my friend.

"I believe that she wants to hear that the grey plaid suit she is now wearing, or *any* suit, will make her appear *older* and prettier!"

"Older? Why, that's . . ."

"Go over and try it," I urged. "Let's see what happens!"

With a pooh-pooh smirk, he joined the little group.

To the surprise of all, my friend, a former salesman, said to her: "That grey plaid suit is not your type!" He hastily glanced at the size ticket, strode to a nearby rack and removed a green suit with an unusual overall woven effect. "This is for you, Miss," he announced, handing her the suit. "It will make you look *older* and even prettier!"

The girl stared at him more than at the suit. She tried it on, pirouetted twice before a full-length mirror and nodded. "This is just what I want," she said. "I'll take it!"

The salespeople almost swallowed their noses!

Obviously piqued, the first saleslady stepped forward. "That suit costs five dollars more than the others, Miss," she smugly remarked from between clenched teeth. "If I had known you wanted something *better* . . ."

I held my breath.

My friend, unfamiliar with the stock, had taken the suit from the wrong rack!

"Oh, that's all right," laughed the girl shopper. "It's what I want, so I'm sure it's worth the extra few dollars! Please put it into a box."

When my friend and I had our late lunch, we discussed the incident.

A newspaper advertisement had persuaded the young-looking customer to come in to the store. Then the persuasion had stopped!

If people in sales do not use the right Emotional Appeals, many sales are lost right from the beginning. Selling is just another phase of communication; it involves people. Where there are people, there are feelings and emotional reactions to words and actions. Even a chance remark may inform you of the whereabouts of the personal key to your listener's emotional treasure box, wrapped in Fatal Four ribbon.

"I may look younger, Miss, but I'm really twenty-one years old!"

A passing remark, but it helped reveal a viewpoint.

This girl's romantic aspirations may have been thwarted because possible "boy friends" thought or said: "She's a swell girl and very pretty, *but I hate to be seen with a girl who looks like a kid!*"

Watch your situations.

Although everyone *is* communicatively related to the Fatal Four Emotional Appeals, or *can* be, it may sometimes require particular understanding.

The reason why the advertising man almost automatically balked when I asked him to use the word *"older"* is that one phase of Self-Preservation in a listener is best appealed to as a *wish* to remain young—the *fear* of becoming older. Here the girl was older but *appeared* younger. It became necessary to think in terms of her *wish* to appear older and her *fear* of appearing younger. On *her* side, this appearance factor undoubtedly had a strong Romance reason.

When she shopped for clothes, she was especially anxious to satisfy her emotional needs for appearing older by seeking out apparel that had Recognition Emotional Appeal to others rather than Self-Preservation Emotional Appeal to herself.

She wanted her emotional needs recognized and satisfied. The words, "This suit will make you look *older* and even prettier," did just that, and the Money-cost was relatively unimportant!

Identifying the emotional cause of a "snap judgement".

Sometimes your words or actions may stimulate your listener to make a "thoughtless" response or "snap judgement."

Alert yourself!

With your knowledge of the Fatal Four Emotional Appeals, you *can* "tell a book by its cover!"

As we shall see, thoughtless remarks and snap judgements are communicative emotional responses. They can be most revealing about the *real* reason for another person's action or lack of it.

A general contractor was exasperated.

Six months had passed and Mr. H. had not paid his bill. The contractor wrote many letters. Some pleaded, others threatened legal action, but Mr. H. did not reply. Twice, the contractor had managed to reach Mr. H.'s wife on the phone. Each time he had been told: "Mr. H. seems to be short of funds. Have patience and he'll take care of the bill."

Still not a word from Mr. H.!

One day, the contractor's 18-year-old son made a suggestion. "Dad," he said, "if you can get Mr. H. to *remember* that he owes you the money, he may pay you before he pays some of his other past due debts."

"Son," sighed the contractor, "how can I make Mr. H. remember?"

The son, known for his sense of humor, told his father to enclose a family photograph in his next letter to Mr. H. It was a picture of the contractor, his wife, the son and two younger sisters. Under the photo, he wrote: *"Here are FIVE reasons why I need the money!"*

Something about the family photo stimulated Preoccupied Mr. H. He made a "snap judgement" and sent a reply.

Mr. H. enclosed a picture of a shapely brunette in a skin-tight swim suit. Under the picture, he wrote: *"Here is the one reason why I can't pay you!"*

The contractor showed his son the reply. "See? Was there any good in trying to collect *your* way?"

"Plenty, Dad," insisted the son. "You received a reply for the first time, didn't you? You've made an impression on Mr. H. at last." He pointed to the brunette's photograph. "The next time Mr. H. thinks of spending more money on this gold-digger, he'll also think of the five reasons why he should pay you." The son winked. "If he doesn't, he's going to suddenly remember that maybe we'll take this picture to his wife!"

The son's prediction proved to be correct.

Soon after, Mr. H. began to repay the debt and also ask for the return of the picture!

The request for money on a family photograph, a Self-Preservation Appeal, set up an emotional chain. It broke Mr. H.'s silence and sparked his "snap judgement" to send the brunette's photo and handwritten excuse.

Most of us are guilty of making "snap judgements" at one time or another. When we "do first—think later," there is always a tie-in with something that is "on our minds." Whatever is "on our minds" outside of a blank vista, is connected with the Fatal Four Emotional Appeals.

This Preoccupation is in every person in every occupation, including the ones in which alertness is essential!

According to Leonard Lyons, in his *Lyons Den* newspaper column, some Chicago detectives made a "snap judgement" that may have embarrassed them more than the brunette's photo embarrassed Mr. H.!

A man named "Champ" Segal was once the manager of Charles "Phil" Rosenberg, flyweight champion of the world. During the Chicago gang wars in the Capone era, some detectives stopped "Champ" in a hotel lobby.

Believing that he was a suspicious character, they swiftly and methodically searched Segal. In one pocket, they found some business cards on which was printed:

CHARLES "PHIL" ROSENBERG

WORLD'S FLYWEIGHT CHAMPION

The detectives promptly apologized.

"Sorry, *Charlie*," they said. "Our error."

They quickly walked away from Segal, who was *six feet tall and weighed more than 200 pounds!*

The activating "feeling" of Recognition Emotional Appeal in the business card had thrown their reasoning for such a loss that they didn't even notice the size of the man they spoke to!

Solving the mystery of your audience viewpoint.

There *are* individual differences.

Not everyone reacts in the same way to the same situation or even to the same story.

Renee, a divorcee with a delightful French accent and a revealing powder-blue dress, tells a humorous story to three women and two men at a cocktail party.

Two of the women are married, one unhappily. The third

woman is 39 years old, wishes she could find a husband and has become tired of hunting.

One of the two men is a widower of means whose spirit is willing but whose flesh is weak. The other man can't stand the woman he has been married to for 14 years; he would rather have an intimate relationship with a whiskey bottle.

Renee's story is about a psychiatrist whose patient complains that she has four husbands and loves each for a different reason. No one husband knows about the others. She has never been divorced and lives in two homes and two apartments with her respective spouses. For three years she has carried on the hoax; now she needs help. Just when she has organized her alibis and her time, she falls in love with a fifth man who wants to marry her. And the fifth, an executive with a missing persons organization, does not know about husbands number one, two, three and four!

Vivacious, 33-year-old Renee dramatizes the story with gestures, facial expressions and swaying body movements. On the outside, the five people in her Audience wear "attentive" half-smiles.

Inside, there are sharp differences in reactions to the story.

Mention of the psychiatrist suggests to the unhappy wife that perhaps her *husband* ought to see one. As this leaves her mind, she wonders: "Who is Renee's hairdresser? I must ask her."

The "happily married" woman thinks: "How in the world would *any* woman want *four* husbands at the same time? Isn't *one* more than enough? Anyway, Renee had better be careful with her motions. That powder-blue dress might *burst* just at the wrong time!"

The bachelor girl exhales deeply: "A woman with *four* husbands and I can't even get *one!*"

The widower can't imagine how one woman can satisfy the needs and attitudes of four husbands at the same time. He doesn't miss any of Renee's form-fitting motions and wishes that twenty years could be dropped off his age.

Now a bit tipsy, the other man silently sighs that Renee could be so "nice to come home to" but would probably "level off and be the same as any other wife!" He takes another swallow and mumbles that he's happier with a bottle than with a woman "because a bottle can't talk back!"

With a mischievous twinkle, Renee stage whispers the story's punch line, and the five listeners appreciatively roar with laughter.

Had they *all* enjoyed the story?

Probably not.

How many could retell it? Perhaps *two*.

How many *would* retell it? Possibly *one*.

Do you know which one *really* listened from beginning to end, but will *not* retell the story?

The unmarried woman, the one who was becoming tired of trying to find a worthwhile husband. There was strong emotional contact for her throughout the powerful—though sad—Romance Appeal in the story of a woman who hadn't been divorced, yet had possessed four husbands and had still been able to find a fifth!

Does this mean that every unmarried woman of thirty-nine has Romance as her *big* Emotional Appeal?

No.

It merely indicates that every group consists of individuals. These individuals differ in the strength and penetration of one or more of the Emotional Appeals of Self-Preservation, Money, Romance and Recognition.

Even though people react to the same story or stimulus in different ways, they will react *only* if sharp enough elements of the Fatal Four Emotional Appeals cut into them.

The Fatal Four Emotional Appeals make up the major portion of *every* desire, fear and attitude. We, as individuals, make up the huge audience that is humanity.

We are part of every plan, every song, story, advertisement, sale, heartbreak or surprise. We are listeners, speakers, observers, readers and writers. The Self-Preservation, Romance, Money and Recognition hopes, wishes and worries are in all of us. They are also in every one of our listeners.

At times, a particular Emotional Appeal has more power for one individual than for another.

Sometimes we do not have the opportunity of knowing anything about our listener or reader until we come face to face. If we "speak" via communication media like TV and radio, newspapers and magazines or advertising, we may never see or meet our audience. This is when Emotional Appeal Technique *must* be a vital part of communication.

We *know* that people are Preoccupied. We *know* that our message can "reach" our listeners when we use the *right* Emotional Appeal. We seek out the *right* Emotional Appeal from the framework of the Fatal Four Emotional Appeals, the Appeals that, in one way or another, affect *every* human being.

Why? Because Emotional Appeal is the ability to motivate and make people *want* to listen—to facts or fancies.

Emotionally, our individual fears, hopes, needs, attitudes and worries are our strongest and weakest points. As individuals, we react differently even though thousands of us are of the same audience.

A woman wrote to the editor of *Living* Magazine, commenting on people who are watching a movie.

"If everyone enthused at the same thing, it would be OK," said the writer, "but consider the difference in the sense of humor of a 14-year-old boy who still thinks love is hooey; a young couple of 21, very much in love; a twosome of 28 on the verge of divorce; an unmarried woman of 35 who is rapidly giving up hope; the overworked 42-year-old mother. Now, give each the right to one good whoop or whistle in the spots they like and a good 'boo' in the spots they don't like in the movie and then, answer this question: 'How much of the dialogue could be heard?' "

Very little, you can be sure. Yet this movie audience, even with its individual differences, contains the *same* instincts and emotions individually and collectively. There are personal reactions even when they are not expressed aloud!

From earliest times the Fatal Four Emotional Appeals have been the Preoccupation-breaking tie-ins between any speaker and listener, writer and reader, performer and audience, teacher and student in every situation. They are the basic approach to the listener's emotional involvement. Whether our audience consists of one, one thousand, one million or more, its attitudes must be treated as emotionally more important than our own, if we wish to communicate successfully.

Perhaps the analogy of "Homer's Riddle" will help impress this fact.

Many centuries ago, there lived a Greek named Homer. He prided himself upon being able to answer almost any question, no matter how complex. As a result, he became known as one of the wisest men in the land.

This acclaim, it is said, made him very happy.

One day, Homer was asked a riddle: "Some fishermen went out in a boat. Whatever they caught, they threw away. All they could not catch they kept. What?"

Homer pondered, but could not come up with the answer. He analyzed the problem, made an on-the-scene investigation by getting into a fishing boat with some fishermen.

His reputation waned. His closest disciples lost confidence in his wisdom. Unfortunately, Homer lost confidence in himself and died without uncovering the Mystery of the Riddle:

"Some fishermen went out in a boat. Whatever they caught, they threw away. All they could not catch, they kept. What?"

The answer was: "FLEAS!"

Although Homer lost much of his reputation because he could not uncover the "Mystery of the Riddle," today we may lose reputation, money, love, life and many enjoyments if we do not successfully uncover the answer to another mystery, the Mystery of Audience Viewpoint.

Can we control, to a larger extent, the emotional reaction to our words and actions in our homes, our marriages, our personal, professional and work relationships?

We *can* if we remember that our own and our listeners' Viewpoints can be found within the Fatal Four Emotional Appeals.

We *shall* when we uncover the *big* Preoccupation-breaking Emotional Appeal that fits a Subject to its Audience.

We *start* by investigating the Fatal Four one by one.

Let's take a look at Self-Preservation *first!*

How to Use Self-Preservation
as an Emotional Appeal

When the hour approached midnight and half the sleepy-eyed audience prepared to leave a club meeting, the chairman presented a speaker by saying: "I now introduce you to a KILLER FROM BROOKLYN!"

The audience hushed and forgot the late hour. Eyes focussed on a grim-faced, sharp-nosed man with heavy black eyebrows who menacingly kept his right hand in his right jacket pocket.

The man rose, removed his hand and smiled.

"I'm a killer, all right," he began, "a COCKROACH KILLER! I've been in the exterminating business for nearly twenty years. My name is . . ."

In less than ten seconds, the Self-Preservation Appeal, "I now introduce you to a KILLER FROM BROOKLYN," backed by a man's expression and gesture broke Preoccupation and changed an audience's mind about going home!

On radio, one afternoon, a literary critic opened a book discussion with: "Would you sometimes like to rock your baby to sleep WITH A BASEBALL BAT?"

Pow!

What a Preoccupation-breaking effect on mothers and others in the radio audience!

One mother, who told me about this attention-getter, said that she had been ironing when she heard the question. She reacted by pressing down harder and vehemently nodding while her seven-month-old baby continued to bawl away in his crib nearby!

A student once started a talk by removing a small paper bag from his pocket. He rattled the bag three or four times.

"In this bag," he announced, "are hours of relaxation, fresh air and good health. With good health, you'll probably live twenty years longer than you expect to right now. Yet," he emphasized, "the contents of this bag *cost less than five cents!*"

The attentive and curious audience watched the speaker pour the bag's contents into his left hand.

"Pigeon seed!" he exclaimed. "You use it when you raise pigeons. Raising pigeons is *my* hobby. Here's why it can be a healthful, stimulating hobby for you."

His audience was vitally interested because of the strong Self-Preservation Appeal!

There's Self-Preservation in every individual and in *every* Audience.

One rainy night, Miss R. boarded a crowded bus, bound for an unfamiliar neighborhood. The rain was heavy. It had come unexpectedly and she had neither umbrella, rubbers nor raincoat.

As she handed the bus driver a one dollar bill, Miss R. said: "Will you please call out at 55th Street?"

Giving her the change, the bus driver sighed. "Look, lady. I'll call out *if I remember*. When I have to make change, keep my eyes on the road and my foot near the brake, it's not so easy. It's a rotten, rainy night and about five other people want me to call out their stops. As I said, I'll call yours *if I remember!*"

Miss R. could have let the matter drop, with the hope that the driver would remember. If he didn't, she would be late for her appointment, possibly get off at the wrong stop and certainly get drenched in the steady rain.

"You'll call out at 55th Street, Driver," she assured him. "They're excavating near that corner. If you don't slow down and stop at 55th Street, *you may get killed!*"

With that, she dropped her fare into the box and pushed her way into the bus.

Although the bus driver must have travelled the route many times that very day without seeing *any* excavation, and although he forgot to call out stops for other passengers, he *did* slow down as he neared 55th Street.

"55th Street, Lady," he bellowed, "but where's the excavation?"

Miss R. thanked him, got off the bus and did not answer. She felt that Self-Preservation Emotional Appeal had done an excellent excavating job on the bus driver's Preoccupied mind!

When some of the other students questioned Miss R.'s application of Emotional Appeal in this instance, her reply was: "I used Emotional Appeal Technique on the bus driver because I didn't want to ruin an expensive hat and coat I was wearing for the first time. The other passengers who asked the driver to call out their stops had *their own reasons* for not wanting to get wet!"

Yes! Individuals *do* differ emotionally, particularly about their feelings of "right" and "wrong!"

Like the others in the essential Four, Self-Preservation Emotional Appeal, properly directed, motivates people to act, feel, or listen. It includes fears, hopes and wishes within attitudes about personal satisfactions, comforts, danger, pain, sickness, health, death or injury.

Self-Preservation Emotional Appeal includes love of parent for child, child for parent, master for pet, and related protective feelings. Desires for personal freedom and fears of imprisonment are in this Appeal; so are most aspects of religious belief and communication.

Within Self-Preservation are the emotional taps for living longer, greater enjoyments, doing things an easier, more pleasant way.

You're a housewife.

You know how much time and effort go into making apple pie. You have to prepare the flour, buy, carry, wash, peel and cut apples. When preparation is completed and the recipe is followed, you set the pie into the oven to bake. This work takes hours, and it *is* work!

Then you see an ad or a grocer or friend tells you about a new, prepared pie mix. "JUST ADD WATER" can be *big* emotional words to you.

These three words have made *millions* of housewives happy to buy or try a product, and they have had an equally good reaction on males.

The words have such Self-Preservation Emotional Appeal that they have been used to sell multi-millions of dollars' worth of pie and cake mixes, headache powders, soft drinks, ice-creams, gelatines, paints, soups, dyes, soap powders, mouth washes, glues and more.

They apply a Self-Preservation Appeal to your need!

They are words that swiftly and emotionally communicate the feeling that a product saves time, fuss, effort. Even to the woman who bakes in order to receive appreciation from her family or guests, a Recognition desire, the Self-Preservation response in the words, "Just add water" can be a big emotional incentive to give the mix a try!

We, as human beings, emotionally seek out the satisfactions more than the contents. This is why there are thousands of Emotional Appeals that can be uncovered to fit services, products and people to the minds of potential listeners, lovers, patients, clients and customers.

When we buy a candy bar, we usually act upon a Self-Preservation wish.

We remove the wrapper and take a first bite.

As we chew, do we reflect: "Mmm. Now I'm swallowing the chocolate . . . Mmm. This tastes like the caramel . . . here go the peanuts and stuff that holds the candy together . . . ?"

No!

If we feel at all, we feel in terms of: "Mmm. Good!" or "Delicious!" or "Satisfying!"

We *bought* the candy bar to satisfy a need. Perhaps we were hungry, needed more pep, wanted to satisfy a wish for "something sweet."

When the facts *actually* satisfy our needs, we get *greater* pleasure!

An elderly man once used the Self-Preservation Appeal on people many years younger.

Eighty-eight-year-old Mr. Y. had an ancient, broken-down country house. It needed painting and was located three miles from town. The steps were rickety and its porch was so small that no more than three people could be comfortably accommodated at the same time. The house was twice as old as its owner, who had asked a number of local real estate men to sell the property for him.

Months went by.

Although the realtors brought more than twenty-five prospects to visit Mr. Y.'s house, no one wanted to buy because of the poor first impression. The asking price was fair, so Mr. Y. decided that there must be something wrong with the way the real estate men did their selling.

Mr. Y. placed a small advertisement in two big city papers and received six replies. Before speaking to the first prospective buyer, he carefully reviewed his sales points. The greatest one about the old house, he reasoned, was the tiny porch, which was so situated that it got direct sunshine most of the day.

Since sunshine and good health usually go together, his first sentence to each prospect was: "This place is only for folks who'll live to be a hundred!"

Attention was immediate.

"Why?" asked each prospect.

"Because that porch *gets more square feet of sunshine per day than any other place in the state!*"

Within a few days, four of the six prospective buyers made offers for the old house!

Mr. Y. did not sell the rickety steps and the need for painting and the small porch. People weren't going to want those things *first*. He was certain, however, that they would be interested in good health, longer life—Self-Preservation.

He sold the sunshine first and the price last, and both he and the potential buyers were happier to talk business!

From a Self-Preservation standpoint, many people *regret* their ages. To others, good health at an advanced age is a personal point of pride.

In Winnipeg, Canada, a 101-year-old woman saw a sign in a restaurant:

```
TODAY ONLY

FREE MEAL TO ANYONE OVER 70

IF ACCOMPANIED BY PARENT
```

The lady pursed her lips, went home and returned with her 77-year-old daughter, Mary. They demanded the best meal in the restaurant, and the flabbergasted restaurant owner gave it to them!

Living longer and putting off death will always be powerful emotional segments in our makeup.

A man was reading a book of vital statistics. He scratched his head and turned to his wife.

"Here's an interesting statistic, Maggie," he said. "Every time I breathe, a person dies."

"Sorry to hear it," replied Maggie. "Whatever you do, please *don't breathe in my direction!*"

Emotionally, death is a fact of life.

We fear death and perhaps have seen death, but we cannot picture our own regardless of our age.

An RN told me about an elderly woman with a severe heart condition who required major surgery. The woman did not seem worried about the operation itself; she realized it was necessary. Her big fear was being anaesthetized.

Each time she was taken to the operating room, she quivered with fear about going to sleep. Because of her heart condition, the surgeons dared not become insistent. Meanwhile, the woman's condition became worse and operating room's time and personnel were wasted.

Upon a suggestion, Dr. S., the anaesthetist, went to the patient's room before another try. "Look at that rain outside," he remarked. "Do you know the thing to do on a day like this?"

The woman looked at him quizzically.

"Close your eyes and have a good, sound sleep. That," smiled the doctor, "is what *I* would do if I were you."

The elderly lady nodded, took a deep breath and closed her eyes.

She was wheeled to the operating room and had a very successful operation because a Self-Preservation desire had been made stronger than a fear!

Self-Preservation and the Fatal Four.

Self-Preservation Emotional Appeal is the reason why people would rather be entertained than educated, why enjoyment of community singing can make a mediocre meeting memorable, why the first few sentences in a play are harder to hear than the last few, why a widow makes men more standoffish than a divorcee, why a conscience-stricken person is frequently accident prone.

Like other members of the Fatal Four Emotional Appeals, Self-Preservation has a huge scope that often interlocks with another Appeal.

When someone holds a gun on you and warns: "This is a stick-up!" you'll react pronto. But a changing situation may overtly change the stimulus for your action!

Four customers and two tellers were in a small bank a few minutes before closing time. A lone gunman entered. "Put your hands up," he ordered. "All of you!"

The frightened customers and tellers complied.

Swiftly, the holdup man herded them towards a wall. He tensed his trigger finger and was about to bark another command when one customer looked at the gun, pointed and shouted: "That's not a real gun. Let's GET HIM!"

Customers and tellers turned instantly and pounced on the holdup man. Knocking the gun to the floor, they pummeled him into submission.

The customer who had made heroes out of six scared men bent over and picked up the gun. "G-gosh!" he faltered. "It's *real!*"

He hadn't been wearing his spectacles when he had said that it wasn't !

But here's what had *emotionally* happened:

"Put your hands up!" was a Self-Preservation Appeal that got an immediate response. Avoiding personal injury, bodily harm or death was much more important than Money loss. When the customer yelled: *"That's not a real gun! Let's get him!"* the desire to save Money and property *then* became *more* important than the fear of getting hurt or killed. So the customers and tellers jumped the gunman!

In our more usual daily living, Money Appeal may interrelate to Self-Preservation in a very different way.

Take, for example, the type of man or woman to whom making Money is of prime importance.

Rufus B. is offered a job that pays twenty dollars a week more than his present employment. He discusses the matter with his wife and a close friend. Both advise him *not* to take the job despite the salary increase; they know the reputation of his would-be employer.

Rufus is adamant, however, and takes the job. His *big* Emotional Appeal is Money. He is a "Money Cow" and wants the extra twenty dollars a week.

Drawbacks in working conditions and responsibilities become quickly apparent. Tenseness, unhappiness and other elements of Rufus B.'s Self-Preservation begin to gnaw as weeks become months. Much of this frustration shows in Rufus' behavior.

But Money is his *big* Emotional Appeal. He re-emphasizes to himself and others that he's "much better off" and "making darn sight more money, and that's the important thing!"

Do *you* know people like this? People to whom making money seems much more important than enjoying life?

Of course you do!

Other types of Self-Preservation-interrelationships concern the millions of us who possess such emotionally powerful wishes for physical satisfactions in sex, food, drink, relaxation and other enjoyments that our health suffers.

Like every one of the Fatal Four Emotional Appeals, Self-Preservation has two sides, the desire and the fear. It is always wise to keep the desire sense on the good health side. If we're too far off center, let's find a competent doctor. Thereafter, controlled communication with Emotional Appeal Technique can help us get much more enjoyment out of *whatever* state of health we have.

A "Money Cow" once proved this to a "Self-Preservation Cow!"

Wealthy Mr. O. was 25 pounds overweight. He loved food, relaxation and was notoriously lazy. Like most Self-Preservation Cows, he was particularly concerned about his health. He worried when he became short of breath after a walk, climbing a few steps or indulging in slight exercise. Although he had been medically advised to lose the 25 pounds and he wanted to he couldn't resist the pleasures of rich foods and overly large amounts of bread, cake, and sweets.

His friend, Mr. E., was a gambler. He disliked working for others and claimed that the only one who could work for him was "Lady Luck." Why did Mr. E. gamble? Because it was the fastest and easiest way to make Money! He was a "Money Cow" who would bet on horses, cards, dogs, dice and anything else that he felt could make money.

One day, Mr. E., the gambler, met fat Mr. O. "My friend," he laughed, "every time I see you I think of a balloon growing bigger and bigger. When are you going to start losing a couple of pounds?"

"Not just a couple of pounds," sadly replied Mr. O. "Twenty-five pounds!" He shrugged. "I can't enjoy what I like to eat and do and lose that kind of weight too!"

An idea occurred to Mr. E. "I'm a gambling man, Mr. O. I'll bet you two hundred dollars that I can make you lose the twenty-five pounds."

"I'll take that bet," chuckled Mr. O. "What are the conditions?"

"Very simple. First, I want to weigh you. Then, you must do exactly as I tell you for eight weeks. At the end of that time, if you don't lose the weight, I pay. If you lose the 25 pounds, you pay me."

Mr. O. agreed.

A small metal valise was padlocked to Mr. O.'s right wrist. Mr. E. retained the key. Three days later, Mr. O. was frantic. "This valise is getting heavier and heavier. I eat with it, sleep with it, even shave with it on. Please take it off. It weighs a *ton!*"

"Not a ton," sighed Mr. E. "It weighs exactly twenty-five pounds, the amount of the extra weight you're carrying. Now, take your doctor's diet and stick to it. Just leave the metal valise on as a reminder!"

Mr. O. was so anxious to get rid of the weight on his wrist that he lost the twenty-five pounds in *six* weeks.

Mr. E. won the two hundred dollars.

Both were happy.

These two people had two different *big* reasons for their different actions in the same situation, yet each was satisfied with the result. Mr. O.'s big appeal was Self-Preservation; the interruption of many of his enjoyments by the weight on his wrist hastened completion of his objective. According to the terms of the bet, he had to wear the valise for eight weeks or lose the twenty-five pounds before then, so he swiftly realized the Self-Preservation advantages of *losing* the bet. Mr. E. had made sure *he* would win the money by using Self-Preservation, the right Emotional Appeal for wealthy Mr. O.!

When there is no physical reason for laziness, the "lazy person" is principally the Self-Preservation type who is rapid with excuses for by-passing chores, helping others or just not working.

I was told about an outside painter whose boss caught him enjoying a nap when he was supposed to be painting a fence.

"Why aren't you working like the other men?" demanded the employer.

Pointing to the lovely Spring sky, the painter philosophized: "Boss, *who but an idiot would try to make money on a day so beautiful?*"

He, you see, acted like a Self-Preservation Cow not a Money Cow!

Words and expressions like "Feet Hurt?", "Instant Relief," "Is a Painful Headache Getting You Down?", "Want to Feel Stronger?", "Babies Wanted," "Need More Pep?", "How to Rid Yourself of that Awful Backache" are all of attention-getting, activating Emotional Appeal when Self-Preservation is the tie-in. Even in dandruff removers, labor-saving devices, safety pins or germ-killing mouthwashes, an adroitly chosen Self-Preservation Appeal may in response make the mind receptive to the speaker, subject, product or service.

Love of parent for child, or child for parent, is part of Self-Preservation.

You're a parent. Imagine how you would react to: "Would you want your child to wear crutches?" or, "Isn't it wonderful when your child says 'I love you?'"

The *fear* approach and the *desire* approach of these two are *both* in Self-Preservation.

Self-Preservation is one of the Fatal Four *b-i-g* reasons why *you* will listen and why others will listen to you! Is there a strong Self-Preservation Emotional Appeal that fits your Subject to your Audience? If there is *use* it!

Let us take the situation of the radio literary critic who had that powerful Preoccupation-breaker for the woman who was ironing.

His *Subject?* A book entitled: "Bringing Up Your Baby."

His *Audience?* Mothers mainly.

Right off, the desires and fears in Money, Romance and Recognition would tend to be of lesser emotional importance than Self-Preservation, which contains "love of parent for child."

Out of the Self-Preservation emotional relationship between Speaker and Listener, he created: *"Would you sometimes like to rock your baby to sleep with a baseball bat?"*

Chances of making his listeners *want* to listen were excellent, because the Emotional Appeal, Self-Preservation, was right!

You have often heard the saying: "Blood is thicker than water." Emotionally, it *really* is!

Perhaps you think your father, mother or child is terribly *wrong* in a particular situation. When an "outsider" says so, you'll tend to defend your parent or child because Recognition will emotionally bolster your Self-Preservation!

Your dog may give you comfort, "understanding" or protection. When there is danger to your pet, or a strange and bigger dog approaches, you'll protect your own, won't you?

You won't fight this desire. It's part of your Self-Preservation!

Religion and self-preservation.

Religionists use Self-Preservation Appeal more than any other.

A "sin" usually relates the possibility of punishment in a *physical* as well as a *moral* sense. There is such a fear of the consequences of doing wrong that religion often brings about a desire to do *right*.

A minister became perturbed, I was told, because of parking in front of his church. He contacted the local police and "No Parking" signs were posted.

This had little effect. Bumper-to-bumper parking continued.

The minister then had all signs changed to read only: *Thou Shalt Not Park!"* and motorists stopped parking in front of the church!

Religion can be a great comfort, because it is emotionally protective. To keep it glowing, it must be lived and efficiently communicated by clergymen.

E. had some interesting thoughts along this line when he took one of my Courses together with his wife. Professionally, he was employed by one of the largest church groups in America.

After a few class sessions, E. came to me and said: "As you have probably noticed, my wife and I are quite devout. We are students of religion and have attended many churches of other faiths. Now we have come to an important conclusion.

"The average clergyman," he emphasized, "doesn't *know* how to make us listen. He needs much more Emotional Appeal! He urges people to go to church or synagogue, but when he gets them there, his sermons seldom break their Preoccupation. He's speaking, but they aren't *really* listening! When they leave church, they shake his hand and often remark: "Nice sermon, Reverend," for their own personal reasons. Actually, the well-intentioned clergyman *hasn't made them listen to anything except what was on their own minds before they entered the church!"*

On the clergyman's side, there may be far more "dozing off" than may be realized.

According to the Associated Press, the minister of a Walla

Walla, Washington, church stated: "Sunday morning we tape-recorded the service. That afternoon, I turned on the recorder and sat down to listen. *I went sound asleep in the middle of the sermon!*"

The need for more Preoccupation-breaking Emotional Appeal in religion and other areas of communication has become more and more obvious. Many of us have, at one time or another, expressed our own feelings.

Two women, evidently returning from a shopping tour, rested their packages on the floor as they stood next to me on a subway train.

"Are you going to church this Sunday?" one asked the other.

"Of course I am. I've got a new hat, haven't I? And anyway, *church is the one place where I can sleep with my eyes wide open!*"

It wouldn't be if *her* priest or minister knew how to say it with Emotional Appeal!

Crime and emotional appeal.

A shapely, 20-year old girl answered a "Help Wanted" ad for a receptionist. She made a phone call and went to a two-room office for an interview.

After a few minutes, her interviewer barred the inner door and tried to attack her.

She pleaded, squirmed, bit and struggled—but could not tear herself loose from his grasp.

Suddenly she stopped resisting and warned: "My real age is *sixteen*. Let me go, or you know what will happen to you!"

The Emotional Appeal in the warning stopped his advances *immediately* and he continued to apologize as the girl ran from the office.

Fear of a statutory rape conviction had instantly changed his mind!

Law-abiding people have innate Self-Preservation fears about arrest and imprisonment; so do criminals. The criminal, in fact, usually devotes more time to planning his *escape* than planning his crime, because "crime does not pay" when he is caught!

A large and busy ladies' specialty store was losing more than fifty thousand dollars a year because of shoplifting. Although store detectives were always on guard and mixed with customers, losses and embarrassment mounted. If a detective approached, detained or followed a shoplifter, other shoplifters frequently made off with merchandise.

The store owner replaced personnel, increased the number of store detectives and bought detection equipment without appreciably reducing his shoplifting losses.

In desperation, he tried a completely different approach to the problem.

He cleared merchandise, racks and displays away from the center of the store's street floor and had these items moved to other locations. Into this large central area, which faced all four sides of the floor, he placed colorful, leather-type sofas and chairs. Smoking stands and ash trays were also made available.

Advertisements were published in local papers and mounted in the store's outside show windows. These invited the public to "Come in and use our comfortable Main Floor Lounge Area. Rest while shopping, meet your friends . . . or just relax!"

Seventy to a hundred people a day accepted the store's invitation. In less than a month, a daily average of one hundred and sixty met, rested, gossiped, stared or enjoyed a cigarette *while commanding an almost unobstructed view of all four sides of the Main Floor, merchandise and people.*

Store sales increased and shoplifting losses sharply decreased!

A shoplifter does not steal when watched.

Like a pickpocket and many other criminals, a shoplifter's biggest fear is getting "caught in the act!"

Because of the large number of people in the "Main Floor Lounge Area" during store hours, it was possible for as many as *fifty pairs* of eyes to be on a shoplifter's movements. Since the shoplifter had no way of knowing *which* eyes belonged to store detectives, shoplifting became a dangerous risk. Rather than take such an "unnecessary" risk, shoplifters stayed away.

In the first eight months alone, this Self-Preservation Emotional Appeal was *worth* more than Fifty Thousand Dollars to the store owner!

Now, let's talk about Money.

Let us *talk.*

The pages that follow will prove that it costs too much to *worry* about it!

Money as an Emotional Appeal in Our Relationships with Others

Have you ever seen an ad like this?

The Reason Why

The reason why I have hitherto been able to sell my goods so much cheaper than anyone else is that I am a bachelor. I do not need to make a profit for the maintenance of a wife and children.

It is now my duty to inform you that this advantage will shortly be withdrawn. I am about to be married.

I therefore urge you to save money and make your purchases at once at the old rate.

O. Kayser

Without frills, the Money Appeal captured attention and stimulated interest. People came to Mr. Kayser's store to "buy bargains!"

A Texas town found use for the Money Appeal in another way. Its Preoccupation-breaking advantages were quick to prevent accidents and stop speeding!

Out-of-area motorists sped through the town in such numbers that local police could not completely control the situation. Investigation showed that the only police warnings to vehicles were signs saying:

```
SPEED
LIMIT
—
20 mph
```

Upon a suggestion, the signs were changed to:

```
20 mph
or
$19.90!
```

The speeders got the idea immediately!

Samuel Johnson once said: "Money and Time are the heaviest burdens of life; the unhappiest of all mortals are those who have more of either than they know how to use."

We mortals never seem to have enough *Time* or Money. We try to get more of each and start by fearing that we will secure neither!

Time is Money to many.

Some of us cheat on one or the other; some cheat on both. Some find such cheating shameful.

Because of our individual emotional differences, we may gain satisfaction, feel guilty, or roll out a conscience-stricken carpet for our Money Preoccupation.

An Oregon woman chose the last.

She worked for the motor vehicle division. During the one year she was so employed, she wasted more time during coffee-breaks than she should have. After convincing herself that this was cheating, she mailed a $95 check to her employer.

This was payment for the time she had "borrowed!"

Bald members of the Ohio Legislature, not too long ago, called for an inquiry into the price of haircuts! They drew up a resolution that said: "It is . . . commensurate with justice, equity and fair play . . . that a reduction of price be effected for those of us who—through no fault of our own—are endowed with that badge of experience and ability called baldness."

Although Money cost was the *big* stimulus, you will again observe that Emotional Appeal is in the lives of everyone, even legislators.

Do you notice a self-justifying desire for Recognition in the words: ". . . those of us who . . . are endowed with that *badge of experience and ability called baldness?*"

In politics or out, making or saving Money will have universal Emotional Appeal.

An organization was formed in Stuttgart, called the *League of the Long*. It consisted of men 6′ 2″ and over, and women 5′ 11″ and taller. Members estimated that it cost 15% more to feed a big man and 10% more for a big woman, as compared to people of average stature and appetite.

The *League* appealed to the government for tax reductions because they ate more than other people!

If *you* had to vote on this, what would your decision be? Would you take your own appetite and size into account?

Emotionally, you would!

At tax time, Money thoughts and actions create many problems.

Tax collectors are *emotional;* they deal with *people* who are emotional!

A man claimed tax exemption for his mother. Internal Revenue men found that the mother had been dead for more than ten years.

When questioned on why he claimed the tax exemption, he sadly replied: *"Mother is still alive in my heart!"*

An anonymous Colorado woman phoned the Internal Revenue Department to secure information about the amount of income tax she would have to pay.

"How much will be due on a $75,000 income?" she wanted to know.

The tax expert did some rapid calculating.

"What about a $150,000 income?" she asked.

The tax man gave her an estimate. "Lady," he wondered, "is there a special reason for asking these questions?"

"Special reason? Of course there is," replied the woman. "I'm trying to decide whether to buy *one* or *two* tickets on the Irish Sweepstakes!"

Money is a poignant attention-holder and attention-getter even via sight and sound.

Want a group of otherwise Preoccupied people to pay attention to you? Wave a handful of paper money in front of them!

Have you ever inhaled a hope of expectancy when you saw a wallet, package, purse or coins lying on a sidewalk? Can you recall your feeling when your last year's coat unexpectedly revealed a forgotten twenty-dollar bill?

How many times has the word "FREE!" taken your attention? Have you ever been activated to turn towards the identifying jangle of coins dropping?

Thousands of other Money reactions are an emotional part of us, even when Money is not our *big* Emotional Appeal. When it *is* we can go to ridiculous extremes.

The "What's in it for me?" person is always among us. He or she happens to have Money Appeal more emotionally inbred than someone else. Sometimes, this Money Cow may be emotionally tempted far away from pasture!

A caterer was locally known as dollar-hungry. Townspeople with whom he had dealt sharply decided to "teach him a lesson."

They engaged an out-of-town actor to register at a local hotel and pose as the affluent head of a cat food company. The "cat food executive" called on the caterer and asked him to plan an elegant banquet for the next Saturday night.

"How many people do you expect?" asked the caterer, taking notes.

"People?" smiled the actor. "There will be no people. This is a banquet for *cats!*"

When the caterer raised his eyebrows, the "cat food executive" instantly lowered them by solemnly counting off one hundred dollars. "This is a part payment," he said. "The balance will be paid immediately after the banquet!"

This made the unusual banquet far more palatable to the caterer. He began to recommend delicacies that cats would enjoy and suggested the inclusion of the "cat food company's own products."

The "executive" agreed and complimented him for ". . . such fine, business-like thinking!"

Before concluding the first meeting with the caterer, the actor also ordered a menu printed in blue and red. These, he claimed, were the favorite colors of the sixty prize cats who were being invited!

The caterer acquiesced and probably saw an additional opportunity to increase the bill.

On Friday morning before the banquet, the "cat food executive" phoned. "I forgot something," he told the caterer. "This will probably cost another hundred dollars or so, but I'll pay for it."

Anticipating an even bigger profit, the caterer accepted a request to "furnish place cards and seat the cats formally, with each male in a place next to a female!"

When the banquet evening came, everything was ready, but only the caterer, his staff and a local newspaperman showed up.

The "cat food executive" had checked out of his hotel and left town an hour before banquet time!

What was the emotional reason behind engaging the actor to pose as a "cat food executive?"

Undoubtedly *Recognition!*

The people who engaged him had wanted to "get even" because their emotional target—the caterer—had probably outsmarted *them* in the past. Now, by outsmarting *him,* they hoped to do some ego-bolstering for themselves!

The caterer was a Money Cow—but "Money Cows" are *not* necessarily unfriendly or dishonest people. Neither are Cows within *any* segment of the Fatal Four. He may have merely made some self-styled "good" businessmen look "bad."

So they hatched this costly "plot" to make themselves look better in their own eyes!

Did the caterer's embarrassment actually "teach him a lesson?"

No.

Neither a caterer nor a cat will change his big emotional spots once they are established!

Our need for money, rewards and possessions.

Money is often the most direct of the Fatal Four Emotional Appeals. It is understood and reacted to by everyone.

Even our over-all way of living communicatively mirrors the depth to which Money motivational strengths and weaknesses are ingrained.

A fifty-year-old man was taken into court, charged with being a bookmaker. The sum of $16,800 had been found in his quarters. When the man told his story, however, the judge and every spectator in the courtroom was convinced by his explanation.

He had made a "fine art of saving." On a $56 weekly salary, he had actually saved the $16,800!

How? By ". . . never dating women . . . never drinking or smoking . . . wearing patched and re-patched underwear . . . using his father's shoes for work . . . wearing the same suit for 13 years . . . borrowing razor blades . . . charging 12% interest on a 15-cent loan to his aged grandmother . . . and never enjoying himself with anything that cost more than 56 cents!"

Despite his miserliness, he admitted that he gained a great deal of satisfaction from the progress he had made in his "fine art."

Money is an emotional need. All of us want to make Money or get its equivalent in rewards, property or possessions, and many people will be quick to tell you how hard they work for the money they get.

When a female star of the Metropolitan Opera was criticized because she made more in a month than the President of the United States earned in a year, she commented: "Well, tell him to sing *Norma* next season!"

Everybody wants Money and the security it seems to promise and we usually try to make Money with as little expenditure of laborious Self-Preservation effort as possible. Some of us want to save it, some want to spend it for desires or satisfactions.

The deep wish, want and desire is to have Money. The fear, hate or uncertainty is to be without Money or to part with it unexpectedly. We are thus emotionally receptive to the person who suggests ways for us to get more.

Late one night, a "practical businessman" supervised some employees who pulled up a section of railroad track on a seldom-used spur of a New York railroad. The men were hard at work with crowbars and acetylene torches, ripping up tracks, when a pair of policemen in a patrol car drove over to investigate.

The businessman, a junk dealer, explained that he had made a contract with a representative of the railroad. He had even had the contract *notarized!*

Investigation revealed that no "representative of the railroad" had authorized the sale, under the terms of which the junk dealer had paid a bargain price for the first eight tons of trackage, with the balance of the spur line trackage available so long as he would pay for it.

Meanwhile, the junk dealer had sold over eighteen tons of the trackage at a handsome profit!

Why had the junk dealer bought the tracks without taking enough time to *carefully* study the matter?

He was a "practical business man." The Money Appeal had top response rate and pierced his Preoccupation. The trackage was a "bargain." Even before parting with his money the confidence man's words and actions made him *visualize* the profit he could make by re-selling the trackage.

His *want* was to make Money. His *fear* was that if he didn't snap up the "bargain," somebody else would!

The confidence man, posing as a "representative of the railroad," knew the junk dealer's most responsive attitude. *It was so much like his own!*

A man who owns his own business tends to be particularly interested in making Money, so the "confidence game" was accordingly set up.

People never change emotionally, so schemes for tapping our hopes and wishes will always exist, with phoney stock promotions, get-rich-quick ideas, fixed sporting events, "sure things," gold bricks and many more hoodwinkers.

Are *intelligent* men and women prey to the confidence man's delusions? Of course.

The Emotional Appeal of Money is intrenched in the rich and the poor, the intellectual and the uneducated, the big crook and the little one.

A lady was supposed to have dropped a dime into the hat of a man who pitifully leaned on a pair of crutches.

"It must be awful to be lame," consoled the lady.

"It is," nodded the beggar.

"Wouldn't it be worse if you were blind?"

"Yes, Lady," was the reply. "When I was blind, people kept giving me foreign coins!"

Can a "successful" criminal utilize his abilities for more honest enterprise? He can, but there is too much *work* attached to being legitimate. Most often the crooked type of person is not emotionally built this way!

The Money Appeal—even in the sense of reward—is planted in children, raised in adults. The most honorable individuals, businesses and organizations have frequently used this Appeal to attract attention, create desire or stimulate buying action.

In prize contests, the communicative emotional power of money and reward is almost unbelievable. Better than forty million dollars worth of prizes are given away in the United States in a single year! These prizes include lump sums of Money, annual incomes, income-producing oil wells, securities, mink coats, ancient fire engines, thoroughbred animals, real estate, products, services and appliances.

Contestants are people from every imaginable walk of life!

A soft drink company ran a national $50,000 Sweepstakes." The winner could have all the silver dollars that he or she could shovel in five minutes. Other prizes included all the silver dollars that a winner could shovel in three minutes and one minute.

Contestants spent over $123,000 in postage just to mail in entry blanks!

To estimate how much money it would pay out for these first three prizes, the contest sponsor used its own shovellers. The expert estimate was that the five-minute winner would shovel in about $13,000, the three-minute winner some $9,000 and the one-minute winner around $3,000. Together, this would total approximately $25,000.

In the given time, the actual three winners shovelled in about $35,000!

One of the three contestants had practiced shovelling iron washers in her basement all winter!

And the soft drink's sales?

Directly or indirectly as a result of the contest, sales jumped up close to 38 per cent!

The fear of money or property loss.

Emotionally, the fear of Money or property loss is as great as the desire for Money or property gain.

Today, it is considered prudent business practice to use experienced credit investigators and agencies in order to check on a company or individual as a credit risk. From the report, opinion is formed, loans granted or denied, business and favors transacted or not.

Multi-million-dollar banks and corporations have these Money-loss fears; so do multi-emotional millions of individuals.

Do you know certain people to whom you would not hasten to lend Money or property?

All through the centuries there have been people like these. However, the fact that a person lacks Money or property is not always a sign that he lacks character!

When Abraham Lincoln lived in Springfield, Illinois, he received a letter from an eastern firm asking for a credit reference on a man he knew. This was his reply:

> Yours of the 10th received.
>
> First of all, he has a wife and a baby; together they ought to be worth $500,000 to any man. Second, he has an office in which there is a table worth $1.50 and three chairs worth, say, $1.
>
> Last of all, there is in one corner a large rat-hole, which will bear looking into.
>
> Respectfully,
>
> A. Lincoln

Money and property-wise, outward appearances do not tell an emotional *inside* story! For good or bad, though, retention of Money or property will always have emotional meaning.

Over a long period, I have asked lecture audiences, student groups, social, business and professional acquaintances for an *immediate* response to this question:

"If a fire broke out in your home and you were alone, what would you do first?"

An overwhelming majority of responses indicated that the listeners would make an effort to save certain personal possessions before trying to escape!

Which possessions?

"I have a foreign stamp collection. It took me more than twenty years to put it together."

"My new fur coat. I wouldn't want anything to happen to it!"

"Three hundred in cash. I've been wanting to put it in a bank for months. This will make me remember to do it!"

"My mandolin. I like to play it, especially when I'm angry. It helps to cool me off!"

"Two of my new suits. I get compliments whenever I wear them."

"My diamond rings. Even if the house burned to the ground and I had to wait for the insurance money, I could raise cash on those two rings!"

"I'd be sure to have my wallet. It's important to be able to lay your hands on some money in an emergency!"

"My boat tickets to Europe. My wife and I have been saving for them for years. Even if my house burned, we'd still go!"

"My book collection. I've never carried enough fire insurance. Some of the books can't be replaced. They'd go up in smoke in no time!"

"I have a certain harmonica. It's my good luck charm and I've been carrying it for three years now. If I ever leave the house without it, I go back—even if I know it will make me late for work. See? Here it is!"

If a fire broke out in your home and you were alone, what would you do first?

Think! Which of your personal possessions would *you* try to save *before* trying to make your escape?

Why waste wins attention.

A man walked into a service station while his car was being serviced.

There, he saw a uniformed mechanic carefully change the oil in a green sedan, test the motor, clean the upholstery after thoroughly scrubbing his hands, check air pressure in all tires including the spare, eradicate four stubborn rust spots on the rear bumper and two on the front.

The man approached his friend, the service manager, and pointed to the energetic mechanic working on the green sedan. "I've been watching that fellow, Mike. He certainly looks like a good mechanic."

"He is," laughed the service manager, "especially when he's working on his *own* car!"

On one side of the Money Appeal, there is the desire to save money and keep our property in good condition; on the other side, we have the fear of unexpected expense, money loss and property damage.

The owner of a parking lot in a large city used this knowledge to fine advantage with his own problem.

Located two blocks or so away from other lots nearer to the center of activity, many transient motorists preferred not to walk such additional distance. Because of this, there were many days when the parking lot was not even half-filled.

To stimulate business, the owner offered discounts, reduced parking fees, passed out circulars and put up larger "P-A-R-K-I-N-G" and "P-A-R-K H-E-R-E" signs.

None of these actions helped until he added a *word* . . . one word with the *right* Emotional Appeal.

All signs were changed to "P-R-O-T-E-C-T-E-D P-A-R-K-I-N-G."

Thereafter, motorists became willing to walk the extra two blocks for "protected parking," and there were days when the lot could not accommodate all the motorists who wanted to park. The Money Appeal "listening factor" of *Protected* Parking" had set up a competitive advantage for the owner of the parking lot.

The negative side of the Money Appeal, fear of loss or waste, can offer as much Preoccupation-holding and Preoccupation-breaking power as the positive side, but care must be taken to control and anticipate the follow-through.

The advertising committee for a famous West Coast fruit crop announced that it was seeking a new advertising agency. Many agencies were screened and the committee's choice narrowed to two.

Both were invited to appear before the full industry committee of fruit farmers.

One agency principal pointed out the danger of selecting an agency which might have preconceived ideas. To illustrate the point, he showed them a beautiful, original oil painting of a bowl of fruit.

Throwing the painting to the floor and grinding his heel on it, he emphatically warned: "Good as this painting may seem, it isn't worth anything. Neither we nor any other advertising agency can create art and copy in advance. We must know your problems *first!*"

His visual approach held the farmer committee's attention from start to finish, but the thought of an evidently valuable painting being thrown to the floor and ruined brought *waste* into the picture.

Emotionally, it enabled the committee of fruit farmers to "feel" this advertising agency wasting *their* money and property! When it came to a decision, the other agency got the contract!

When Money-waste is properly directed, it can retain Preoccupation-breaking advantages of Money gain, even as a mass Appeal.

Cecil B. De Mille, one of the most successful Hollywood producers, showed this in making many of his films.

He once started work on a motion picture that he thought was destined to be a box office smash. Although he liked the story and the star, as time went by he was not entirely convinced that the movie going public was being given enough advance reasons to remember and see the film.

He bought a chinchilla-trimmed nightgown for $1,500. In the picture, he had the star hold it for a few moments while dragging it across the bedroom floor!

Even Hollywood people were aghast.

Such waste! Such unheard-of extravagance!

Newspapers and columnists picked up the story. Some editorialized on wastefulness and used De Mille's $1,500 nightgown as a classic example.

Movie goers took sides; many who had private arguments on the subject went to see the picture.

When the box office gross was totalled, it was discovered that the Preoccupation-breaking, discussion-holding Emotional Appeal of a wastefully lavish $1,500 nightgown had added an estimated $250,000 to the motion picture's income!

Waste can win as much attention as economy.

Both are phases of Money, one of the Fatal Four Emotional Appeals that undercoat the reasons why we act, "feel" or listen!

Thoughts that help stifle money worries.

Even with the comparatively small percentage of people who claim they have enough, Money is a four star general Preoccupation-breaker-and-holder. It is so indelibly woven into our living pattern that more adults worry about Money than most other phases of their existence.

"O Money, Money, Money," wrote Ogden Nash, "I am not necessarily one of those who think thee holy—but I often stop to wonder how thou canst go out so fast when thou comest in so slowly!"

The Emotional Appeal of Money refers to saving, buying, winning, investing and earning. Money wishes, fears, and desires embrace property ownership, economy and feelings about personalized phases of "future security."

To many of us, Money is the *big* Emotional Appeal, despite various degrees of sprinklings of the other three Appeals.

Individualized Money beliefs and attitudes flow from our lips and bodies in words, actions and reactions that range from a purchase of eggs to the more complicated aspects of daily living.

With objective observation, you can readily ascertain whether Money is the dominating communicative Emotional Appeal in any person.

Mrs. B. is a housewife, mother and Money Cow.

Her late parents had been poor. Her father was a seldom employed, frustrated actor, whose most animated performances were given at home while standing on the three-foot, circular pink stage that was their kitchen table. Whiskey was his prompter; wife and daughter were his most frequent "captive audience." Mrs. B.'s mother had been a breadwinner who had so exhausted herself as a laundress that little time or money remained for her daughter's physical or emotional needs.

Mrs. B. had worked since the age of twelve. She had married at nineteen.

Long before her marriage to Mr. B. she had resolved to give her own family "some of the things I never got when I was growing up!"

She had inadvertently hastened her marriage on the day when she showed Mr. B.'s mother how to economize on scrambled eggs.

"Use soaked white bread as a stretcher," she had advised. "Just cut off the crusts. The scrambled eggs taste just as good, look so fluffy. Remember how much can be saved when you have a large family!"

Mr. B.'s mother, father and two older sisters soon found themselves boasting to neighbors and friends about the "smart manager he's keeping company with. She makes her own clothes, re-makes old clothes so you'd never know. She lives on a strict budget and even knows how to save on soap. Can you imagine how wonderful she'll be running a house? You just don't see girls like her around."

They urged Mr. B. to "marry her before somebody else does!"

Mr. B., an easygoing Self-Preservation Cow who had usually acceded to his family's whims without a whimper, asked her.

So they married.

From the outset of their honeymoon, Mrs. B. emotionally evidenced the *big* Appeal with which she had become overpossessed. She became a penny-pinching, bargain-hunting, corner-cutting do-it-yourselfer.

When a grocer, druggist or seller suggested the larger size and said: "It costs a few cents extra, but see how much more you get!" . . . she took swift action. Any "Money Back Guarantee" instantly broke her Preoccupation and took her a long way along the path towards decision. Sales that screamed anything along the line of "ONCE-IN-A-LIFETIME CHANCE TO BUY AT THESE PRICES!" made her do a double-take!

One of her clothes closets was filled from the bottom to the top with boxes of paper napkins that she had bought at a "sensational bargain!"

Her 12-year-old daughter had often asked for permission to move her clothes to this closet and had suggested that the napkins be given to relatives and friends as gifts.

To this, Mrs. B. had retorted: "You mind your business. I paid for those napkins. They didn't come *free!*"

The growing child's desire to have more room for her clothes was completely disregarded.

With aggravating repetition, Mrs. B. had tried to instill economy and avoidance of waste into her daughter, nine-year-old son and husband. To all of them, she had become tense, taut and fretful. As with many such people, living on a budget and being economical had become compulsions, not necessities. Mrs. B. was allowing her attitudes to close her open-mindedness, self-center her outlook, harm her health, and lessen her husband's respect and desire for her.

Mr. B. found himself losing his easy going temperament.

He loved his children, but hated his home. Three nights a week, he ate in restaurants. Such dining was followed by "club meetings and card parties" to avoid coming home to his wife's harangues on economy. He owned a retail store and earned an ample living, but he and Mrs. B. had not enjoyed an intimacy for at least two years.

"All she wants to talk about is money, even when we're in bed," he once sighed ruefully. "She sleeps next to me, but she could just as well be a hundred miles away!"

Like thousands of husbands and wives, the B.'s were merely "going through the motions." Life was a breathing-in, breathing-out monotony. Sundays and holidays were merely "other days in the same old week."

The B.'s had little zest for living, because they weren't using words and actions to effectively communicate, motivate and emotionally understand each other.

After listening to Mr. B., my image of Mrs. B. was that of a tall, thin, scroogey woman with a long, thin face and a bun on her head!

The woman I met for the first time was a neatly dressed, pretty brunette minus makeup and style additives. She was about thirty-six, of medium height. Her lips were tight and stonily creased in a pair of corner puckers.

Mrs. B. was furious.

Why had her husband spoken to me about their worsening relationship? Merely because Emotional Appeal Technique had helped so many others in problems of communication was no reason why it could help them! On she blazed.

After nearly three memorable minutes of staccato criticism and voice crescendos, she burst into tears and spoke a half-whispered apology.

She admitted that Money was her chief concern. Much of this Preoccupation had been created by childhood and early work experiences.

When she married and became a mother, she had her first continuous opportunity to direct her Money attitudes at people who could not help but "captively" listen. She had been enjoying this more and more, while her husband and children had been reacting less and less favorably.

From time to time, any person may become Preoccupied with Money fears and desires, because Money is one of the Fatal Four Preoccupations against which there is no immediate emotional defense!

When, however, our Money Preoccupation repeatedly reveals itself in behavior that has a bad emotional effect on others, it is certain to damage us too!

In Mrs. B.'s situation and multi-thousands more, such emotional damage may frequently be stopped almost as soon as it can be uncovered.

By understanding and applying Emotional Appeal, you can provide yourself with *Two Thoughts That Help Rid Yourself of Money Worries:*

1.–MONEY VALUES AND ATTITUDES ARE BETTER LEARNED BY *SPENDING* THAN BY SAVING!

Want to be more economical? Consider *first* what you have . . . *then* how to expend it for your best emotional benefit.

Save by curbing spending on small items. Since there is a tendency to attach less emotional significance to these, such behavior will rarely cause stress, and small items soon add up to big savings.

When worried about buying a *large* item, seek out opinions of others while getting facts for yourself. These opinions may not agree with your own attitudes, but they are certain to enter your Preoccupied mind.

If you do *not* make the purchase, you eliminate causes for attached Money worries and feel that you are doing the *right* thing. When you *do* buy, you will enjoy the purchase *more—* because you have increased confidence and assurance.

Either way, you learn economy by spending—even if it is only the expenditure of Time. And, by the time your actions culminate in decision, your Money worry will usually have left!

2.–*"LIVING ON A BUDGET" IS GOOD ONLY IF YOU CAN ENJOY IT.*

Budget "living" is meaningless unless you can adjust your emotional needs to your budget's limitations and objectives.

If this adjustment does not assure a fair measure of pleasure, you may emotionally lose far more than the money or property "gain."

The individuals who can enjoy "living on a budget" start with a strong drive and intensify their hope for achievement as they go along. This makes the desire for Recognition a powerful motivating ally and removes all or most of the feeling of frustration that may arise. With this approach, it will be more pleasurable to "live on a budget" and more emotionally profitable to accomplish what you are after.

Otherwise, why suffer frustration and upset?

"Living on a budget" is *good* living only if you can enjoy doing so!

Through the years, I have recommended these Two Thoughts that Help Rid Yourself of Money Worries. They have made many people aware that Money attitudes must be communicated on the basis of their own motivations and those with whom they interact.

Often a listener may have far more or less Money desire or fear than a speaker—another reason why it is so vital to uncover and identify the *big* "listening factor" when you communicate. If you do not, you will neither "reach" your listener nor understand yourself and you can unnecessarily intensify a Money worry.

How Emotional Appeal Technique rapidly rids you of fears, worries, and upsets will be discussed at greater length in Chapter Eight. Meanwhile, it will be wise to make a careful note of the aforementioned Two Thoughts about Money:

1.—Money values and attitudes are better learned by *spending* than by saving.

2.—"Living on a budget" is good only if you can enjoy doing so.

They will help rid yourself of Money worries and provide emotional "first aid" when you want it!

Applying Romance Emotional Appeal to Our Dealings with People

Thirty-two-year-old James D. was a "50-50" partner in a small factory. He carried more than his share of the work and had invested most of the capital.

When it came to management decisions, there was little mutuality. His "equal" partner insisted upon the final word and got it by hinting that the partnership might otherwise dissolve. Such a dissolution could wipe out nearly all of James' assets, since the business was still very young.

James conceded to his partner's whims and brooded.

He found a pair of pretty ears to listen to his woes when he found Grace, an attractive 28-year-old blonde. In less than six months, they decided to announce their engagement at a party to be given by her mother.

"They're not married yet," confided Grace's mother to some of her friends, half in jest. "James shouldn't be given extra opportunities to turn his eyes in the wrong direction. There won't be another pretty and unmarried girl at the engagement party. I'll see to that!"

Grace's "noncompetitive" cousin Barbara was invited.

She wasn't married; she wasn't pretty. Very plain, neat and unglamorous. Except for a semitransparent, scalloped lace collar, the jacket above her navy blue skirt resembled a white middy blouse.

Age-wise, she was three months older than Grace; with her

straight, flat Buster Brown haircut, she appeared three years younger!

Grace held James' right hand possessively. "When we're married," she said so that all could hear, "it's going to be a 50-50 partnership in every way. Right, James?"

Barbara spoke up before James' automatic nod had lowered his chin.

"That's not how it's going to be when *I* get married," she announced, having heard about the aggravation that James was having with his "50-50" partner. "In my home, my husband is going to be the boss and make the decisions!"

James pursed his lips and appreciatively raised his brows.

Grace looked shocked.

The guests became more attentive!

Barbara continued: "And when I'm married, I won't say 'No' to my husband. What I have and can give will be his—whenever and however he wants it. That includes my financial help, my physical help, my love and my *real* understanding of his problems!"

The expression on James' face sounded like applause.

Grace didn't know what to say.

Her mother changed the subject to: "Have you *all* tasted the engagement cake that Grace baked?"

Unobtrusively, James removed his hand from Grace's. He sparkled with a glow he had never known.

The next night, he phoned Barbara for a date.

They were quietly married a month later. A month after that, James told his "50-50" partner that he wanted to dissolve the partnership. Instead, the partner sold out to *him*.

And it had all started *emotionally!*

Barbara had heard about James' "50-50" partner and Preoccupation-holding problem from passing conversation shortly after the guests had arrived at the "engagement party."

Romance was on Barbara's mind, but it didn't just sit there! It helped her frame the right Emotional Appeal for James.

She had fit her words to James' emotional needs with well-aimed Recognition Appeal, aided by communicative dippings of other Appeals. As a result, James felt that he would be on much more secure ground with her than with Grace.

Why had James reacted to Barbara's words *at that particular time?* Because Grace had never really "reached him" with his most emotionally responsive chord, his Recognition desires and his Money fears. She had not truly been the "only one," not even at the engagement party!

He was still wide open and waiting for the "right" woman to come along.

No woman can be the "right" woman for a man unless she can use the right motivating Emotional Appeal in her words and actions!

Sex attraction and desire for marriage.

Any girl, plain or pretty, can get a husband.

Whether or not she attracts one has little to do with face, form, age or financial state. If she can meet the available man she wants and use the right Emotional Appeal, she can succeed in getting a mate!

Any man, handsome or hesitant, will get married, stay married and be happy-though-married when his words and actions have the right Emotional Appeal for his woman!

Romance is a pocket in our emotional clothing that may be picked when we least expect. It is a pocket that we can "pick" in others, because Romance is one of the Fatal Four groups of emotions that make up every individual's attitudes.

Like the others in the Fatal Four, Romance Appeal in communication is as ancient as Time and as certain. It can bring pleasure or pain from early Preoccupations to late frustrations.

Romance as an Emotional Appeal consists of:

1.—Sexual attraction and desire for Marriage.
2.—The Future Promise.
3.—The New Experience.

Sex fulfillment and satisfaction are in Self-Preservation; sex *attraction* and *desire* are in Romance.

Romance fears and lacks are as important as desires and wishes as prepotent Preoccupation factors. Like the positives and negatives in all the Appeals, they are in our lives every day.

Pick up a large circulation daily newspaper, for instance. Turn to page 3.

You'll see all sorts of headlines.

A four-column story screams: "PRESIDENT SUBMITS NEW BUDGET." A two-column story reads: "TWO PARADES ON SUNDAY." One column is headed: "FIGHTER FIGHTS FOR LIFE." Half-column is topped by: "STRIKE TALKS ON."

A smaller two-inch story carries the headline: "NUDE RED-HEAD FOUND ALIVE."

Which story will most readers read *first* and remember *best?*

You're right! The story of the "Nude Redhead!" It has higher attention-getting impact than the "bigger" stories on the page. For women readers, too!

In headlines, as in life, it's not how big you are, but how strong you are EMOTIONALLY!

Now, turn a few pages to a group of news pictures. Your eye wanders, but where does it rest?

On the "cheesecake" photo of two shapely beauties sitting with their legs crossed and skirts draped two inches above their knees!

If the cross-legged beauties happen to be on the same page as one blonde lovely in an abbreviated dancing costume, your eyes will stray to the blonde. Comparatively, she has more Romance Sex Appeal.

The *promise*, mind you, *not* the fulfillment!

Let's say you're an Office Manager.

Your boss is standing in front of you, explaining some important details about a new and complicated office machine. You must learn its operation in order to train others in its use. You know that your boss does not like to repeat instructions, so you stare off, wrinkle your brows and give *complete* concentration to his words.

You do, until you see Tessie, the receptionist.

The boss is still explaining, but you notice that Tessie is wearing a tight, pink sweater that pinpoints her bust when she walks.

The boss is talking, but are you really listening?

You may be the most refined, cultured man or woman; you

may like or dislike it; but you will not resist a Preoccupation-breaking Sex Attraction, unless *another* Emotional Appeal has higher attention-getting and attention-holding value at the moment!

A tall, superbly built lady thief could have been much more successful if she had known this!

With a plunging neckline down to h-e-r-e, she posed as a customer in jewelry stores of various cities. Her method of operation was essentially the same wherever she appeared.

Stylishly dressed, she would walk over to a showcase containing diamond rings. When a salesman came to serve her, she would smile invitingly, part her coat, and bend over as if to look more closely at the rings in the showcase. This brought the salesman's attention to her plunging neckline.

With his eyes and thoughts so diverted, she would ask to see one of the trays that contained stock-size diamonds set in platinum. Certain that he was concentrating on her bosom, rather than on the rings, she would "palm" a real diamond ring and substitute a paste imitation in the tray.

After a promise to return within the next few days ". . . with my husband," she thanked the salesman for his "trouble" and left. She disappeared and so did the real diamond. Because the "paste" substitute was now on a tray with many similar rings, the "switch" often remained unnoticed for weeks after the lady thief's visit.

For more than a year, the woman continued her criminal career. With the Preoccupation-breaking neckline as her chief accomplice, she was said to have stolen some $50,000 in diamond rings.

One day, she walked into a jewelry store and began her well-rehearsed approach. This time, she was attended by the 72-year old owner of the store, who held his hands on his hips and wriggled while he waited on her.

When she bent over to distract him and switch the rings, he saw the "switch," gave the alarm and she was arrested.

The strange part of her undoing was that the 72-year old jeweler had a local reputation as a "woman chaser." Ordinarily, he would have given instant attention to her plunging neckline.

When the woman entered his store, however, he had a severe backache. To lessen the pain, he pressed his hands into his hips and back.

Preoccupation with pain, a part of Self-Preservation, was at the moment more emotionally important to him than the Romance sex attraction of the neckline so he wasn't diverted.

If the shapely jewel-thief had chosen a day when the jeweler had been in better spirits, she might easily have added him to her list of victims!

As an Emotional Appeal, Romance is something we *want*, and *fear* we may miss. It may be a force to be used *on* us or *by* us!

Here, Sex desire was the attention-getter to a man. Might it be such to a woman?

Yes.

Where sex attraction is involved, women are as interested in women as men are!

In the follow through, however, sex attraction may not be in an individual's *big* Emotional Appeal. It may mean much to many, but it is not the everything to everybody, woman *or* man.

Note the *particular* differences in your listeners.

Use them as emotional indicators.

You will discover various individual reactions to Romance and sex promptings even when you tell a joke or relate a story. You will find differences in feelings and approach towards Romance Sex desire just as you will find different reactions to politics, a moustache or a pair of earrings.

To some, sex attraction adds a delightful surge towards Self-Preservation satisfactions. To others, it is Recognition for personal charm or physical attractiveness. Many declare that one of its best functions is to help close a business deal for money and profit. There are those who claim it is most effective for clearing a path to love and marriage.

Overshadowed by other Preoccupations, our sex desire in Romance Appeal will silently slumber. Because it is emotional, we cannot see, hear, or touch it.

Once awakened it throbs, pulsates and pushes out all other Preoccupations!

Romance is a prime Preoccupation-holder that can unlock

padlocks of reason. On target, it can outperform and outpersuade other Appeals.

A small photography studio in a densely populated business neighborhood had many office girls come in during their lunch hours. They were "shopping around" for prices on portrait photographs.

Cost was a big factor; competition was keen.

The owner of the studio had too small a sales volume to compete price-wise. He was about ready to close his door when Emotional Appeal, the response-awakening ability to get people to *want* to listen, entered his life.

He suddenly realized that nearly every female who "shopped" for prices on portrait photography was *unmarried!*

How did he learn this?

By looking at their marriage ring fingers and discovering no marriage ring!

For the first time, he had unearthed a *big* emotional portion of his listeners' attitudes!

Swiftly, he put this knowledge to work so he could enter the minds of his customers and make them react the way he wanted.

When unmarried girls came to his studio, they would ask: "How much do you charge for portrait photographs?"

He did not respond immediately. Instead, he smiled and beckoned them towards a small desk.

Opening the top drawer, he asked: "Do you know why we are called 'the lucky photographers'?"

While they wondered, he removed four bridal photographs, face down. Turning them over, he quietly remarked: *"These girls posed for us less than a year before they were married!"*

It made unmarried females buy again and again!

This phase of Romance Emotional Appeal, an unmarried woman's desire for marriage, was made more important than Money cost or the Recognition desire for a flattering photograph. The Romance *Future Promise* further intensified the Appeal!

Before applying Romance Appeal or any other, keep your eyes and ears open. Never overlook the obvious in your attempt to uncover the *big* reasons why your listeners *want* to listen!

Even people who have 20-20 vision are so Preoccupied that they can look at something very clear and see nothing!

An unmarried female of marriageable age *does* want to get married!

Unmarrieds, a thousand at a time, reminded me of this some years ago.

I was invited to lecture at a large summer hotel on a Sunday at 3 P.M. My lecture was to be titled: "Emotional Appeal—Key to Happier Living."

Three days before the lecture, the man who had arranged the engagement phoned me. He was very anxious to change the title.

"More than 80% of our guests are known as 'two week wonders'," he explained. "These are the unmarried girls and women who spend their two week vacations at a summer hotel trying to attract a husband. If your lecture title can tell them the one thing they want to hear," he insisted, "we can publicize it and you can double your audience!"

When I asked him what lecture title he suggested, he told me and I chuckled. Without question, it had far more Emotional Appeal to the audience than the original one. I thanked him and re-planned my Subject to better fit the Audience emotionally.

Sunday turned out to be a beautiful, cloudless day.

I arrived at the hotel shortly after the midday meal. Not only were many of the guests discussing the forthcoming lecture with animated anticipation, but nearly 300 people from nearby hotels had also come to attend!

By 2:45 P.M., the hotel changed its plans about holding the lecture in the large Social Hall.

The audience was asked to assemble on the wide concrete walk beside the huge swimming pool. Folding chairs were provided, but the number was inadequate and standees began to gather on grass knolls. Soon the need for a public address system was evidenced, and this caused another delay.

By 3:35 P.M., some 1300 people, including more than 1100 unmarried women, sat or stood near the swimming pool impatiently awaiting the speaker.

The new lecture-title, which had been widely publicized via

the hotel's newspaper, bulletin boards, special announcements and a tiny item in the just-published edition of the local paper, had not doubled the expected audience; it had quadrupled it!

The lecture title?

"How to Use Emotional Appeal Technique . . . and Get a Husband!"

Because the Romance Appeal in the title told unmarried women of all ages *what they wanted to hear,* they were emotionally anxious to listen!

Even available vacation occupations like tennis, golf, archery, sun-bathing, lake swimming and other Self-Preservation enjoyments became less important!

This audience did more than merely attend. Nearly half had paper and pen or pencil for note-taking!

They learned that Romance and marriage need pass no woman by if she can use the right Emotional Appeal to secure a competitive advantage in the Preoccupied mind of an available man!

What is her important *first step?*

She must uncover the most emotionally responsive chord that makes her prospect *want* to listen or *fear* to!

Once he listens, he *can* be persuaded!

Is he mainly a Self-Preservation Cow? Is Money his emotional mainstay? Romance? Recognition desires and fears?

Many examples were given, illustrating words, actions and incidental behavior that might indicate what made him want to listen.

Mention was made of the fact that whether a woman can or cannot attract a husband has little to do with appearance, financial set up or physical let down. It basically depends upon her ability to reach a man's responsive chord via emotionally effective communication.

It can even have to do with the way she says: "Good night!" after a date!

You're a marriageable female. For some time, you have yearned for a date with "B." You get one.

The evening is now over and B. takes you home.

"Thank you for the nice evening, B.," you say sincerely, "I enjoyed it very much."

"I'm glad you did," replies B. courteously. "Good night!"

"Good night!" you reply.

And that's it.

You go in and he goes home.

Do you *really* want your relationship to end on such a final note?

When you and thousands of other marriageable females close the door behind you do you *emotionally* close the door on a male's further interest?

You don't have to.

You *can* have Romance when you know how to say it . . . with Emotional Appeal! Here's how:

When B. takes you home, *don't* say: "Thank you for the nice evening."

This has far too much *finality*. You can provide a delightful Romantic New Experience and do far, far *better* if you care to.

Say: "Do *all* your lady friends have such a lovely evening when they're with you?"

Watch him smile, glow, blush a bit, then splutter. You can almost count off the seconds it will take him to think of an answer.

The powerful Recognition appeal in your question will *instantly* give you an advantage. There is no finality yet you have said "Thank You!"

But now something vastly *different* has happened.

You have rocked your gentleman friend *emotionally!* You've said something that has made him tingle.

He is now beginning to *warm* towards *you*.

It's much easier to be certain that his "Good night" will *not* mean "Goodbye!"

"Do *all* your lady friends have such a lovely evening when they're with you?"

One of my students, a bachelorette of 36, created this Emotional Appeal after a specific assignment. She used it at the "right" time on a date with a man she thought was "right" for her.

It was the first time she had "reached him" emotionally, and it was the first step towards her marriage.

It can be *your* first step too.

The difference between a spinster and a bride is a fellow who *wants* to hear *what* he wants to hear . . . *when* he wants to hear it.

So say it with the Emotional Appeal that will create the right response.

During the six or seven months after the lecture, I received 92 "Thank You" notes from unmarried girls in the audience who got husbands!

Three of these girls had sat in the audience as had the fellows they married!

Two years later, I was guest on a daytime network radio program. In response to a question, the incident was mentioned. Within a week, the network, its local stations and my office received nearly 1500 letters, cards and telegrams from all over the United States.

One letter came from an unmarried, 28-year-old who lived in one of the Western states. She wrote: "My brother heard you on radio. Will you please send me the Emotional Appeal sentence that is sure to start Romance? I certainly hope that it helps me get a husband, preferably a cowboy!"

The sentence was sent to her, along with some words of caution about the timing.

Four months passed and the lady sent another note.

"Dear Mr. Garn," she wrote. "I used the Emotional Appeal and I have the cowboy. The Emotional Appeal works, the cowboy doesn't. What do I do *now?*"

The attention-compelling advantages of the future promise.

Earlier in this chapter, we talked about two expressions:

1. The Future Promise.
2. The Desire for New Experiences.

Both are portions of the overall Romance Appeal and can be utilized as omnipotent message carriers.

The Romance "Future Promise" and Desire for New Experiences have potent Preoccupation-breaking ability. To many people they are as emotionally strong as boy-wants-girl, woman-needs-man sex attraction and desire for marriage.

"Future Promise" is emotionally ingrained.

Many predictions are made about the future. Actually, no one truly knows—unless the future is an anticipated portion of an exact, premeditated and controlled plan.

How many plans are like this? Few, indeed.

Usually, the future is only an unknown quantity to wish for and wonder about where people, products, services and situations are concerned.

When an undergarment, perfume or reducing method *promises* to make us appear more attractive or feel better, it frequently has more Emotional Appeal than how much it costs. If a skin cream or vitamin plan can help eradicate wrinkles, it may be more emotionally important to us than factual information about its contents.

A savings plan that promises "future security" can emotionally stimulate us to save regularly despite the effort required; it will also induce many of us to avoid making necessary withdrawals!

Whether in love, health, money, appearance, satisfaction or recognition, we all strive towards some form of perfection. Those whose words and actions help us move mentally in the direction of our personal preferences offer us more of the happiness we seek.

So we listen.

Individuals with a desirable "Future Promise" that *can* be fulfilled will encounter little difficulty in getting us to *enjoy* doing what they want!

On our side, we must fit what we say and do in terms of our listener's needs.

This need can often be initially contacted by a Romance "Future Promise" Appeal!

This is so whether you are a teacher, preacher, dachshund-stretcher, millionaire, fellow named Eustace, or lady called Jill.

Let's say you're a millionaire.

You have a lucrative business, many investments, much property. Your annual income is over one hundred thousand dollars a year.

Will you be interested in becoming *"rich?"*

You will *not!* Such a thought may seem insincere or ridiculous to *you* so you won't really listen.

In the Money sense, you're rich and you know it!

Will you positively respond to words that tell you how to become "rich?" No.

Will you agreeably react to words that suggest how you can become "richER?" You *will!*

This is a Romantic Future Promise *you* want to hear!

A girl may be physically beautiful. She has a stunning figure. Her skin texture is just perfect.

Do you feel that she will be interested in becoming "beautiful?" Does she have a desire for a "good" figure? Is she seeking a "clear" complexion?

Not at all.

She already has these advantages and you may feel certain that she knows it!

Yet, she and every other gorgeous girl will become emotionally attentive to becoming *more* beautiful, having an *even better* figure, or a *lovelier* complexion!

This is Future Promise, the hope for the unknown tomorrow that lives in everyone *today.*

Forget about most colorless adjectives and superlatives! Carry the COMPARATIVES with you always!

Why say *rich, good, nice, pretty?* There's far greater Preoccupation-breaking value to adjectives like *rich*ER, *nic*ER, *bett*ER, *pretti*ER!

These and other "E-R" adjectives have Emotional Appeal at all times! They contain two little letters that can spell the difference between belief and ridicule!

What if an "e-r" word isn't on the tips of your lips? Use similarly effective Future Promise words! Words like *more* or *extra.*

"Wouldn't it be wonderful to have *time* to relax?" No.

"Wouldn't it be wonderful to have MORE time to relax?" Yes, this is a far stronger attention-getter!

"How would you like to have a *twenty-dollar bill* in your pocket right now?"

You may have one handy, and the question can seem ridiculous. You're more certain and you have far more activating Emotional Appeal when you do it this way:

"How would you like to have an *extra* twenty-dollar bill in your pocket right now?"

The Future Promise part of the Romance Appeal can give additional persuasive impact to any of the Fatal Four.

When the owner of the photography studio told the unmarried girls: "These girls posed for us less than a year before they were married!" the Romance Future Promise packed more power into the Romance Desire for Marriage.

"How would you like to become the biggest man in the mail order business?" was a Future Promise that interlocked Money and Recognition Appeal.

Remember the well-dressed woman who climbed to the top of the bridge to commit suicide? The policeman's reminder that she would jump into "filthy water down there," emotionally steered Future Promise into Recognition.

"Do you know that over 60% of the wealth of the United States is in the hands of widows?" This was a Future Promise that meshed with Self-Preservation and Money Appeals. You will recall that a student of mine used it to get a job as assistant to the company president who didn't mind if he "worked seventeen hours a day, every day."

When the younger-appearing 21-year-old girl was undecided about buying that suit, my friend had said: "This suit will make you look older and even prettier!" This Future Promise beribboned her desire for Recognition and wrapped up persuasion.

"This place is only for folks who'll live to be a hundred!" smiled old Mr. Y. when he showed prospective buyers his ancient house with the porch that "gets more square feet of sunshine per day than any other place in the state." This Future Promise was pointed in the direction of Self-Preservation.

You'll find thousands of other ways to use the Romance Future Promise in your human relationships. One of its great advantages is the fact that it can establish instantaneous "emotional contact."

Without control of "emotional contact" you cannot successfully communicate!

With such control, you can use Emotional Appeal Technique in *any* communication situation and be more certain of the outcome!

A large company sold quality aluminumware on a door-to-door basis. Its salesmen worked on a commission-only basis.

Each salesman had a supervised territory where he knocked on doors and rang doorbells. When he secured orders, he turned them over to this superior, the territorial Sales Manager. There-after, it took a week or ten days for the order to be delivered and payment collected from the customer. After this, the sales-man received his commissions.

In order for a new salesman to start earning a fairly good income, he had to record plenty of daily calls, refuse to become discouraged over his "No-sales," and stick to his job for at least a month. After that, he had an excellent opportunity to build a remunerative future with the company.

To get salesmen, the General Sales Manager placed classified ads in newspapers and trained local Sales Managers to handle interviews.

Turnover of these door-to-door salesmen was extremely heavy.

Out of every ten such men engaged, six dropped out during the first week. Three quit before the end of the second week. The other one either turned out to be a "find" or dropped out before the fourth week had passed.

Despite the offer of additional incentives and benefits, the General Sales Manager was unable to reduce such wasteful and costly turnover of new personnel, most of whom continued to quit after working less than one week!

Investigation revealed that the interviewer's words and ac-tions at the first interview lacked "emotional contact."

The interviewer stressed the company's reputation and facili-ties, showed samples, charts and pictures and assured the ap-plicant that he could "make a lot of money if you make a lot of calls and do things our way."

This approach was not emotionally persuasive to the job-applicant. He had heard too many similar stories at other interviews for "commission salesmen."

The interview procedure was changed.

Right after the would-be salesman came in, the interviewer would introduce himself, motion him to a chair and ask: *"Will you gamble five months of hard work to set up a steady future income of over $6000 a year?"*

While the job-applicant concentrated on the idea of "five months of hard work on a commission basis, in order to set up a desirable future income of over $6,000 a year," the interviewer spoke the facts to a mind that had been *emotionally contacted* and made more receptive to the proposition.

This "Future Promise" Appeal, established from the beginning of the interview, caused a huge decrease in turnover of new personnel!

Out of every 10 new salesmen interviewed this way, approximately four remained, surmounted the initial "rough times" and built their way into a future with the company.

Of the remaining six, two lasted up to three months. During this time, they received earned commissions and increased the company's overall sales. The others stayed on an average of two-and-a-half weeks, more or less rarely "under a week" as before.

This phenomenal decrease in turnover prompted valuable character training and stick-to-itiveness in the men who pushed on!

Some of these men became executives with the company. Such opportunity would never have materialized if the "Future Promise" lead-in to Money and income had not created the initial emotional contact and incentive!

Someone once said: "Today is the tomorrow you were talking about yesterday!"

Tomorrow always comes and so does your opportunity to enjoy the many benefits of Romance "Future Promise."

Now that you know its secrets, use it sincerely.

It can make exactly the response-compelling Preoccupation-breaking emotional contact *you* want, time after time after time!

So can the fears and desires related to New Experience, the last phase of Romance Emotional Appeal, which we shall look into next.

How romantic new experience melts mental monotony.

Some years ago, Miss S., a student, spoke on the subject: "Why a Lady Wears Perfume."

She requested a young woman and a man to come forward from the class. As they stood side by side, she asked the fellow: "Notice anything unusual about her?"

He shook his head negatively. "She's kind of pretty," he grinned. "That's about all I can say right now."

Miss S. smiled "Thank You," and led the blushing young lady out of the classroom.

"Wait!" she told us. "We'll be right back!"

They reappeared half-a-minute later.

Miss S. placed the girl beside the young man once more. "Anything different? Anything unusual?"

The chap's nostrils quivered. His eyes sparkled and he said: "Now she smells *swell!*"

One visual demonstration and a few words concentrated our attention upon the *big* idea that Miss S. wanted to get across: *Women wear perfume for very personal reasons—often romantic ones!*

Three years after this incident, she greeted me on the street.

"I don't know *your* name," I confessed, "but I recall that you are a former student of Emotional Appeal who once delivered a talk on "Why a Lady Wears Perfume!"

She was astonished. "You've had thousands of students since then, Mr. Garn. How could you possibly remember *me?*"

I chuckled. "You gave me something to remember. Many of my other students did *not!*"

What's different about *you?*

In the things you do, do you pass unnoticed because your words, actions and personal tastes seem the same as ten thousand other men or women of your age and achievements?

With some initiative, creative imagination and personal show-manship, you can make yourself easy to remember and hard to forget!

Little differences are often the ones that really count, if these differences have Emotional Appeal to your listener.

Girls with a desire for marriage make a "play" for the same man. Which one convinces him to put the ring on her finger? The one who helps him do what he always wanted to do!

This girl's words and actions have led him to feel that he has convinced himself!

She made herself seem *different* to him! She *individualized* herself! She knew that her biggest competition was the competition to enter his mind! She realized that his mind was Preoccupied! She told him what he wanted to hear—*not* merely what she wanted to tell him! She uncovered his *big*, most emotionally responsive chord!

She made emotional contact!

He liked these little differences and he came back for more and more.

She gave a New Experience that sprinkled sparkle into his otherwise dull existence!

"Love is when a man thinks one woman is different from all others," wrote H. L. Mencken.

Love is communication. To communicate successfully, you must use Emotional Appeal. Without well-directed Emotional Appeal, you have no Love!

Men of similar background apply for the same job. One gets it.

Is this because he has such unique knowledge from prior jobs that he overshadows the other applicants! Rarely!

Mr. Successful Applicant most often enters the mind of his interviewer with a Preoccupation-breaking "something different" from his competitors, an emotional "something" that the employer or interviewer is seeking personality-wise.

In the letter of application, in the personal interviews, this *difference* gives Mr. Successful Applicant a competitive advantage that keeps him remembered. Most often he projects a refreshing, Romantic New Experience into a going through the motions, routine filled mind, the mind of his interviewer.

He uses the right Emotional Appeal. He breaks Preoccupation. He gets the job!

"Help Wanted" ads elicit thousands of replies. Those who

screen such letters agree that almost all are run of the mill, lacking in originality and winsomeness. After a while, one looks the same as another.

Then one says: "I have been searching for an employer who is worthy of my intensive know-how, loyalty and merry disposition. When may I come to see *you?*"

The young lady who wrote this in her letter of application received an interview and *the interviewer actually looked forward to meeting her.*

This letter provided an attention-arresting New Experience and Recognition of this employer as "worthy of my intensive know-how, loyalty and merry disposition."

She had emotionally balanced the odds in her favor even before the interview!

Middle-aged Mr. C. had had a prolonged illness. It had become necessary for his long-time employer to replace him. Upon recovery, Mr. C. received an excellent reference but no job.

Hundreds of unemployed people of his own age and up to twenty years younger also possessed excellent references! They were his competitors!

An advertisement in a morning paper offered a job with: "Permanent opportunity. Peanuts to start. Fine salary and benefits after six months of training."

Others hurried to the "personal interview." Mr. C. corralled a competitively advantageous Emotional Appeal and then went to the interview.

When Mr. C.'s turn came, the interviewer was bored. He had already gone through the same motions with some eleven applicants for the job.

Mr. C. entered the interview room, stood beside the desk, and waited for the interviewer to finish writing some notes on the previous applicant. When he looked up, Mr. C. smiled warmly and laid a small bag of peanuts on the desk.

"Your ad said 'Peanuts to start,'" he quietly remarked. "I brought some along to doubly assure you that I want your consideration." Tearing off the top of the bag, he said: "Have some peanuts. Perhaps they'll help you remember me and make your decision easier!"

The interviewer laughed, thanked Mr. C. and reached for the peanuts.

When he made his decision, he "reached" for middle-aged Mr. C.

Mr. C. and the New Experience of the peanuts had dabbed a dash of delightful color into the interviewer's colorless day!

The Romance Appeal of the "New Experience" is emotionally desired, sought after, and hoped for by *everyone*. Another power packed portion of Emotional Appeal Technique, it is *yours to use!*

Carefully conceived, you'll find that it will better the outcome of your dealings with people and assure you of a competitive advantage, no matter how old you are or how young.

Mike had to find a daytime job that would help support his mother and two younger sisters. His father had died suddenly in an accident. He secured "Working Papers" and began his job hunt.

It was early summer. School was "out" and thousands of boys were available.

He went to a well known factory that sought an errand boy. Although he arrived at 8:45 A.M., nearly fifty boys of high school age were ahead of him, lined up in single file in front of the door to the interviewer's office.

A uniformed guard was stationed beside the door to keep order.

Young Mike walked up to the guard so he could read the name of the interviewer, lettered on the door. The boys on line started a howl; they thought that Mike was trying to get ahead of them. When the guard ordered him to the end of the line, Mike assured himself that the name on the door was the name of the interviewer inside.

With so many boys ahead of him, Mike realized that the interviewer would either reach him by mid-afternoon or later or make a decision before interviewing all the applicants.

The line moved slowly. By 11 A.M., ten boys impatiently left.

Mike counted his fare and lunch money. He didn't have much but he did have an idea.

After having waited at the end of the line for more than two hours, he was quite sure that he would not lose his place if he walked off for a little while. He rushed over to a telegraph office three blocks away. Following a discussion about cost, he sent this cryptic telegram to the interviewer at the factory:

"PLEASE DON'T GIVE JOB UNTIL MEET FRECKLE-FACE MIKE END LINE."

The interviewer received the telegram. It was a ray of sunshine that interrupted an unrelenting rain of high school boys!

He popped his head out of the door and asked the uniformed guard to bring him the "freckle-faced boy named Mike."

Mike's individuality was such a much-desired New Experience to the interviewer that the boy was cordially welcomed into the interview.

Emotionally "presold," the interviewer liked him immediately.

And Mike, who had initiated the emotionally advantageous Preoccupation-breaker, made a superb follow-thru!

Once again, the Emotional Appeal of a Romantic New Experience had melted the mental monotony of a listener!

Projecting your own personal touch.

A lovely girl won a beauty contest and came to New York City expecting fame and fortune. But, no!

New York had plenty of beautiful models, so she became one of many who job hunted the agencies. Disillusioned and discouraged, it was said that she was about to return home.

Then she added a "personal touch."

She chose an unusual, memorable name and began to wear peppermint striped clothes. She had calling cards printed, peppermint candy style. She left the cards with modelling agencies and distributed them wherever she appeared.

From calling cards to clothes and name, she became a Romantic "New Experience."

The phenomenal modelling career of "Candy Jones" was launched!

A man named Cooper sold costume jewelry for more than ten years. He called on small and medium sized stores with a line similar to that carried by a dozen other salesmen who covered the same territory.

Income-wise, he barely eked out a living; employment-wise, he was constantly at odds with his boss because of his poor sales record.

One winter, he caught a severe cold and his doctor advised him to wear spats to help keep his feet warm. Reluctantly, Cooper bought a pair.

The next day, he called on a small storekeeper who took notice.

"Spats! Hah! I haven't seen them in years," satirically commented the man. "From now on I'm going to call you 'Spats' Cooper!"

"Call me anything you want," hollowly grunted Cooper, "but call me when you need costume jewelry!"

As he left, his customer waved cheerily and repeated what he considered a good joke. "Goodbye, Spats. Too bad I have no order for you today."

Two weeks later, Cooper re-visited this store and the merchant was most cordial.

"It's my friend, Spats Cooper. How are you, Spats?" He extended his hand, which Cooper shook. "Look who's here, Harry," he remarked to one of his salesclerks. "It's Spats Cooper!"

Cooper got a small order and a big reaction.

At no time during the five years that he had called upon this merchant had he been so nicely welcomed. He had even received a voluntary handshake!

Thereafter, he took great pains to introduce himself to customers as "Spats" Cooper. "See?" he would say, pointing to his feet.

The nickname caught on. Sales volume began to increase and so did his income. Soon he was outdistancing most of the dozen competitive salesmen who called on the same customers.

When time passed without a visit from "Spats," his customers or their personnel would remark about his absence!

When warmer weather came, a problem came too. "To wear 'em—or not to wear 'em?"

"Spats" Cooper decided to "wear 'em!" He had light-weight spats made, and he could now afford such custom-makings.

He had established a very "personal touch," a Romantic "New Experience," that emotionally set him in a more advantageous light than his competitors.

His customers had something to remember and enjoy gossiping about!

Tall H. was representative of a small New Jersey plant that designed and manufactured chemical process and heat exchange equipment. He called on executive, engineering and purchasing departments in the multi-billion-dollar Chemical Process Industries.

Few were receptive. Although Tall H. had intensive experience in calling upon such prospects for a previous employer, they had famous name suppliers with many times the facilities of Tall H.'s company.

Tall H. needed more business.

How could a break-through be made with purchasing agents of the big companies?

Emotional Appeal Technique was put to work and Romance Appeal emerged—in the form of a RABBIT!

When Tall H.'s employers saw the rabbit, they flipped!

"We're in the chemical process industries," they objected. Our kind won't go for rabbits. They're engineers and technical people. They're used to charts and they want facts! This rabbit, created as our company symbol, hasn't got a chance. It's unusual, but it won't sell our kind of buyer!"

After a short discussion, however, they agreed to go along with the plan "against our better judgment."

Tall H. followed instructions.

Wherever he made a call, he referred to himself as "The Rabbit." He would leave a business card or literature featuring the rabbit pointing to his company's name, number and list of services.

Whenever possible, he would raise his right index finger and wink: "I'm the one rabbit that outperforms them all!"

Receptionists, secretaries and executives soon became friendlier and more inviting when Tall H. came. He provided them with a momentary "change of pace" and they got a "kick" out

of thinking about him as "the tall rabbit who makes heat exchange equipment."

After a month or so, eagerly awaited phone calls began to
trickle in to his company, asking for Tall H. and estimates.
Usually, the caller would jest with the operator by saying something like: "Will you please connect me with your representative,
the tall one we all call 'The Rabbit'?"

It wasn't long before Tall H.'s company began to add some
of America's best known industrial corporations to its growing
customer list.

When Christmastime neared, the company used a novel Santa
on its Christmas Cards, the rabbit in costume, with a fluff of
white absorbent cotton on its chin!

Tall H. told me that it was the longest-eared Santa he had
ever seen, and one of the best ever!

On a number of occasions, his employers repeated their amaze-
ment that Emotional Appeal had proved so successful on "people
who work with facts."

There is nothing "amazing" about this.

People in every business, occupation and situation may claim
a "right" to expect the facts, but here is a *fact* too:

*Facts are never acted upon unless a prepotent Emotional Ap-
peal opens a Preoccupied mind to receive them!*

Because minds are so Preoccupied, the Romance New Experience portion or another properly communicated phase of Emotional Appeal Technique can *always* be applied to a personal,
business, sales or professional problem—even to dentistry!

Are you a "dentist-shopper?"

Thousands of us are. When we need dental care and do not
know of a dentist, we may go from one to another "just looking"
and asking about cost for dental work.

Those who do so are termed "walk-ups" or "walk-ins."

We often waste a dentist's time and never return, despite
promises to do so. Worse, we go to one dentist, have him ex-
amine us, then misquote another dentist's comment and quo-
tation.

Some dentists try not to accept any but recommended patients, but most agree that the "walk-in" provides an excellent potential for a practise.

Unfortunately, though, many dentists do not use Emotional Appeal Technique on "walk-ins" and a large percentage of these become permanent "walk-*outs*"!

Dr. Z., a dentist, had a so-so practise for years. He was quiet, extremely shy with a person he met for the first time. Located on a busy thoroughfare, much of his work originated from "walk-ins." Extremely interested in dental craftsmanship, he failed to observe that his patients had emotional needs too.

As a result, he had too few patients who remained with him through the years and too many "walk-ins" who walked out!

A "New Experience" was created that would help Dr. Z. overcome his shyness in meeting people for the first time. Simultaneously, it was to be used for all patients who came in for new dental work or periodic examination. It was evolved with Dr. Z. and titled: "Personal Case-History-Chart."

Regular and recommended patients, as well as "walk-ins," were immediately introduced to a "Personal Case-History-Chart" even if they came to Dr. Z. for the most minor dental work, or periodic examination.

The word "Personal" has an intimate Recognition Emotional Appeal and means *confidential* to everyone.

Thus, Dr. Z. instantly established his genuine professional interest in the patients.

Then, and only then, did he place the patient in his dental chair. Thereafter, he and the patient returned to the "Personal Case-History-Chart" and itemized the why and wherefore for the needed dental work.

By doing it this way, neither "walk-ins" nor regular patients could misquote his advice or fee, since they could rarely remember the complex breakdown of professional service, laboratory work or materials.

With the "Personal Case-History-Chart," Dr. Z. retained privacy and professional pride. At the same time, he added an advantageous "personal touch" that kept him respected and remembered.

"Walk-ins" were instilled with a desire for better dentistry rather than "better price." Emotionally, they *wanted* their relationship with their dentist to be truly personal, and Dr. Z.'s approach gave them greater satisfaction here too.

For Dr. Z. himself, the "Personal Case-History-Chart" provided an eloquent conversation starter. Because he was so conversant with its subject matter, he rapidly rid himself of his shyness and words flowed easily. He became better able to reveal his personality and professionally project such emotionally potent companions to dental cost as appearance, pain and comfort.

Today, most of Dr. Z.'s patients come by recommendation, and the "New Experience" Emotional Appeal of his "Personal Case-History-Chart" continues to help turn nearly every "walk-in" into a "stay-in"!

Out West, another dentist created ONE WORD with such Emotional Appeal that it attracted thousands to his offices!

A man named Parker set up his office in a neighborhood where there were many dentists. They, too, had "Dr." in front of their names. From the outside, one dentist seemed the same as another.

To establish a competitive advantage, attract "walk-ins," and give all patients something to remember, he changed his signs to " 'Painless' Parker, Dentist."

So many people came for dental work that he had to engage other dentists to help handle the overflow! Soon, he opened a "chain" of dental offices under the name: "Painless" Parker, Dentist. The offices prospered to such an extent that Parker stopped doing dentistry in order to concentrate on executive supervision.

"Painless" Parker spotlighted a "New Experience" to people seeking a dentist. His name was "different." Its unusualness broke Preoccupation, piqued curiosity, started remembrance, pointed to Self-Preservation.

It was what the "listener"—a patient—emotionally wanted to hear about a dentist BEFORE sitting in his dental chair!

By the time that anyone objected to the word "Painless" as nondescriptive of the service rendered, I was told that Parker legally changed his first name to "Painless."

He had been called that for so many years that he had almost forgotten his *real* name!

The Romantic New Experience is a much desired emotional condiment that can heighten the flavor of any person, product, company, situation or act, to *any* audience or individual listener. It has a refreshing, response-activating Emotional Appeal that attracts attention, opens the mind, and makes for a repeatedly recalled memory.

A pet expression, gesture, method of speaking, type of wearing apparel or hair-do, even a trademark, letterhead, or calling card may be enough to start other people's interest if it is enough of a New Experience!

Two fellows went into the photostat business. They might have continued merely to be "two fellows in the photostat business." Then they added a couple of delightful-looking kittens to their letterheads and calling cards. Next to the kittens, were the words: "We're copycats—and proud of it!"

The attention and remembrance values of their trademark provided a business building New Experience that uniquely described their service!

In education, the professions, personal and family relationships, commerce—even show business—the Romance New Experience provides a challenging *extra* for students, customers, clients, patients and listeners to see, hear, think and talk about!

Bing Crosby, Frank Sinatra, Perry Como, Nat "King" Cole, Pat Boone and others will long be remembered because of the *different* way each sang his songs.

Stop now! Visualize that "something to remember" in their styles.

It's there, isn't it?

When Al Jolson performed, it wasn't necessary to see him or have his name written across his chest. Audiences could close their eyes and *know* it was Jolson—not Horsewhistle! He gave out with an individualized, *identifying* Emotional Appeal!

A singer named Edith Piaf built a devoted following and performed in such top spots as the Waldorf-Astoria.

With super-expensive-looking costumes? Hair brilliantly

coiffed? Bosom pushed-up from under? Glittering high-heeled shoes?

No. Too many night club audiences *expect* such things.

Edith Piaf sang in a *plain* black dress. Hair? Mostly mussed. Bosom? Flat. Shoes? Usually open-toed, low-heeled sandals.

Accompanied by a superb choral group and formally-dressed musicians in near-symphonic musical arrangements, her performance could enthrall audiences into whispered breathing!

The unforgettable dance bands and stars in entertainment have given unique expression to the advantages of the "personal touch."

Picture Ted Lewis and his battered top hat, sing-talking "Is Everybody Happy?" Recall Eddie Cantor's roly-poly eyes, bouncy manner and stories about his daughters? Jimmy Durante's lengthy nose and individuality of comedy style swept him to fame. Guy Lombardo's distinctive musical bounce made his orchestra known to millions. Lawrence Welk's accent and "a-one . . . a-two . . ." way of cueing on the "champagne music" of his orchestra broke many of the "rules for success" in TV—but made him and his performers among the top crowd-pleasers in show business.

When an announcer said: "Swing and sway . . ." untold thousands would add: ". . . with Sammy Kaye!" For years, George Gershwin's *Rhapsody in Blue* introduced Paul Whiteman better than a personal calling card.

Every individual involved has profited by creating and adhering to a "personal touch" that offers a New Experience to others. Occasionally, the Romantic New Experience can be made even more memorable by "naturalness" or "imperfection."

Perfection is commonplace. Rarely recalled, it blithely blends into Preoccupation.

Imperfection can seize attention and open the mind.

Socially, you have known Doris for years. Her lipstick is always "just so" . . . her hair is "exactly right" . . . face powder "perfectly applied" . . . clothing and accessories "like a carefully-checked department-store manikin." She has such sameness in her perfection that she has somehow seemed "cold."

One morning, you happen to drive past her home. You see super-perfect Doris emptying a garbage can! Her hair is in a bun atop her head. She hasn't a dab of cosmetic.

Can this be *Doris?*

It *is*—and you suddenly *stop* feeling that she is a "too-perfect" clothes-horse and *start* feeling that she is a far more *human* being. The unexpected *imperfection* has made her seem "warmer" too!

A bit of *imperfection* in a person is as memorable as discovery of imperfection on the front page of a newspaper.

"BIG BANK ROBBERY!" Sounds interesting.

"BIG BUNK ROBBERY!" . . . and HUH? We become far *more* attentive!

The radio or TV announcer who refers to billowy suds as "sillowy buds" or to the Iron Curtain as the "Curtain Iron" breaks our Preoccupation immediately.

Sponsored programs boost sponsor's products. Most "commercials" have become a going-through-the-motions routine to listeners and viewers. When Arthur Godfrey *chided* his sponsors and their products, he not only sold more because his audience listened *better*—but he also helped himself become one of the biggest attractions on Radio and TV!

There have been many fine performances of the opera *Aida.* The one I remember best had a glaring *error.*

Trumpeteers lined up on stage. The conductor led his orchestra into the famous *Triumphal March.* Vocal performers *failed to appear.*

The conductor stopped the music and tapped his baton. He started again and again. The march was replayed four times before the vocalists came onto the stage!

Sometimes the suggestion of an *impossible* situation can be high in Romantic New Experience.

Pedestrians and motorists pay constant heed to a small truck that moves about in a large Eastern city. The back of the truck bears the sign: "A BLIND MAN IS DRIVING THIS TRUCK!"

It is so unbelievable for a blind man to drive that hundreds of people daily turn their eyes to the driver.

When they do, they see a sign on the *front* of the truck with the name and address of a *venetian blind company!*

Most of our living pulls us deeper into the mire of mental monotony.

We are so Preoccupied with doing things that are generally considered *right* that we have little time to find out whether they are emotionally *right* for *us!*

We rise the same way, brush our teeth and comb our hair the same way, eat the same foods at just about the same time. We leave and return home the same way, cuss the same way, spend nonworking time doing the same thing.

Sameness so whitewashes our outlook that beautiful horizons appear blank.

When you upset this sameness with a "personal touch" as an emotionally-appealing New Experience, you power-up the desire to like, agree, accept, act or decide to buy.

Life Magazine once carried a fascinating article about twelve of America's leading models. In it, David Scherman wrote: "Although the twelve have fine teeth, they rarely smile. While they possess lovely skins, it is the aristocratic European bone structure that makes them famous. It may be un-American, but . . . they have sold more soap, soup, radios, nail polish, carpet sweepers, jewelry, perfume, cars, shampoo and other products than any 12 women in America!"

Americans are used to Americans. Expose them to a person with "foreign" appearance and there is immediate interest.

One of my students was very anxious to lose her French accent. I advised her not to. By losing the accent, she would lose an individuality that could provide a Romantic New Experience to others! And more Preoccupation-breaking Emotional Appeal for *herself.*

In the Eastern part of the United States and elsewhere, a Southern drawl can be emotionally advantageous. A Western twang, hitched to a Western "touch," can add a dab of brightness to drab lives!

Call upon your initiative and creative imagination! Do *new* things. Make them a New Experience to others!

Create and add your own *personal touch!* Dare to be *different!* Try *new* foods, ways, styles, people, thinking!

Use this Emotional Appeal *intentionally*.

Notice how much it will do to refresh your attitudes, personality and ability to persuade.

"There is little difference between one person and another," said William James. "What little there is . . . is *very* important!"

Make *your* "little difference" your ability to use more Emotional Appeal.

Give yourself a *personal touch* . . . a touch of *individuality*.

In little time, providing a Romantic New Experience for others will make a great B-I-G difference in *you!*

Now that we have more insight into the three underlying phases of Romance Emotional Appeal:

1. Sex attraction and desire for marriage
2. The Future Promise
3. The new Experience

We are better able to approach the motivations, attitudes, fears and desires that undergird Recognition—fourth of the "Fatal Four" Emotional Appeals that prepotently reside in our Preoccupation.

Using Recognition Appeal to Achieve Personal Success

During the first years of *Theatre* Magazine history, Paul Meyer, the publisher, was frequently low in funds. To economize, he cut down on many personal expenditures.

One enjoyment that he would not forego was attendance of Metropolitan Opera performances.

Known internationally as "Friend of a Thousand Stars," few knew his financial state. They were acquainted, however, with his evident French accent, sparkling wit, characteristic cane and love of theatre and opera.

Paul Meyer told me that, in the first decade of the twentieth century, opera was almost entirely attended by people of wealth and "cream of society."

"No so-called 'gentleman' would attend unless he wore immaculate full dress, silk hat and white gloves," said Mr. Meyer.

With the ladies, it was often a case of trying to outdo one another in glittering, competitive display of expensive and exclusive evening gowns, jewelry and furs.

Once a gown had made its impression, the "lady" would either discard it or give it to her personal maid. The maid, in turn, usually tried to outdo other maids on occasions when she wore the now "second-hand" dress!

Never would the upper-stratum lady be seen wearing the same evening gown twice. This would provide too juicy a morsel for gossip!

And . . . oh . . . those hapless evenings after a society woman had spent many weeks and more dollars being fitted for an unique creation only to discover another lady wearing the same 'original' sitting a short distance away! These, according to Mr. Meyer, were unheralded performances when two pairs of crimson ears shimmered more brightly than the costumes on stage!

The stage performances were superb and lavish. "Even the women watched these occasionally, because the darkened house prevented them from watching each other!"

Everything conformed to the luxurious atmosphere of the Metropolitan Opera House except the program. This was a one-sheet tabloid, poorly printed on cheap paper.

One evening, resplendent in a carefully brushed, borrowed full dress suit and customary white gloves, Paul Meyer attended a Metropolitan Opera performance. While he sat fingering the program, his white-gloved fingertips turned gray.

By the end of the performance, they were coal-blackish.

He placed his hands on his lap, palms down, so that the smudged portions would not be apparent. While he did this, he noticed that many other meticulously dressed men in the audience had taken similar action.

Mr. Meyer complained to John Brown, the Assistant Manager. "These gloves were white when I came in. Look at them now!"

"You're a publisher, Paul," smiled Mr. Brown. "Do you think you can publish a *better* program?"

Mr. Meyer nodded.

The next day, he phoned Otto H. Kahn, Chairman of the Metropolitan Opera's Board of Directors, and made an appointment for the following week. Meanwhile, he worked out a new program format.

When Mr. Kahn studied the presentation, he was delighted with what he saw, but what he said staggered Paul Meyer's hopes. He told Meyer that, since the new program would carry advertising, the Metropolitan Opera would require $27,500 a season for the publishing contract!

Paul Meyer's face dared not mirror his disappointment. He

assured Mr. Kahn that he would give the matter prompt consideration.

Alone with his thoughts, he exhaled defeat. He had urgent financial problems of his own. How could he raise $27,500 and publishing costs? The publication was new and untried.

Would advertisers be willing to spend money on such a program?

He knew that he had to plan swiftly or inform Mr. Kahn that he wished to drop to entire subject. The Board of Directors of the Metropolitan Opera Company would not do business with any dilly-dallier, he was sure. The Metropolitan Opera was too exclusive for that.

Exclusive!

This was the best one-word description of Metropolitan Opera House audiences of the time. This was the same audience that would read the Metropolitan Opera programs!

Hurriedly, he made appointments with every well-known advertiser he could contact. Briefly, he told about the program.

In each case, he gave this advice: *"You know what an exclusive organization the Metropolitan Opera is—so only the most outstanding companies are being invited to advertise. This is your opportunity to be included—or left out!"*

Results came quickly.

Knabe Pianos, Aeolian, and Hardman Peck signed up. Gorham Silver, American Tobacco Company and many more promised to buy space. Phonograph companies like Victor, Columbia and Brunswick went along. On the basis of the commitments he received, Paul Meyer was able to raise the money required to secure the publishing contract.

The first issue of the new Metropolitan Opera House Programs was distributed on the opening night of the 1911-1912 season. It caused such comment that reporters of the day mentioned that glittering society figures temporarily forgot to stare at each other!

Paul Meyer's financial future took a tremendous forward step and he continued to publish the Metropolitan Opera programs for ten years.

The program itself sparked a new era in program publishing. Its basic makeup has been followed by almost every opera company, symphony hall and theatre of today.

Beneath the surface, every firm solicited wanted to be *recognized* as ". . . *one of the most outstanding companies in America!*"

This Emotional Appeal broke Preoccupation, got quick attention.

Action followed.

The desire for Recognition is in every company. It is an essential ingredient in every individual's wish for personal success.

It intensifies from the moment we became old enough to communicate with a cry, a smile or a frown.

As we age, Recognition becomes as necessary as breathing; as personal as pride.

Recognition is an inner, *emotional* portion of everyone. Proper communication of this Emotional Appeal can assure achievement in limitless ways.

A hand-lettered sign fronting the driveway of a house in New Jersey once made me very curious. I watched two lads with shovels trot past the sign to the rear of the house.

There, they joined four other boys who readied themselves to shovel into a sand pile while a grinning man raised his hand for silence.

The man later told me that he had to remove the load of sand in order to replace it with topsoil. Because of an ailment, he could not do the work himself. He had placed a sign in front of his house offering a dollar to anyone who would shovel the sand behind his garage.

There were no takers.

He had raised the offer to a dollar and a half, then up to two dollars without receiving any response.

One day, he watched and listened as a group of neighborhood boys competed against one another in running, spelling, jumping and feats of strength. After this, he removed his sign and replaced it with the one I saw.

This read:

```
┌─────────────────────────┐
│   75¢ TO THE BOY        │
│   WHO MAKES THE         │
│   BIGGEST PILE OF       │
│   SAND BEHIND MY        │
│   GARAGE TODAY—         │
│   SATURDAY—AT 3 PM      │
│   —AFTER I SAY "GO!"    │
└─────────────────────────┘
```

Among the neighborhood boys, the desire for Recognition had more Emotional Appeal than the amount of Money offered!

Underlying every subject, there is a "listening factor" that can be discerned. With proper choice from among the Fatal Four reasons why people listen, communication can become more successful, more pleasant, and more persuasive.

Well-directed, motivating Emotional Appeal in words and actions can save time—even prevent an upset. Objective observation of the person you want to "reach" often indicates that the *right* choice lies in the realm of Recognition!

A milkman learned this truth just as he reached the end of his patience.

In the darkness before a dawn, the milkman prepared to deliver two quarts of milk to a small, well-landscaped house owned by a middle-aged widow. He lifted the lid of the milkbox with his left hand and placed the bottles in with his right. As he withdrew his hand, he screamed.

A jagged piece of metal, extending into the box, had unexpectedly scratched the back of his wrist!

He reached for his flashlight before removing the empty bottles and walked back to his milk truck, licking his wound.

He wrote a note to the widow and placed it in the box: "Please fix the milkbox. I cut my hand on it this morning. (Signed) Milkman."

Two days later, he made his next delivery. Lifting the lid of the milkbox, he set in the bottles of milk.

"Oww-ww!" he screeched, whipping his hand to his waist. The jagged metal had slashed the backs of two fingers on his right hand.

The lady had *not* fixed the milkbox!

He wrote another note and attached it to one of the milk bottles.

"The poor milkman," she sighed after reading the note. "I have so many things to do today. I must remember to have that box fixed."

But she didn't.

Peeved, the milkman decided to visit the woman after completing his route. When she saw his bandaged hand and heard his story, she was extremely sorry. She assured him that she would have the milkbox fixed that very day.

The milkman thanked her and left her tastefully decorated house.

The next morning, when he made his usual pre-dawn delivery, he did not use his flashlight and "Ow—OWW!"

He rushed back to his truck, muttering dire thoughts about the lady. He covered the new gash on his right pinky with a handkerchief and reached for a cardboard carton on the floor of the truck. In thick, emphatic four-inch letters he began to print another reminder.

The day sun-brightened and he stared at the lady's house. He noted the carefully trimmed lawn, choice of shrubbery and exterior paint. He recalled the meticulous inside decoration and he tore up his vengefully written message on cardboard.

Instead, he left this note: "Dear Mrs. A.: *I am your Milk Box. Please fix me. Everything else is so pretty in and outside your house.* (Signed) Your Milk Box."

The lady read the note, reproached herself for forgetting and had the milkbox repaired!

Two mornings later, the milkman timorously approached the box, with flashlight carefully poised.

In one of the two empty bottles, he found a message. "Thank you for reminding me, Mr. Milkman. The box is all right now and I hope you like the color. I tried very hard to match the outside trim. (Signed) Mrs. A.!"

How to make yourself better-liked.

One of my students, a tall, dark-haired, handsome fellow with roguish black-brown eyes, had been a paratrooper in World War II.

His name was Michael.

When a lecture and class demonstration had proved the singular advantages to the person who could offer a rememberful, Romantic New Experience to others, he had permanently changed his name to "Smiling Mike."

Smiling Mike lived his name. He told me that the change had calmed him, aided his outlook.

Apparel-conscious, even an occasional flamboyancy in Mike's attire tended to blend tastefully. He was proud of his appearance, choice of clothes, sense of humor and wealth of anecdotes. He prepared class assignments with originality and care and was ever-anxious to perform before an audience.

The other students liked Smiling Mike. He hastened to note changes in dress or hair-do . . . he was sincere about compliments . . . he avoided criticism . . . he was alert to appreciate the tiniest favor.

When he spoke, he trained himself to peer deeply into the eyes of his listeners; when *they* spoke, his eyes and inviting smile spotlighted attentiveness.

Smiling Mike was one of the most popular students in the class.

One Tuesday morning, he told me, he rose after a wonderful night's sleep and felt "like a million." The sun was shining; it was his day off and he had a luncheon date with his favorite girl friend, a stunning model named Marie.

He showered, leisurely enjoyed the delicious breakfast that his mother had prepared and began to dress for his date.

He decided to wear a deep purple suit with a lavender pin-dot that he had long admired in the window of an exclusive clothing store. Peering into his bureau mirror, he knotted and re-knotted a pale purple tie with large, intertwined white X's until it made a perfect dimple in the collar opening of his pastel purple shirt.

Before leaving his apartment, he re-checked his grooming in a full length mirror, made a slight adjustment of the tie with the white X's and bade his mother goodbye.

Downstairs, he opened his mailbox. There, he saw a thickish white envelope, hand-addressed to his name. It bore neither postage nor return address.

Curious, he opened the envelope and found four fifty-dollar bills inside of a folded sheet of looseleaf paper on which was written:

> Michael:
> You will be surprised to receive this money, I know, but you can guess how many years this matter has been on my mind. You were kind enough to lend me the two hundred after I just about lost my shirt in that poker game at Mickey's place during the war. Thanks again. Sorry it took me so long to find out where you were living, so I could repay the two C's.

Smiling Mike's eyes blinked as he recalled the fellow and the incident.

A radiance wreathed his being like a recircling gesture of joy!
Found Money!

Two hundred dollars—and all *his!*

What a day! All mankind was marvelous! *Wowie!*

He whistled while he walked the street. His left hand squeezed and re-squeezed the two hundred dollar windfall. His smile magnified into a halo of happiness.

Fred, his long-time friend and neighbor, came towards him, carrying a huge bag of vegetables. "Hello, Smiling Mike," said Fred.

"Hi, Fred," beamed Smiling Mike. "Beautiful day, isn't it?"

"It's a beauty, all right," answered Fred, halting. "I wish I could say the same about that outfit you're wearing. I saw you coming from a half-a-block away. Holy Mackerel! A tie with big white X's!" Fred shook his head disdainfully. *"You sure do know how to pick the doozies!"*

Smiling Mike stopped smiling.

His mood *instantly changed!*

Ann Lande

Dear Ann Landers: Regarding your recent column in the Dallas Times Herald:

When did I stop beating my wife? It was when I realized she provoked me because she wanted to suffer. Slapping her around seemed to satisfy her temporarily, but it wasn't a permanent solution.

In answer to L.T.L.'s recommendation that "a bit of battering can be a good thing," don't be suckered into it. Some women drive a man up the wall because they know they'll get hit. Then they can feel sorry for themselves and make HIM look bad. I know all about this sort of thing — first-hand. I'm signing myself — 'H.I.N.O. (Husband In Name Only)

Dear Husband: Sounds like a gorgeous marriage you two have. As my grandmother used to say — there's somebody for everybody.

Dear Ann Landers: My husband and I enjoy a wide range of friends — some social, some business. The diversity adds spice to our lives and to theirs. More than a few are plenty overweight.

Surprisinlgly, many of them have one thing in common — the ability or unconscious desire to em

Horosc

By CARROLL RIGHTER
GENERAL TENDENCIES: A goo
day to put in motion a new plan of a
that can provide a greater
ersonal advance
sit long-t
re.

fire kills 41

Coast said, although some bodies
through were so badly charred that
is West identification could not be
early made quickly. There were
people no immediate reports that
es de- any Americans were
sys- among the victims.
an   A fire brigade command-
rench er said later Thursday it
      was possible there were
vere more bodies under the
ate wreckage.

r days are
on trees

As Fred walked past, shaking his head derisively, Smiling Mike *cussed*.

He has disliked Fred ever since!

More, he has stopped patronizing the supermarket where Fred owns the fruit and vegetable concession!

The positive and negative sides of Recognition Emotional Appeal lash out suddenly.

Of all people, the Recognition Cow is the quickest to erupt or seethe with a simmering "slow burn" that can last a lifetime.

Since Recognition fears and desires are such a vital part of everyone's feelings, Recognition-charged words and actions must be kept under control at all times. Haphazardly chosen expressions having the wrong Recognition Appeal for a person or group can cause dislike, hatred, lost friendships or violence.

In human communication, the Emotional Appeal of Recognition can instantly break Preoccupation, enter a mind or change a mind. It relates to pride, opinion, appreciation, identification with clothing, appearance, behavior, events, people, products or organizations. It embraces emotional tie-ins to loneliness, popularity and the way you appear "in the eyes of others."

Looking "good" to others is important to *us*.

There is far more emotional fact than fable in the actions of a 53-year-old "bachelor girl" who told her aunt about her shock at finding four empty whiskey bottles in her garbage can.

"I was so embarrassed," she primly pouted. "I removed them immediately. Would it be nice to have the garbage men think that I drink?"

"No, it wouldn't," agreed her aunt. "What did you do with the four bottles?"

"Well, there's a minister who lives next door," she confided. "I put them in *his* garbage can. *Everybody knows that he doesn't drink!*"

Recognition desires make millions of people falsify inner facts by outer expressions and appearances. These "false fronts" may include name-dropping, exaggeration, "showing-off," imaginary adventures, or living beyond one's means.

It is not unusual for the person to whom Recognition is particularly important to pour a less expensive whiskey into a known-to-be-more-expensive brand bottle. He often knows that this is illegal, because the words: "Federal law forbids the sale or re-use of this bottle" are *on* the bottle—but he wants to impress his guests!

For related Recognition reasons, countless people foster "label switching."

A man or woman buys clothing or furs at a discount or low-cost store. Thereafter, he or she will obtain a label purporting to come from a store or supplier well-known for expensive or exclusive creations. This emotionally-identifiable woman may hand a fur coat to a hostess with the expensive label *up* just to make an impression.

The man who wants to "show-off" will purposefully open his jacket, turn out his inner jacket pocket where the label is sewn and reach in so that the expensive label is directly seen by the one he wishes to impress!

Untold millions express their Recognition desires and fears by similarly extreme actions. Is there anything *wrong* with these people? Rarely. These are the people who live with you, work with you, meet with you. They are just human beings doing what comes *naturally!*

If you sincerely want to be better-liked by them, show that you ARE impressed by their words, actions or possessions.

It's as simple as that!

When you help a Recognition Cow "look better," you pave the way towards being better liked; when your words or actions help a Recognition Cow "look bad"—watch out!

The Recognition emotional component can be a dangerous word or action explosive or a powerful drive towards attainment. It may make us complimentary or catty; idolize or criticize.

In the fuss of an argument, we may impatiently remark: "You're crazy! You don't know what you're talking about!"

Or, "What a foolish thing to say. You ought to have your head examined!"

"If you had any sense, you would never say things like that!"

Sense? How insensible *we* are! Such remarks give us little chance to motivate, persuade, or to be better-liked by our listener.

Are we using good Emotional Appeal? We are *not!* This talk violates vital Recognition desire.

When we make ourselves smarter, saner or *more* sensible than those with whom we are communicating, we minimize our chances to convince, be respected or appreciated.

Emotionally, our attention must be concentrated upon the needs of others, not upon ourselves!

Use your ears. Teach yourself to *listen* to others when they speak to you. Their words and actions will repeatedly reveal the direction of their *big* Preoccupation-breaking, Preoccupation-holding Emotional Appeals.

Listen with your eyes. This much-desired bit of Recognition will *always* serve you, and you need not say a word!

Your depth of interest is mirrored by your eyes and your surrounding expression. It is what every speaker seeks from you.

"Attentive silence" is impressive, expressive, and activates emotionally-satisfying contact between listener and speaker!

Remove your worries, operations, children, failures and complaints from your communication with others. If asked about these, keep your answers smiling, courteous and brief.

Telling about physical handicaps, sorrows, bad luck and bad health often begets a negative Recognition reaction. You may derive pleasure from such self-pitying subjects, but they're so personal that your listeners can feel neglected and promptly become Preoccupied.

Attention is being concentrated upon you instead of upon your audience!

"I shouldn't have come to your party, Harriet," you declare to your hostess as two other guests look on. "My nose is running and I've been sneezing all day. Look at this pimple breaking out on my chin. I should have stayed home in bed!"

How do Harriet and the other listeners react? Individually, they feel: "I wish you *did* stay home. I have my own troubles. I didn't come to this party to listen to *yours!*"

To be better liked, those with whom you communicate must be made to feel *more* important, not less important.

No speaker is more important than his or her listener.

The listener is the *reason* for the speaker, the reader is the *objective* of the writer, the customer is the *target* for the sales-person, the attorney is the *emotional sounding board* for the client. In all cases, the attempt to communicate works the other way, too.

When we require an attorney's services, we want to protect ourselves, our money, property, or the well-being of those dear to us. As plaintiffs, we want the satisfaction of being in the right and suing successfully. As defendants, we fear loss of the action; such loss may affect our health, finances, prestige or aspirations.

The alert and successful attorney plays a strong Recognition hand of understanding. He will uncover and act upon our emotional viewpoints and make us feel important. By gaining our cooperation and confidence, he can usually present a better case.

We will *like* him.

The Emotional Appeal in his words and actions can make us happier, better satisfied clients who will recommend other clients, *regardless of the outcome of the case!*

Adroitly directed use of ears, eyes and Recognition Emotional Appeal can make *any* attorney and *any* person better-liked and more successful in *any* relationship.

A handyman-house painter contracted with a luxuriously-appointed dancing school to take dancing lessons for a year. After starting the course, he realized that he could not afford the $3,100 he was committed to pay. He consulted an attorney, who pronounced the contract ironclad and thoroughly enforce-able. Sadly, the grime-stained client rose to leave.

"Just a moment," said the attorney.

He rapidly reviewed the Fatal Four and realized that the dancing school would not be receptive to Self-Preservation, Romance or Money Appeals. As a matter of fact, Money was un-doubtedly the main reason why it wanted to enforce the con-tract!

By elimination, Recognition had to be the handyman's strongest Emotional Appeal, *and it had to be made more im-portant to the dancing school than making Money on the con-tract.*

The attorney instructed the handyman to attend the next two dancing sessions wearing his work clothes!

The dancing school's management became so upset by the lowered tone that his appearance lent their dance studio that they admitted defeat, tore up the contract and saved the handyman some $3,100!

Recognition is the fourth major emotional indicator that governs our attitudes, wishes, achievements or reactions. Since there is always an emotional factor behind what we say or do, words and actions of Recognition can be the Preoccupation-breaking stimulus that makes others receptive to welcome, agree, reject or like.

Projected with foresight, persistence, and favorable emotional identification, Recognition represents an omnipotent power for improved Personality and Persuasion. Thoughtlessly used, it can swiftly create conflict, change of outlook and attitude and lasting distress.

Control your words and actions. If you don't, they may have the wrong emotional effect when you communicate.

Remember that your listener is a Very Important Person.

Even if you ask a 10-year-old neighborhood boy to take your dress or suit to the cleaner's, you must see *his* side of the situation. If you don't, he may promptly yip, "Aw, take it yourself."

If your personality has not had proper Emotional Appeal to him in the past, he'll probably refuse you the favor anyway, dime or no dime!

Another way to use Recognition to increase your likeability is to rid yourself of long-winded apologies, excuses and alibis.

Almost all alibis and excuses are lies.

Most often, we alibi in order to emotionally "save face" to others; occasionally, we alibi to "save face" to ourselves.

The alibi is part of Recognition. Few people avoid making an excuse unless they are so obviously wrong that they do not stand a "fighting chance." If they *do* have the chance, they'll bluff it out—because they hope for the satisfaction of *winning* the bluff!

Depending upon the emotional makeup of the individual, the extent of his imagination and the particularity of the situation, lies will always be with us and so will liars.

During the baseball and racing seasons, lies flourish as a national sport.

"I'm awfully sorry, Boss," moans Arthur. "My ears are ringing. It must be a bad cold coming on. Will it be all right to leave the office early?"

After gaining permission, thousands of "Arthurs" join friends at race tracks and baseball parks!

Unfortunately, each of us has a Recognition desire to "look good," to have others want and like us. Such emotional needs overshadow a good deal of truth telling, and we fear *opposite* reactions.

We lie, try to protect appearances and stay in the good graces of others, according to the extent of our private conceptions of right and wrong.

While lies and alibis are within personal desires and fears concerned with Recognition, successful use of this Emotional Appeal emphasizes the need to concentrate upon others before concentrating on ourselves. By telling more *truth* about ourselves, we can give more Recognition to others and become better-liked. *Once we are better-liked, we gain in initiative and personality.*

Soon, we become more persuasive.

Sometimes our tongues twist and words come out garbled. We start again while our listener laughs.

Why go into a profuse excuse? Laugh right along! The joke is on you. You're facing up to a fact. You're acting like a human being, with faults. That's the way you were emotionally meant to be, so act naturally.

I once heard an excellent lecturer garble a half dozen words.

Despite the seriousness of his subject, the audience roared. Instead of starting a weak-kneed apology or alibi, the speaker joined the laughter. As it quieted, he told a story.

A lady went into a butcher shop and pointed to some meat in one of the showcases. "Let me have a pound of those KIDLEYS," she told the butcher.

"Er," hesitated the butcher, "I'm sure that you mean KIDNEYS!"

"Why, that's what I said," screamed the lady. "DIDDLE I?"

The tale received a resounding chuckle—and the audience loved the speaker for telling it. No apology or alibi was given, yet the listeners knew that the lecturer was admitting that he had made an error.

He made the audience feel *big;* he made himself seem small. It *is* human to err, isn't it?

When you're late for a date and it can't be avoided, let the extent of your apology be: "Sorry I inconvenienced *you.* I know I'm late."

Change the subject as soon as possible letting the listener retain the advantage.

He or she *wants* this Recognition!

When you have a severe headache and want to make a good impression on others, don't call special attention to your problem. Your listener, customer or client *wants* to be more important than you, so allow him to fulfill this Recognition desire!

Why emphasize a physical disability, fault or weakness?

Dwell too long on your hard-to-wave hair, unshined shoes, shiny nose or mussed appearance and your listener feels overlooked.

Eliminate excuses, apologies and alibis!

Every listener has at least as many hard-luck stories as a speaker!

If eight-year-old Mathilda is subtly shoved over to the piano in order to give a special recital for Aunt Ophelia, don't apologize by saying: "Mathilda's only been taking lessons for three years, you know!"

Aunt Ophelia doesn't need any excuses for Mathilda's sournotes. She's a courageous woman to listen smilingly in the first place. Say nothing and Mathilda's mistakes won't sound so bad!

Coughing, clearing your throat, loosening a collar, glancing into a mirror for a check-up, adjusting clothing and such are all natural gestures that are strictly personal. They are *not* strictly personal when you have an audience.

These personal mannerisms are mistaken for nervousness, lack of confidence, fear or lack of good manners. They focus the wrong kind of Recognition.

If you think that you're too fat, too skinny, too tall or small, why act "self-conscious?"

If you have weaknesses, apologies and excuses only highlight them. When you must draw attention, emphasize your *strong* points, your "listening factors," your Emotional Appeal.

Make your listener important—not yourself!

You end a joke. "So the three-headed monkey didn't know which head to scratch! Ha-Ha!"

You laugh as you deliver this punch line, but your listeners stare blankly. You try again.

"Now, three heads on *one* monkey would surely seem strange. Get it? . . . So the pay-off is: He 'didn't know which head to scratch!' "

Your listeners sigh and you feel colder than the floor of a deep freeze. Your joke has fallen flat and you feel awful.

You have placed yourself into this position because you have violated an important principle of Recognition. When your joke or story doesn't get the laugh you expect, why explain it?

As soon as you start explaining, your listeners believe that you are understimating their ability to comprehend. Once they believe this, they will *not* think well of you.

Your listener wants to be recognized *for* intelligence not the lack of it!

If you have a feeling of "inferiority" use the motivating power of Recognition Emotional Appeal to cure it. *Tell* others that you feel inferior to *them.*

They'll like you and thank you for the compliment, and your feeling of "inferiority" will soon begin to *disappear!*

Don't call attention to yourself. Every time you do you belittle your listeners!

Allow your words and actions to fertilize your *listener's* hunger for Recognition, not your own.

In Providence, Rhode Island, shortly after the Civil War, a political candidate did this with a few words and won an election.

Two men were candidates for a seat in the United States House of Representatives. One had been a general during the war; the other, a private.

On the day before Election Day, each delivered his final campaign speech to the assembled voters.

The general was emphatic. "You all know that I was a general, a man of great responsibility. If my worthy opponent is worthy of taking the responsibility of representing you in Congress, why wasn't *he* a general? Tomorrow, vote for me—the general!"

The crowd applauded loudly and he sat down.

Meekly, the former "private" rose. Could he controvert the general's reasoning?

"The general told you the truth," he began. "During the war, he was a general and I was a private. Tomorrow is Election Day and you are entitled to vote." Dramatically, he raised his right hand and his voice. "All those among you who were generals— vote for him; privates—vote for me!"

The "private" and his Recognition Appeal won the election by a huge margin.

Oliver Wendell Holmes once listed those he disliked: "People who know everything; loud people; people who talk about their aches and pains; people who affect the grand manner as if we were insects; people who gush."

Perhaps you would add others to Dr. Holmes' list; perhaps you would focus a talking picture of people you know,

Dr. Holmes especially disliked people who made themselves more important than their listeners!

Now *another* secret can be yours.

The reason why many people will like you is because they feel a sense of importance in your company! You will be interested in them . . . *their* troubles . . . *their* children . . . *their* successes.

You will show your interest by your *words* . . . your *truths* . . . your *actions* . . . and *the way you listen.* You will make yourself an *emotional part* of those with whom you communicate.

Such Recognition of the feelings of others will gain more Recognition for you.

It is the surest way to make yourself better liked by more people!

The power of praise.

A glib, 29-year-old applied for a job with a tool manufacturer. His interviewer was a business-like, well-dressed woman in her mid-thirties, with a pocked chin and a growth of black hair over her upper lip.

"First," she pointedly asked. "How old are you?"

"On the right side of fallen arches and withered illusions," he quipped, smilingly. "Just like you!"

The lady laughed. "You mean that you are the *same* age as I?"

He nodded. "Just about."

Quietly, she queried: "How old am I?"

He squirmed.

"Come, now," pressed the interviewer. "Why do you hesitate?"

"I'm hesitating," he purred, "because I can't decide whether to guess ten years younger *because of your beautiful face* or ten years older because of your cleverness!"

The lady interviewer blushed and changed the subject. In a few minutes, she ended the interview.

Be sincere about compliments. Offer them sparingly. Base them upon the person and situation.

"Take from a woman all mirrors," said Madame Pompadour, "and glances of men will tell her that she is pretty. Take from her the glances of men and those of women and children will tell her. A pretty woman and one who is not pretty are so dissimilar that all nature presents itself under different aspects!"

The lady interviewer did *not* have a beautiful face and she knew it. To her, the contrived compliment was an insult and a jibe at an obvious physical portion of her emotional self, her face!

Words of praise are a universal Recognition need, but individualized reactions must always be anticipated.

Few experiences are more emotionally pleasing than a well-deserved compliment; few occurrences are more emotionally distasteful than words of deflation or criticism.

One reason why some people won't speak to one another is that they have no one to talk about.

Most of us *like* to find fault with others. We rarely realize that we inflate our own importance when we belittle someone else. If we unduly seek out and comment upon the faults of others, we often reveal a lack of confidence in ourselves.

When we prepare a project, we hope for appreciation.

When we prepare a meal, test for taste, expend time and effort and serve with pride, we expect some complimentary comment. If it is not forthcoming, we feel hurt and rightly so. Our desire for Recognition has been by-passed.

Often, the difference between a good hostess and a bad one is a sincere compliment!

Irritability and argument may be our way of righting this "wrong." We may implant a grudge that waits to spout venom.

If we did not actually flare up, it was probably because others were around, and we wanted to *appear* unperturbed for reasons of Recognition.

When words and actions violate Recognition desires, they can stimulate emotional conflict. Such conflict may evidence itself in sudden anger, unexpected obstinacy, dislike, physical violence.

Between marital partners, it frequently carries over into a refusal to kiss or make love!

One woman has disliked her sister-in-law for years because she overheard the sister-in-law telling a neighbor: "*I wonder how her husband can put up with her silly moods!*"

A man refuses to welcome a brother who once remarked: "*I'd hate to wake up in the morning and find his wife's face looking at me in bed!*"

Emerson said: No man has a prosperity so high and firm but that two or three words can dishearten it."

So many times, these words and actions run contrary to our feelings for Recognition.

Think, for example, of a green-and-purple dress that a wife chooses to please her husband; recall a gray-black topcoat that a husband is positive his wife will like—one with a checkerboard design; remember a square hat an unmarried girl purchased to please her boy-friend.

Now, imagine hubby ridiculing the way his wife looks in the green-and-purple dress even before he sees the bargain price! Envision the wife's snide snickering when the husband seeks her approval of the checkerboard topcoat! Picture the unmarried girl's fury when her boy friend greets her on a Sunday, so Preoccupied with a mud spot on his coat that he doesn't even notice her new hat. When she asks how he likes it, what does he say?

"A square hat, eh? Honey, it would look better on a mule with a square head; not on you!"

What a reaction she has!

And how about the time you invited your friend Anna over, after you put up those maroon-and-blue drapes and nearly fell off the ladder?

Can you forget how you felt when Anna stared at the drapes, wrinkled her nose and commented: *"They're all right, I suppose, but solid blue would have been a much better choice for your walls and carpeting!"*

You don't invite Anna in as often as you used to, do you?

When a friend selects new clothes, hairdo, apartment decoration or wife, rest assured that it required personal taste and time. Your friend has feelings and *wants* Recognition.

As it is deserving, show your approval with a compliment! Ask your friend's opinion on some of *your* problems!

Your power to praise can make people *want* you . . . *admire* you . . . *defend* you . . . *agree* with you.

People *need* appreciation for their work, choice, appearance, attitudes and actions.

Appreciation is a slumbering silhouette often wrapped in Recognition.

Since we differ emotionally as individuals, appreciation may be translated in ways that range from "Thank you! That's a good idea, Frank!" to "I must compliment you upon your ability, Cynthia. This is an excellent report!" or "I love you!"

Outside of intimately personal instances, when praise is presented in the presence of others it has even greater Emotional Appeal.

To secure any pure form of appreciation, persistence is a vital virtue. When we half-try to achieve objectives in friendships, love, family, marriage or business, we rarely capture the appreciation we require. When we *fully* try with the *right* Emotional Appeal, appreciation and desired Recognition can come!

"Nothing can take the place of persistence," wrote Calvin Coolidge. "Talent will not do it; nothing is more common than unsuccessful people with talent. Genius will not; unrewarded genius is almost a proverb. Education will not; the world is full of educated derelicts. Persistence and determination are omnipotent!"

"This day," penned Christopher Columbus in his log, as he sat in a frail ship on an unknown ocean, "despite imminent threats of mutiny and storms, *we sailed West because it was our course.*"

To hasten appreciative reactions from a person, emotionally identify him or her from among the Fatal Four Emotional Appeals and be sure to keep a tight rein on your Power to Praise.

But be sincere.

A story was told about Clarence Darrow, the famous attorney. He once advised a friend that a provision in his will called for cremation of his body, with ashes strewn from a hill overlooking Jackson Park in Chicago.

"*If such an event comes about,*" sighed the friend, "*a man will have to walk all over Jackson Park to get an outstanding legal opinion!*"

Clarence Darrow must have blushed with pleasure and glowed with pride. The compliment embodied a depth of sincerity.

The desire for praise is locked in every listener; unlock it and it will reward you *and* your listener.

A student, L., was a travelling salesman.

Barbers who served him during his trips knew that they would neither see him again nor make him a regular customer, so they tended to "get the job over with."

Neat in appearance, one of L.'s biggest problems in travelling was: "*How can I get a good haircut from a strange barber?*"

When he used Recognition, the *right* Emotional Appeal, he usually got the *right* haircut!

Before sitting in the barber's chair, he would smile and nod to the barber. The barber, in turn, smiled and nodded to him.

Shortly after the barber started snipping, L. would say, "*You have such light hands. Why, I can hardly feel that you're giving me a haircut!*"

Flattered, the barber would thereafter *outdo himself* to be worthy of the compliment. L. told me that barbers would put such time and care into their work that they often kept their *regular* customers waiting!

If you want a *better* haircut. try this Emotional Appeal on *your* barber, *even if you know him well!*

Praise, given in advance, can make a person *prove* that he deserves it.

If criticism *is* necessary, train yourself to express it with related *good* comment about your listener. You will be more persuasive and much better liked.

When Betty is late again, a comment like: "Can't you ever keep an appointment on time?" has far less persuasiveness and shows less self-control than *"You're dependable in so many ways, Betty. Why do you have trouble keeping appointments on time?"*

Seek out the good in another *before* talking up the bad. Why build an emotional wall between yourself and your listener? With Emotional Appeal Technique, you can just as easily build a *bridge!*

As you practise the art of paying compliments and giving deserved reassurance and appreciation, you will discover that it is far more difficult to say *nice* things than to find fault. Being *nice*, you know, involves use of words and actions with the *right* Emotional Appeal.

No matter how many compliments you may feel like paying, the people you communicate with will not be around long enough to receive the *full* amount they deserve.

Neither will you.

Take Berton Braley's word for it: "If you think that praise is due him, NOW's the time to slip it to him . . . for he cannot read his tombstone when he's dead!"

Make the Power of Praise a powerful portion of *your* ability to motivate and make others want to listen. You'll truly say it with Emotional Appeal!

Riding the recognition train to attainment.

During the many years I have taught and lectured on the subject of Emotional Appeal, I have gained great satisfaction from the almost innumerable ways that students have been able to apply the Technique in order to better understand themselves and communicate more successfully with others.

Ninety-nine percent of the time, people do not *truly* communicate; they *attempt* to communicate. And what a difference there is between *trying* and *succeeding!*

This difference is in the emotional contact made. When the *big* "listening factor" within each of us is properly tapped, it is possible to *enter* our minds and *change* Preoccupation-holding attitudes! If emotionally wrong communication contact is made, or there is no contact at all—neither minds nor attitudes may be changed.

The first forward step in communication contact lies in your ability to uncover the *big* motivating Emotional Appeal from among the Fatal Four of Self-Preservation, Money, Romance and Recognition. Once this "listening factor" is identified, it becomes easier to "reach" a person with words and actions containing the *right* Emotional Appeal.

How do you identify the *big* Emotional Appeal in a person? By knowing the definitions and inclusions of the Fatal Four, then, by objectively observing the words and actions that characterize the Self-Preservation, Money, Romance or Recognition "Cow."

We *all* have these emotional characteristics and we exhibit them when we communicate. When you use Emotional Appeal Technique, you can emotionally identify your listener.

Even in extremely individualized communication situations, this is truly your train to attainment!

One of my students, Ralph, had a close friend named Tom who had become an alcoholic.

Tom, an accountant, had tried personal and group therapy without success.

Ralph and his wife, June, wanted to help Tom. They felt that the experts he had consulted had not "reached him" in terms of his deep-down *emotional* reasons for drinking or not drinking. In general, they were *attempting* to communicate; in particular, they were not communicating with Tom according to his personalized emotional needs and feelings.

To uncover Tom's BIG listening factor, Ralph tried to recall as many situations as possible when he and Tom had been boyhood buddies. He remembered wartime and more recent experiences and made a list.

He knew that Tom had an ultra-strong ego.

Through the years, Tom had argued and fought physically with those who had offended it. As a youth, he had become overly jealous and upset when attentions were paid to his girl friends by other fellows.

In selecting a girl friend, beauty had been of paramount importance; he *wanted* to be seen with an attractive girl and had constantly made certain that others knew that the girl was *his*. In selecting apparel, individuality of design and enhanced appearance had always been more important than cost and Tom thoroughly enjoyed being complimented upon possessions, adventures and "names" he knew.

Ralph knew that Tom had started his overindulgence in liquor while in military service. On each drinking occasion he had tried to out-do those around him, both capacity-wise and as a center of attention.

Weighing these and other indications, Ralph decided that Tom's BIG Emotional Appeal was Recognition. If he could be emotionally reached via Recognition, thought Ralph, Tom might begin to become more emotionally aware of himself and possibly curtail and control his alcoholic tendencies.

With the cooperation of June, Ralph developed a unique, *particularized* communication approach.

June and Ralph invited Tom and five other friends to dinner. Cocktails were served. After the first drink, Ralph removed the liquor and June announced that dinner was ready.

There were eight settings at the table. Each place had a dinner plate, silverware and napkin—except Tom's.

His setting consisted of one glass.

Tom looked at the other settings and reddened. He called to his hostess: "June, did you forget me? Where is my dinner plate?"

"We *eat* our dinners, Tom, so we use plates," replied June

steadily. "You usually *drink* your meals. That's why you were served a *glass!*"

Tom winced. He lowered his eyes and peered at the table-cloth in a sub-zero hush. "I promise," he choked, "I promise that you will never again be ashamed to have me with you. Now, may I *please* have a plate and some silverware?"

The incident was the initial step towards changing Tom's drinking habits. For the first time, he had been *emotionally* reached by communication that performed deep surgery on his *feelings*—not his thinking—about the right or wrong of his actions. A Recognition *fear* had been uncovered that was stronger than a Recognition desire . . . in a Recognition Cow.

Because the communication was correctly *particularized* emotionally, it reached its target—Tom. And the emotional reaction *remained* in his memory, because the "listening factor" was *right!*

Ralph and June told me that Tom remained a close friend and kept his promise. He also remained a Recognition Cow—and a wonderful one—with his words and actions. About three years after the "glass incident" he married. Although he joined them in a drink or so on occasion, he had no recurring problem with overindulgence that had ever again come to their attention!

Miss T., a high school teacher, enjoyed a vastly different mass communication attainment via Recognition Emotional Appeal.

Her problem?

"How can I use Emotional Appeal Technique to increase the grades in my poorest French class?"

Miss T. had become quite exasperated by the poor showing of a class of 38 teen-agers. Marks had been as low as 40. From these facts, she sought out the most important Preoccupation-breaking Emotional Appeal that would fit her suggestion to her students. After an emotional search into the other three Emotional Appeals, she decided that her answer rested within Recognition.

She went to the blackboard, turned to her class and asked: "Do you know the passing mark in French? It's 75," she said, writing the number on the board.

"Do you know what grades many of you received in yesterday's French examination?" she continued. "Marks were as low as 40, 55 and 60. Suppose I write these numbers, too."

She did. "Is there anything terrible about such low grades? No. There is a shame, though, in having such a low mark *stand next to your name*—because we should all be proud of our names. Imagine! M. Brown—40; J. Gramme—55; O. Zipey—60," she lamented, printing a name next to each low grade.

"Isn't your name important enough to have a *higher* number next to it? A number like 95 or 85 or 100? If you think it is, I'm going to give you a chance to prove it!"

"There will be another French test on the day after tomorrow. *The number next to your name will show everyone in the class whether your name is important—or not worth very much!*"

Miss T. reported that this *en masse* Recognition Appeal increased the grades of her class by 26 per cent!

The wish for Recognition and the fear of going on without it will always be emotional drives that result in individual and group achievement—despite financial, educational, social and physical handicaps. Often, Recognition desire has been the emotional motivation that has nurtured unrelenting initiative and ambition.

Beethoven was deaf; Lord Byron had a club foot; Helen Keller was deaf, dumb and blind; Glenn Cunningham, one of the greatest runners in history, had withered leg muscles from severe burns during childhood; Demosthenes stuttered, had weak lungs and a grating voice, yet became one of the most persuasive orators; poverty-stricken George Washington Carver achieved fame for his scientific brilliance; popular singer Perry Como was a small town barber.

These and other individuals were so imbued by their desire for Recognition that they gained greater emotional command over themselves. You can too.

If Recognition is *your* BIG Emotional Appeal, you will hasten your attainments by remembering that: *"To gain Recognition, your words and actions must give Recognition!"*

Although degree of determination differs from person to person, hope for accomplishment is often impatiently imbedded.

The woman or man who has particularly powerful desires for Recognition usually isolates such hopes and repeatedly pushes them forth. In many instances, fulfillment follows—even against seemingly insurmountable odds.

Pitcher Carl Derose of the Kansas City Blues had a recurrently ailing arm. He was warned that his baseball career was almost over, but he refused to accept such physical and emotional defeat. Diligently, he practised and pleaded for a chance to pitch.

Touched by his persistence, his manager started him against the heavy-hitting Minneapolis club on June 26, 1948.

Inning after inning, Derose pitched masterfully. By the fifth, his arm became increasingly painful but Minneapolis remained hitless.

Motivated by a desire to prove his prowess to the doubters, he summoned up every iota of ability and judgement. Although excruciating pain accompanied every pitch, he relentlessly reached towards his objective.

Inspired by his efforts, his team slammed in five runs and played errorless ball.

When the last Minneapolis batter struck out in the ninth inning, "washed up" Carl Derose had pitched the first *perfect* game in the history of the American Association.

No hits, no runs, and not a Minneapolis man reached first base!

Confucius said: "If I am building a mountain and stop before the last basketful of earth is placed on the summit, I have failed!"

When Recognition drives, determination thrives!

People in the creative world, writers and show business folk are particularly susceptible to and motivated by the Emotional Appeal of Recognition. There have been tens of instances in which actors, actresses, and entertainers have sought and made appearances and participated in "publicity stunts" because of their desire for Recognition.

Often, too, many people in less glamorous occupations regard the amount of their pay as indicative of the "amount" of their Recognition!

Like individuals who are principally motivated by—or receptive to—each of the other Emotional Appeals in the Fatal Four, the Recognition person repeatedly reveals himself in his communication with others. These emotional indicators include conversation, actions, appearance and personal habits.

Whether or not he is a "nice person" to *you* depends upon your own emotional makeup and needs and his reactions to *your* words and actions when you communicate!

He possesses all Four Emotional Appeals, of course, along with their positive and negative factors. Recognition, however, is his BIG Emotional Appeal—his most important motivating and "listening" factor. As a result, the user of Emotional Appeal Technique can readily identify the Recognition "Cow" and communicate more successfully for mutual satisfaction, respect and understanding.

The communication characteristics of the one whose BIG Emotional Appeal is Recognition cover a wide variety of emotional indicators—but all move in the same direction. He may assure himself, before facing others, that his suit, pocket handkerchief, tie or shoe shine is "just so" . . . He may habitually pull at his trouser creases and sleeves after sitting—particularly after he has held something on his lap. Why? Because he doesn't want the wrinkles to show! How "old" he looks will usually be important to him. Bald spots and grey hair will bother him—if they are *his*.

He exaggerates somewhat and occasionally enjoys "namedropping." At social functions, he likes being seen with the more attractive or important people. When others are attentive to his remarks, he glows. He steals a higher-than-average number of glances in mirrors or window reflections. Might he perhaps comb his hair *back* very, very carefully—then finalize with a tender *forward* pat to create the most flattering effect? Yes.

He is most often the impeccably uniformed pilot. Pride is his takeoff and landing!

The female in whom Recognition is a "super-must" evidences similar habits and communication characteristics.

Often she is the "This dress makes me look too fat" woman . . . the lady who brushes off imaginary dandruff or dust with a reassuring flick . . . the "Is my stocking seam straight?" wonderer. Sometimes she is the "permanent resident of a beauty parlor" who frequently *feels* to be sure that every curl is in place. More extreme examples include the "I must make an impression" overplayer who can wear slacks, shorts or denims and "forget" to remove her diamonds! Some tend to sharpen their ears when they powder their noses. Many gossip because of the sense of importance it gives them.

The Recognition Cow is easily "hurt"—and possesses an "I-won't-forget-this" attitude in wanting to "get even." Often, she feels deeply "indebted" until she returns invitation-for-invitation, favor-for-favor!

Individuals whose BIG Emotional Appeal is Recognition, more than the Self-Preservation, Money or Romance Cows, mistakenly overuse the pronoun "I"—a word that can emotionally minimize *any* listener. Good Recognition communication represents the "YOU" in a speaker's words—not the "I!"

To be more listenable, likeable and persuasive, the pronoun "I" should be *dropped* whenever possible. Instead, use pronouns with instantaneous Recognition Appeal; words like YOU . . . WE . . . US . . . OUR problem . . . YOUR family and mine. They will *always* help you ride the Recognition train to attainment!

People with a fine "sense of humor" have strong Recognition tendencies.

Why do so many like to tell jokes? Because they seek the Recognition that a laughter response assures! Emotionally, however, laughter can be a road of action . . . and *reaction!*

The young daughter of an internationally famous comedian attended one of her father's movies. While the audience roared with glee, she *cried.*

When her mother asked the reason, the child said that she thought the people were laughing *at* her father—not *with* him!

The individual who frequently interrupts when you speak may irritate you or seem discourteous. Most often, he isn't. He is just indicating that he is ready for Recognition.

He can't wait to let you finish *your* thought because he is emotionally anxious to have you listen to *his!*

Alert yourself to the interrupter; communicate *successfully* . . . with Recognition words and actions!

These are all strongly indicative clues to the person we call the Recognition Cow. There is a wealth of other evidence that you can identify and use with your present interpretation and understanding of Recognition as a prepotent motivator in yourself and in your listeners.

Recognition is principally an Emotional Appeal to the "ego" —or an upset of it.

Each of us has ego. Each is a big "I am" underneath. Many of us who aren't would certainly like to be! Here are two more ways we can heighten our attainments with well-directed Recognition Appeal:

1—*No matter how important you think you are, let somebody else tell you!*

2—*Emotionally "build" yourself d-o-w-n; emotionally*, such communication will *"build" your listener U-P!*

Attendance at regular monthly meetings of a community organization had fallen off. The president and his committee wrote letters to the members and made personal phone calls, but were unable to improve the situation.

They suffered particular embarrassment on an evening when a prominent speaker was featured and addressed a mere handful of people!

For the next meeting, they engaged another speaker. This time, they preceded his appearance by enclosing an individualized letter and lapel badge for each member.

On the evening of the meeting, there was a packed house. More than two hundred members and guests attended.

Over half this number conspicuously wore a blue-and-gold paper badge bearing the member's name imprinted with the title:

```
┌─────────────────────────────────┐
│                                 │
│         Vice-Chairman           │
│    RECEPTION COMMITTEE          │
│                                 │
└─────────────────────────────────┘
```

Recognition had attracted and multiplied an Audience!
No matter who you are, belittle yourself—not your listener.

Admit that you're *not* very smart and most people will like you, because you confess *their* superiority. It is then emotionally *easier* for them to agree . . . do what you want them to do . . . or enjoy having you.

When General Eisenhower was first welcomed to New York City, he said: *"New York cannot do this to a Kansas farmer boy and keep its reputation for sophistication!"*

He made a huge number of people prouder of *themselves.*

As President, Franklin D. Roosevelt repeatedly opened his "Fireside Chats" with the words: "My friends . . . !"

You and I and all people listening—FRIENDS of the President of the United States!

Recognition is constantly at *your* emotional fingertips to help you gain attention, remembrance and attainment.

Speaking on the subject: "Dick Tracy, My Favorite Comic Strip," one of my students began by asking: "How would you like to walk down the street and have people point you out as the smartest, bravest detective in the country?"

This Recognition Appeal broke Preoccupation and immediately stimulated interest!

Like the other three of the Fatal Four Preoccupation-breaking, Preoccupation-holding Emotional Appeals, Recognition is a powerful emotional component that is omnipresent in every person and every group.

By understanding the impressive importance of Recognition, you can *identify it* in yourself and others and better *control* the reaction to this Emotional Appeal when you use it in your words and actions.

With such understanding and control, the Emotional Appeal of Recognition can truly be a Train to Attainment.

Won't *you* climb aboard?

How Emotional Appeal Technique Rapidly Rids You of Fears, Worries and Upsets

It was 6:30 A.M.

"Gladys" popped her blue eyes wide open and turned quickly as the alarm clock sounded its sandpapery screech. Her right hand reached out in a familiar arc and her fingers closed on the alarm hammer.

Silence . . . and the chirping of early morning birds.

Gladys felt vitally refreshed. She bounced out of bed, brushed the window curtain aside and merrily smiled at the sunlight.

She stretched. "Wonder what I should wear?" she mused. "Something nice and bright—just like this day."

Swiftly, she slipped into her peach-colored nylon robe. Twice, she whirled around in graceful pirouettes and hummed as she tip-toed into her frilly slippers.

At 7:20, she patted her red straw sailor onto her brownish-blonde hair and tunefully whistled. Five minutes later, she boarded the big green bus and sang out a cheery "Hello" to Gus, the driver.

"Swell morning, Miss," grunted Gus to his first and only passenger. "But it won't be good for everybody. It's *Friday, the thirteenth, you know!*"

Gladys stopped fumbling for change. "Today? *Friday the thirteenth?*" Horror splashed over her oval face. Her eyes widened. Her left hand tightly gripped the guide rail as she dropped her fare into the box.

"Please, Gus," she begged. "Drive slowly. Be *extra* careful!"

Timorously, she sat directly behind him. Perspiration bubbles formed trickling beads above her brows. Her lips quivered.

She rose and walked to the center exit door as Gus slowed down for the corner stop.

"What's the matter, Miss?" he called, half-turning. "Forget something?"

"No—it's something I just *remembered!*" Glady's voice was husky, urgent. "I sang before breakfast and whistled before leaving the house." She sighed. "I always take my first step with my *right* foot; this morning I used my *left!* A sob choked her. "Today's Friday, the thirteenth. Gus, I'm going back. I'm *doomed!*"

How superstitious are *you?* Does "Gladys" seem like an "extreme case," or does some part remind you of yourself or some person you know?

Are you the black cat worrier? Does the three-on-a-match fear suddenly break your Preoccupation?

Millions of us are superstitious or believe in luck charms. Because of individual differences, some of us prefer one superstition to another and attach personal meanings to things that "just happen."

Superstitions are fear-filled fancies.

Why is a "black" cat unlucky—when cats of other colors are pretty much "all right?" Black—since ancient days, has represented darkness and the unknown. The "cat" idea, you will recall, has been connected with all sorts of nursery rhymes and witches. So—like other memories that emotionally "grew" into our experience, "black cats" grew along too!

The "witch" has always had dramatic definition—and a "villain" can draw as much attention as a hero. Even William Shakespeare played up this theme in "Trouble! Trouble!" . . . spoken over a boiling cauldron of witches' brew!

The "three-on-a-match" fear, we are told, was created and publicized by a match magnate who wanted us to use more matches!

Our fictional "Gladys" may have seemed super-superstitious

when she so fearfully reacted to the day being Friday-the-thirteenth.

Friday is not the shiver-giver; the number "thirteen" *is!* Today, many buildings in New York and other large cities "leave out" their thirteenth floor. Renting agents have too frequently found it a bar to rentals!

Many airlines omit a "13th seat" on planes.

In a New York Medical Center, psychiatrists once studied the "Number 13 Fear." While doing so, they worked in a multi-storied building. *The floor between the 12th and 14th was designated as "P Floor!"*

What is thirteen? Just another number!

A London restaurateur claims it's his luckiest. He won a tax-free equivalent of $392,000 in Britain's national soccer sweep-stakes. Said he: "The street number of my house is *thirteen*. I mailed the winning entry on Friday, the thirteenth—and it was the thirteenth line on my ballot that gave me the prize!"

The desire for "good luck" has brought about huge buying audiences for such items as luck charms and rabbits' feet. It seems that the only thing *unlucky* about a rabbit's foot is the *rabbit!*

Worried because you broke a mirror? Seven years' "hard luck?" No! No! Thousands of people will swear that SEVEN is a very *lucky* number. Listen to the dice player's call: "Come on, you *lucky* seven!"

Are you superstitious about opening an umbrella *inside* your home or office? Any umbrella expert will assure you that it's hard to find a better way to dry it and preserve the fabric!

Believe in fortune tellers? Better than $150,000,000 is annually spent for fortune telling, tea-leaf readers, palmists, card analysts, horoscopists . . . even mystically-garbed "swamis."

Dream books? Luck-and-love potions? Salt for throwing-over-your-shoulder-after-walking-under-a-ladder?

These and hundreds of variations *do* exist and *will* continue, because "good luck" emotionally means many things related to the Fatal Four Emotional Appeals in each individual.

Due to our particularized emotional identifications, almost everyone possesses a "pet" superstition.

A Romance Cow I know is particularly careful to leave by the same door she enters! If she doesn't, she'll worry about it until a more enjoyable emotional stimulus breaks *this* Preoccupation and puts her mind on her preferred Preoccupation with sex attraction, a future promise, a novelty, an unusual person or a New Experience!

Superstitions can be *enjoyable* when you treat them lightly and laugh about them. They do you no good when they close your mind, start arguments, paralyze your opinions or get you upset.

The mere fact that a hanging street sign drops and misses your head *on the very day that you first wear your brown tweed suit* doesn't have a hidden meaning.

You will only *prompt* future fears, worries or upsets when a particularly "bad day" comes along and you are *not* wearing the "lucky" brown tweed suit!

Look into your emotions. *Face up to the Fatal Four groups of "feelings" within you.* Learn their Emotional Appeal Technique inclusions so you can readily identify each. You will better understand *yourself*—and the way *others* will emotionally react to the Emotional Appeal in *your* words and actions!

Fears wear many cloaks other than those sewn with the thread of superstition.

How you fear whatever you fear can be impossible for others to detect.

They do not notice your spine tingle . . . your lips imperceptibly purse . . . your eyelids flutter . . . your nerve endings tickle the nape of your neck . . . your heart jump . . . the self-pity that reverberatingly re-echoes . . . or the fact that you deliberately avoid certain people, places, or situations.

Most fear reflexes are not what you would undergo if a gruff voice behind you hisses: "Watch out. I have a gun!" Nor are they a flickering fluttering as you flee at midnight through an animal-infested jungle. You will rarely have the opportunity to freeze with fright, and there is not much chance that you will be at ease while on a 70-mile-an-hour roller coaster.

Fears are distinctively personal.

They restlessly remain in our Preoccupation as penned-up

worries that are directed by the emotional individuality that blankets them. This individuality depends upon the *personal* activations of the Fatal Four Emotional Appeals within you.

Our main fears consist of attitudes that seem unimportant to others, but are important to *us*. They relate to our emotional being and are a part of our personality.

Even such a general fear as the possibility of being rain-drenched without the protection of a raincoat, umbrella or rubbers can create individual differences in response.

Some of us may worry about what the rain may do to our appearance when others see us; many will concentrate upset upon the chance of catching cold or pneumonia; certain people will focus inner apprehension on "ruined clothes," cost of cleaning, pressing or medical care; a good percentage may damn the rain for spoiling an opportunity to "get away from it all."

And there will always be those whose rising anxiety is in the desire to save a new straw hat that gives an unaccustomed air of good looks or confidence!

To each, the fear is *emotionally* important.

Fears enter our minds and grip us in thousands of ways.

The bashful young man goes to a party. He summons up enough courage to introduce himself to the petite girl in the black-and-yellow dress.

Hesitantly, he remarks: "Haven't I seen your face somewhere else?" She frigidly replies: *"Certainly not. It always remains right here between my ears!"*

He crimsons.

The unexpected response shatters his confidence.

At a loss for words, he backs away, rebuffed.

He speaks to his host and acidly refers to the girl as "that sassy tomato in the black-and-yellow dress!"

If Recognition is his biggest emotional factor, the bashful young man may suffer a deep emotional slash. Confidence with the opposite sex may desert him for months or years. A deepening fear can drill into his personality—the way others emotionally react to *his* words and actions!

Fears are inadvertently reflected when we communicate. They are emotional indicators.

Parents fear about children, their careers, well-being, the influence friends hold over them. Will their daughter be an "old maid?" "Why doesn't she try to meet a nice fellow? She's past twenty-eight and hasn't had a date in nearly a year!"

Wives and husbands fear loss of love, by-passing of emotional desires, onset of age, lack of earning capacity, ill health, money problems. Worry-causing upsets are derived from stature in the family, business and social community, unfulfilled sexual desires and satisfactions, suspected impotence, spite, irritability, coldness and regret.

There are fears of job loss . . . an unwanted conception . . . war . . . death of a loved one . . . sickness or injury . . . bad publicity . . . criminal investigation . . . deprivation of money . . . waste of investment . . . imprisonment.

Such actual happenings could very seriously affect us.

Still, we daily distribute equal or greater emotional weight to upsets that plague us when we anticipate an unpleasant task . . . when we are about to repeat a much-disliked routine . . . when we become exasperated because we cannot afford something we want . . . when we fret about how others may react to our looks, friends or choice of clothing . . . when we are compelled to "face-up" to certain people or circumstances . . . when we worry about doing something for the first time . . . when we are perturbed about someone accepting an invitation that we do not want to be accepted . . . when we tense in an overt experience.

"A telegram? B-but we don't expect a telegram. I hope nothing happened to Jim!" . . . *"What can be wrong? Mildred is nearly an hour late for dinner!"* . . . Or, *"The phone is ringing and it's 3 a.m. There must be trouble!"*

Emotional needs originate fears!

The fear that people will make uncomplimentary comments after we have left their presence . . . the fear of a reprimand from a marital mate, parent, employer, or friend . . . the fear that our pot roast will not be praiseworthy . . . the fear that someone will notice that we have "aged a lot" . . . the fear that a certain person is going to cheat us . . . the fear that a chore will take longer than we have time for . . . the fear of exam

questions for which we are not prepared . . . the fear that
Romance will pass us by . . . the fear that a run may develop
in our stockings "at just the wrong time" . . . or that our husband, sweetheart or wife will not welcome our advances tonight.

Fears . . . fears . . . fears that fill Preoccupation, cloud thinking and emotionally entangle facts!

Except in the on-the-second immediate, there is no such thing
as fear. There are only *anticipations* within the Fatal Four when
we *think* about words, actions or situations that we *may* be
exposed to.

Why look forward to fears? You only invite unhappiness, a
Number One cause of illness, trouble and personal failure.

Look *backward* on fears and you will find that they were
mostly silly and unnecessary!

With Emotional Appeal Technique, you can rapidly rid yourself of fears—and worries and upsets too—by following these
Three Guiding Principles:

1. Quickly identify your fear in terms of the Fatal Four Emotional Appeals!

Isolate fears for what they are and what they are doing to you!

Is the fear related to health . . . injury . . . enjoyment? Parent-child situations? Sexual satisfactions? Death, personal freedom, religion, or another phase of Self-Preservation?

Does the upset have to do with possible cost or income? A
possession? Property damage or loss? Waste? Some other form
of Money worry?

Is the fear in the realm of sex attraction . . . desire for marriage . . . future promise? Is it akin to monotony, routine, or
need for New Experiences? Other elements of Romance as we
now know this powerful motivating and "listening factor?"

Does the fear tie-in to pride, appreciation, popularity? Need
for reassurance or aspects of Recognition feelings?

Is it a *superstitious* fear within the Fatal Four, like: "Forget
to drink the bubbles in a cup of coffee and you will lose money?"
. . . "Walk under a ladder and you'll soon after get hurt?" . . .

Or, "Miss the bride's bouquet when she throws it and you'll never get a husband?"

Identify your fear. Make this the *first* step towards *understanding* your fear feelings. And remember: *We fear what we do not understand far more than what we do!*

Uncover the cause of your fear in terms of your own interlocking emotional distribution. *Know your Fatal Four.*

Whatever the fear, worry or upset, identify it quickly!

2. Concentrate your attention elsewhere.

Direct your feelings to other things!

Get more work done each day. If you have not previously done so, make a written list of your daily objectives; if you already do this, *change* your schedule—even if only a *slight* change is possible.

Seek New Experiences . . . new friends . . . new ideas . . . new skills that stimulate your creative imagination. Hobbies like soap-or-wood sculpture, woodworking or painting should be acted upon. If you build things or bake, create an *original* approach for the edging or topping.

Look for new places . . . new entertainment . . . new ways to do things. Dare to experiment with your appearance, hair style, colors and type of wearing apparel. Choose a different way for traveling a familiar route.

Read more. Satisfy your curiosity about subjects you like—but "never got around to."

Suppose the subject is "dogs." Read up on the breeds you are most interested in . . . their origins and abilities. Make inquiries about shows that feature your favorite breeds. Attend them.

Or, let's say you have long wondered about judo. Is it possible for an unarmed man or woman to overcome a twice-as-big armed assailant? Is judo truly a defensive sport? Read! Attend classes. Watch demonstrations. Ask questions. Yes—even participate.

When you concentrate your attention elsewhere, you concentrate attention *off* your own fear feelings!

3. Play "opposites" emotionally.

Each of the Preoccupation-breaking, Preoccupation-holding Emotional Appeals of Self-Preservation, Money, Romance, and Recognition has two *opposite* sides—the *fear* and the *desire*. These are the emotional activators in every person.

By identifying and understanding more about your fear, worry or upset, you can assure yourself that there is no valid reason for it. Then, by concentrating your attention *off* the fear, the fear starts moving *off* your Preoccupied mind.

These are the first two steps. Now, take the third, if necessary.

Eliminate the fear by substituting a *desire*—the opposite emotion within the same Emotional Appeal. For example, if you identify your fear as a fear of Money *loss*—take affirmative action for Money *gain!*

A man, W., rapidly neutralized a deep-set Money fear when he used this approach.

W. owned and managed an apartment house-and-store property. It was his only investment and chief source of income. For months, he had been unable to cover his operating expense and fear began to fretfully fill his feelings.

Little by little, he visualized both his income and investment dwindling away.

He worried, brooded and communicated his pessimistic attitudes to his wife and two children. Gradually, they too began to seethe with worry and upset.

When he seemed almost overwhelmed by his ever-deepening Money fear, W. was called to my attention by a former student who defined the fear as ". . . a personal communication problem for Emotional Appeal Technique to solve!"

The fear was readily identified for W. Then, he was reminded of the many ways that he could remove his attention from it. Finally, he agreed to concentrate his feelings on a desire for Money *gain—not* a continuing fear of Money loss.

W. sought out a firm of managing agents. If they could assure him that their efforts would be income-producing by the end of a mutually satisfactory trial period, they would be retained and offered an incentive bonus based upon results.

The firm made an analysis for W. and recommended certain supervisory and procedural changes. Under their management, the apartment house and related property began to earn a better income for W. than he had ever thought it could.

Meanwhile, by playing "opposites" with his fear of Money loss, W.'s *affirmative* actions and attitudes began to eliminate the emotional negatives that had unnecessarily implanted themselves in his feelings and those with whom he communicated!

The rule of emotionally playing "opposites" can also be followed for other fears, worries, or upsets.

Is the fear a Romance fear? Move ahead with *desire* for Romance.

Communicate and accomplish this desire by putting the Romance chapter, Questions and other Chapters to work for you!

Is a *disagreement* "getting you down?" Take action with "opposites." Seek *agreement*.

Edmund Burke once said: "To concede is *not* to belittle one's self." Say it with the *right* Emotional Appeal and you can "give in" . . . without "giving up!"

Self-Preservation worry about ill health? Do something to help achieve *better* health.

See a medical doctor, a dentist or an oculist—as your situation demands. Get professional advice, then build up what you cannot physically help by training the Emotional Appeal in your words and actions to zip out with a vigor and energy what bad health cannot hold back!

This is another one of the many ways you can play "opposites" . . . emotionally!

Recognition fear?

Use your *desire* for Recognition as your motivation to *achieve* Recognition.

Others have done it; you can too. With Emotional Appeal Technique on *your* side, you have the "listening factors" that *reach* listeners!

Play "opposites" . . . emotionally.

You'll emerge with more energy and greater confidence every time you face yourself in the eyes of those with whom you communicate.

Whoever you are . . . whatever you do, Emotional Appeal Technique provides you with the understanding and prompt action that will make *any* personal problem more endurable.

Happiness is vital to your health, outlook and success. Let fears, worries and upsets *out* . . . and you bring more happiness *in*.

The problem of "emotional problems."

Today, more than ever before, men and women of every age and occupation are plagued by unnecessary "emotional problems."

Tensions . . . anxieties . . . conflicts . . . fears . . . frustrations and all sorts of upsets have attained unprecedented priorities in our Preoccupation. These emotional stresses cause huge losses in happiness, health, earning ability, production capacity and personal outlook.

A beautiful model with a child by a former husband falls in love again. The man tells her that he "wants her, but does not want the child!" She allows herself to be duped into thinking that the child is the barrier between herself and her chance to remarry. She turns her motherly love into multi-faceted hatred for a five-year-old boy who spends more time crying than sleeping!

An engineer believes that his supervisor unduly "picks on him." He becomes tense, quick to battle with his wife and slap his children. When there is little conversation, he rages; when there is a lot of conversation, he is tempestuously touchy. His wife has become sexually unreceptive and he has beaten her. He copes with the situation by venting venom on those with whom he believes he is secure. Now, everyone's unhappiness is more deeply imbedded by the emotional pounding and he is about to lose his job!

An executive abhors the irritability, loud voice, and "rotten disposition" of his wife. In the morning, it carries over into his business life and he finds himself making errors; an hour before leaving his office, he starts anticipating unhappiness upon arrival at home. He is so Preoccupied by his problem that he devotes many business hours to inventing excuses and planning ways to stay away from home. For religious and family reasons, he cannot consider divorce; for personal reasons, he is contemplating murder!

"Emotional problems" are a major cause of psychosomatic and physical diseases, personnel turnover, marital difficulties, financial troubles, spinsterhood, dejection, suicide and crime.

A man with a rich, attractive wife has a poor and plain-looking secretary. The wife finds more time for social obligations than marital ones; the husband receives more kindness, attention and understanding from his secretary. He demands a divorce. The wife shudders with shock and suffers intense upset. A partial paralysis sets into her face. The real reason for her upset is *"How will I look to the people who know me?"*

A lovely young lady in her early thirties has passed up marriage proposals because both she and her parents regard her suitors' occupations as too lowly. She meets a man and becomes fascinated when he reveals that he is a resident physician in a city hospital. Because of the assurance of his medical background, she participates in an intimate, pre-marital relationship. Although he is unreliable about appointments, he convinces her that *"Once we can afford to be married, it will be the only necessary evil about being a doctor's wife!"* One evening, he is two hours late. Against his request, she phones the city hospital. They assure her that there is no such doctor on the staff. Further check-up shows that he is married, father of three children and not a doctor at all. Since her discovery, she has become curt, introvertive and will not believe *any* man!

J. works for a firm for ten years. A promotion seems assured. Expecting the promotion, he assumes obligations that can only be met on the basis of the increased income. J. faces what he believes is an insurmountable financial burden when the job is awarded to a man from outside the company. He steals from his firm and makes false bookkeeping entries. After a conscience-stricken month, he convinces himself that the new man is beginning to suspect. Each day he palpitates with a mushrooming anxiety. On three occasions, he wants to leap in front of an approaching subway train but loses his nerve at the last moment!

The person who has a deep-set "emotional problem" is particularly Preoccupied. Such Preoccupation can cause embarrassment, mistakes, accidents on the job, at home, while eating, walking, or driving a motor vehicle.

A teen-age boy's father is "too busy" to interest himself in his son's activities and friends. The boy neglects homework and repeatedly alibis his reasons for coming home late. The father becomes numb with regret when his son is picked up by the police and suspected of a teen-age gang crime. Formerly a careful driver, the father remains so Preoccupied with his upset that he receives two traffic summonses for reckless driving within a few days after his son's arrest. On the first occasion, he miraculously misses a head-on collision with a police car; the second time, he narrowly avoids killing two children!

Inattention to the "emotional problems" of executives and employees costs American business multi-millions of dollars a year. And thousands of supposedly "successful" people are becoming increasingly aware that emotional stresses can cause a pronounced lack of success in their personal lives.

K., for instance, devotes a year-in, year-out, seven-day work week to his growing business. He conquers obstacles, takes some risks and becomes wealthy. From time to time, he remembers his wife and gives her expensive furs and diamonds. Mrs. K. accepts these graciously, then uses them to attract other men. She wants to be *wanted* by K., but K.'s overwhelming Preoccupation is with making more Money. His outlook crashes in on him when she insists upon ending the marriage. The property settlement costs him almost as much as he has gained—but he knows no way to make up his emotional loss!

Some people talk about their "emotional problems"; few do right by them. Progress frequently proves too lengthy, complex, costly and uncertain.

When embarrassment rubs a right index finger over a left one in a "s-h-a-m-e! s-h-a-m-e!" motion, the situation becomes even more difficult.

Most people suffer their "emotional problems" in silence.

They sap their happiness, frustrate their enjoyments and blacken the horizons of those with whom they come in contact!

Despite such "silence"—it is impossible for people *not* to communicate.

When we do, our words and actions can cause emotional reactions that will affect our lives for better or for worse . . . and similarly affect the lives of those with whom we interact!

The person who says: *"Oh, you musn't let yourself become upset"* doesn't know what he is talking about!

Big or small upsets are natural reactions.

You cannot fight them!

Repeatedly wrong Emotional Appeal in words and actions can cause despair and unhappiness—the major cause of many physically painful and medically puzzling diseases.

Unhappiness depends upon the individual's strengths and weaknesses within the realm of the Fatal Four.

It may refer to job or money situations, neighbors, noise or environment, unwanted relatives in the home, jealousy, arguments, nagging, marriage curtailment of personal freedoms, overwork, loneliness or boredom, sex fears or dissatisfactions, lack of appreciation, "days when nothing goes right," even personality clashes.

Often, the body translates this emotional distress into physical distress.

"Emotional problems" are medically known to contribute to heart and circulatory ailments, joint and muscular pains, skin disorders, allergies, digestive difficulties like peptic ulcers and colitis, headaches, high blood pressure and more.

A young woman's family and friends take continuous advantage of her time and good nature. She complains that her pent-up unhappiness is "too much to swallow!" *Seemingly out of nowhere, she begins to have difficulty in swallowing.*

When a doctor eventually discovers and removes the emotional cause of this psychosomatic ailment, the swallowing difficulty stops!

A person who is a mental "pain-in-the-neck" to man, it has been found, can truly be the origin of the man's *physical* pain in the neck!

In a host of other ways, emotional dissatisfactions may emerge as painful, aggravating or noticeable symptoms that unwittingly elude medical diagnosis.

A nutritionist related the case of a man who had a rash on *one* finger.

The man consulted with doctor after doctor. Food tests revealed nothing and the rash remained.

One doctor, alert to emotionally caused illness, questioned the man about his marital situation. He learned that the patient despised his wife and had been doing everything possible to obtain a divorce. Again, he looked at the rash. *The rash was on the third finger, left hand!*

"Emotional problems" are principally problems of communication. They arise because we do not know enough about our own motivational makeup and the emotional components of the people to whom we communicate . . . *before* we communicate.

Experience with thousands of men and women, including the physically handicapped, convinces me that we lose more opportunities for fun, satisfaction and happiness because of what slips through our lips—rather than what slips through our fingers!

"Emotional problems" begin when, as children or adults, we get upsetting reactions from certain people. After steady emotional hammering, we become more solidly nailed to the wall of frustration.

"Emotional problems" are not caused by emotions in general. They are specifically created by the way our emotional needs are directed or disturbed.

"Emotional problems" are not problems that hit "one out of every ten" . . . "one out of every twenty" . . . or similar impossible ratios.

"Emotional problems" affect TEN out of every TEN people! So long as people use words and actions to communicate, there will always be emotional reactions that can originate "emotional problems"!

On an individualized basis, people must decide just *what* means the most to them *emotionally*.

With Emotional Appeal Technique, we can more rapidly make

this decision after delving into the relative weights of the Fatal Four Emotional Appeals that contribute to our personality.

Once we understand more about motivating ourselves, we will find it easier to fit our needs to the emotional needs of others. Thereafter, we can direct our communication more successfully, become better-liked and more persuasive.

At the same time, we can better prevent the onset of "emotional problems."

How do we start?

By indelibly pinpointing the fact that our most valuable personal asset and our best "preventative medicine" is Emotional Appeal, our ability to motivate and make others *want* to listen and react more favorably to what we say and do!

CHAPTER
9

Command Situations with Power-packed Emotional Appeal Questions and Attitudes

If we merely spoke for the sake of moving our lips and listening to the sound of our voices, we would certainly be wasting our time, wouldn't we?

And yet, how often have we "listened" while our minds were far, far away?

How many times have we been so Preoccupied that we have suddenly "come back to earth" with *"Er . . . what's that?"* . . . or, *"Will you say that again, please?"*

And what about the hundreds of conversations in which the extent of our participation was a *nod . . . "Yeah!" . . . "Yes!"* . . . or merely *"Uh-huh"?*

Others were speaking, but were we *really* listening?

Might we not have found their company more enjoyable if their words had kept us alert and attentive? Would we not have *learned* more and *remembered* more if we had *listened* better?

Questions with Emotional Appeal, properly timed, *instantly* make others *want* to listen.

Emotionally power-packed, they can command situations, improve Personality and Persuasion and help others remember *you . . .* your *product . . .* your *service!*

In a short time, we shall learn six Rules for Asking Questions. First, however, let us understand the activating Advantages that Questions offer:

1. Questions break preoccupation and get immediate attention.

Even *"Nice day, isn't it?"* breaks Preoccupation and asks for a reply. *"Is this the 2nd floor?"* . . . *"Do you like getting pushed?"*

For better or worse, the simplest question gives you this advantage!

2. Questions put your listener or audience on the defensive.

"Is your name 'Connie'?" . . . *"Which do you prefer—tea or coffee?"* . . . *"That's a lovely bracelet. May I get a closer look?"* . . . *"Why is this one more expensive?"*

Before replying, a listener must *think* of the answer.

This puts him on the defensive, gains time for you and gives you the opportunity to organize your next thought or action.

The *time* it takes to get answers can be decisively advantageous. You may enlist this time to direct, identify, confuse, delay, save life or property—even change a criminal's mind!

One of my students was held up in daylight by a gun-wielding man with a handkerchief over his face.

While complying with his requests, she remained calm and smilingly prodded him with questions. *"Is this the only way you earn your money?"* she asked . . . *"Isn't it dangerous to use a gun in your work?"* . . . *"Have the police ever caught you?"* . . . *"Is that the kind of gun the nice cowboys use?"*

Trying to hasten the robbery, speak the answers and reprimand her *all at the same time,* the holdup man became confused. He backed away, muttering: "Damn you, lady. You've got me all mixed up!"

He took nothing from her.

Her questions had kept him on the *defensive.* She had emotionally upset his *offensive*—the commission of the crime. By making him think of the answers, she had *gained* time—while he *lost* it!

She *entered* his mind . . . but *he* changed it!

Criminals are usually ordinary people where emotions are concerned. They cannot *do* two things at once and cannot *think* two thoughts simultaneously.

Questions can put a listener on the defensive—and keep him there!

3. Questions allow your listeners to speak.

People usually love to do this, especially when they know the answer.

"Did you have any trouble finding our place?" . . . *"Where would you rather live? Big city? Small town?"* . . . *"If you had another son, would you want him to be a teacher, too?"*

The Rules for Asking Questions will demonstrate how this Advantage of Questions heightens the persuasive power of your Emotional Appeal and often makes the obvious your irrepressible ally!

4. Questions sustain interest in your subject.

By stimulating responses, they hold or recapture attention even when your conversation, speech or sales talk is weakening!

"Have you noticed that this little gadget contains only three cap-nuts?" "Isn't it one of the smallest you have ever seen?" "How much would you guess it retails for?"

"Why did you folks decide to go to Hawaii?" . . . *"Was it also because you don't see so many beautiful hula dancers in the States?"* . . . *"By the way, is dining very expensive in Hawaii?"*

5. Questions cut resistance by bringing objections into the open.

By eliminating guesswork, questions shorten the time needed for persuasion. They direct your words and actions towards what is *really* on your listener's mind!

Question: *"Why don't you want to have dinner at Eleanor's?"*

Answer: *"She's only inviting us because she wants her daughter to meet our son!"*

With this reply, you have uncovered the real objection and can chart a far more persuasive course for your comment.

Controversially potent as any situation may seem, it would be much worse if you had to *guess* that the answer might be: "I hate to go out on such a cold night!" . . . "It will cost too much to buy her a gift!" . . . "She's seen me in every one of my dresses!" . . . "My jewelry is in the vault!" Or, "Her husband is such a bore!"

6. Questions lead your listeners towards the conclusion you want.

"When you don't move ahead, it's easier to fall behind. That's true, isn't it?"

What do your listeners say or feel?

"Why, of course!"

You ask: *"How many of you have heard of the Golden Rule —'Do unto others?'"*

Individually, your listeners' minds or lips reply: *"I have!"*

"Shall we sit back and do nothing about this situation?" you query a large audience. *"We know that such negligence can mean death or serious injury to our children and to ourselves, don't we? Shall we placidly sit back and do nothing?"*

Your questions are leading your listeners to answer "No!" . . . "Yes!" . . . then, "Certainly not!"

You are letting your Audience "lead themselves into" the course of action you have been leading them towards.

Once they start "leading themselves into" . . . they will start agreeing.

You have *entered* and *directed* their minds with Questions; your listeners will *change* their minds with Answers!

7. Questions give your listeners credit for the thinking.

By eliciting replies, you ensure *mutuality*.

Why is this so important?

Because it *proves* that you are emotionally *reaching* your listeners!

Recognition is a prime pinnacle in the Fatal Four. With questions, such a pinnacle can be reached.

You reassure your Listener . . . and your Listener reassures *himself!*

People *want* credit for their thinking. Questions *give it* to them!

8. Questions bypass distractions.

A distraction is a Preoccupation-breaker that does not help you. *You can make it help you with Questions!*

When your interview is going well . . . your love scene is getting him ready to pop the question . . . that important dotted line is to be signed . . . BOOM!

Out of the blue comes a telephone call . . . or a lamp crashes . . . or a knock on the door changes the mood and situation!

While convincing hesitant Susie to become local fund-raising chairman for your organization, her 5-year-old son rushes in, screaming about a sock on the head that his playmate has just given him.

Your listener's *mind* is on the distraction. You must bring that mind back to *you!*

What to do?

Don't fight the distraction; blend into it with a question!

"Aren't telephones wonderful—even though they sometimes ring in the middle of an interview?" "Do you know what I was thinking the moment I heard that knock on the door?" "Were you particularly fond of that lamp?" "Susie, do you realize that raising funds and raising children have somewhat similar problems?"

A tactful question *instantly* helps you recapture the attention of your listener. Often, it will promptly prevent the onset of an upset!

Another question or two and you can almost always reactivate the previous high note.

To swiftly regain control of situations, by-pass distractions with blend-in Questions!

9. Questions take the "edge" off a direct command.

Five people are before you.

"*Give me your book!*" you say to One. "*I'd like to try your watch on my wrist. Please let me have it!*" you tell Two. "*Pick up that paper!*" you remind Three. "*May I see your ring?*" you ask Four. "*Hand me the pencil!*" you order Five.

Four of the five people will take offense, even wonder: "Who in the heck does he think *he* is?"

Number Four, however, will take no offense and will even *like* you. She was the only one you *asked!*

You *told* the others what to do.

Don't tell people what to do; *ask* them!

Asking is good Emotional Appeal; your listener is making the decision. *Telling* means that *you* are making the decision.

Make your listener feel *more* important by *asking*. Why create resistance and conflict by ordering others around?

In speaking, the question mark is far more persuasive than the exclamation mark!

Emotionally, your listener *wants* to be asked, so he'll tend to *do* what you ask.

Let Questions take the "edge" off a direct command. You'll Say It With Emotional Appeal and you'll be better liked and more persuasive!

10. Questions build your confidence in yourself.

Questions can *start* a conversation, *control* one or suggest a next meeting. They can begin friendships, romances, sales, jobs, opportunities, satisfactions, and speeches.

When you know how to opportunely project Questions, you immediately increase your self-control and confidence in every phase of your communication!

Even when an unfamiliar subject arises, ability to use Questions with Emotional Appeal will rush to your rescue.

You are with four others, one afternoon, enjoying coffee and conversation. The conversation veers to books.

Although you are a well-read person, you have only perused a review of Skipdunk's newest novel: *He Came Home in Seven Parts.*

Unexpectedly, you are asked: *"What do you think of Ophelia, her fifth husband's maid?"*

You do not know much about Ophelia, but you are anxious not to "lose face" in front of the others—especially since flap-tongued Minnie J. is sitting next to you. Wisely, you reach for the first aid that Questions always offer.

"Ophelia, the maid? I don't know yet," you reply. *"I wonder, though, can you answer another important question?"*

"What is it?" volunteers Minnie J.

"Do you think that 'He Came Home in Seven Parts' is Skipdunk's best novel?"

This will turn the discussion in another direction, but use of Questions provided you with a wonderful "face saver." You followed a Rule, took advantage of the obvious and made yourself *seem* to know more about the book than you actually did.

Emotionally, such "face saving" can be very important to you!

Carefully conceived and directed, Questions will help you build confidence in yourself quickly and surely in hundreds of ways.

With the Rules for Asking Questions that follow, they will assure you of a wonderfully persuasive 'round-the-clock weapon too!

THE RULES FOR ASKING QUESTIONS

It's true that you will continue to use words and actions to communicate, isn't it? Would you like others to be more responsive when you do?

Use Questions.

With Questions, you *can* get people to do what you want. But, you must remember the Rules.

These six Rules for Asking Questions with Emotional Appeal should be *memorized, interlocked* and *kept ready* at all times.

Ask the *right* Questions and prepare to emotionally discover a newer *you*. Even your most difficult listeners will begin to "see things *your* way"!

Here are the Rules:

1. Word your question in such a way that you get the answer you want.

To a young mother: *"Wouldn't it be wonderful if you could have more time for relaxation?"* This question is certain to elicit a "Yes" reply. It has Self-Preservation Appeal too!

To that mail order executive: *"How would you like to become the biggest man in the mail order business?"* No mail order executive will say "No!" Notice the Preoccupation-breaking Appeal of Money and Recognition as extra-power behind this approach?

Remember the opening Question of the sales manager interviewer to the commission-salesman job applicant? *"Will you gamble five months of hard work to set up a steady future income of over $6000 a year?"* The job applicant thinks "Yes!" The Romance Future Promise has made emotional contact and is directing the Money Appeal into a receptive mind!

2. Be sure your audience knows the answer.

It bothers people to be asked a question they cannot answer. On the other hand, it is excellent Emotional Appeal when they can impart knowledge. When using this Rule, *always* take advantage of the obvious!

To a trout fisherman: *"Do you have a favorite bait for trout?"*

To an executive: *"Which qualities do you believe are most important for a man to be successful?"*

To an advertising agency interviewer: *"Are you the regular interviewer?"* "No," he replies. "I work in the art department." The girl job seeker again acts upon the obvious. "Do you feel that stylized animated art is more attention-getting than photography in an ad?" Busy as he is, he smiles and accepts this opportunity to express his opinion to ears anxious to listen. Does *he* know the answer? He sure *does!* As a result, he remembers her better than the other applicants *because she has emotionally given him something to remember!* She gets the job! *Careful use of this Rule interlocked with some of the other Rules for Asking Questions had created a vital competitive advantage for her.*

3. Use leading questions wherever possible.

A "leading question" puts the answer into your listener's mind and gives *double* impact to what you are saying. A "leading question" is easy to work with. You simply make a statement and turn it into a question.

"You want a man who knows your local problems, don't you?"
"Mighty good choice, wouldn't you say?"
"This is Tuesday the 16th, isn't it?"
"You were wearing a tailored maroon suit the last time we met, weren't you?"

4. Objectively relate your question to the situation, time and listener.

"How would you like to keep weeds, bugs, and insects out of your garden forever?" This is a sales-compelling question that includes most of the Rules for Asking Questions. It is extremely effective when used on transient customers in the seed and garden section of a department store. When asked of a transient customer in the ladies hat department or in a shoe shine parlor, it would fall flat on its face!

The Swiss Republic, last nation in Europe that bars women from politics, voted on a constitutional proposal to allow women to vote in federal elections. The voters were all male. Before Election Day, posters bearing two persuasive questions were hung throughout Switzerland in areas with high visibility. The questions were: *"If a woman is happy, what do politics mean to her?"* *"If she is unhappy, will politics make any difference?"* The male voters overwhelmingly voted against the proposal and women still do not vote in Switzerland. As previously remarked, Emotional Appeal remains a force for evil as well as for good!

Do you recall the Romance example of the owner of the small photography studio where the unmarried girls "shopped" for prices on portrait photographs? His success came because he *interlocked* this Rule with some of the others. When the girls walked in, he said: *"Do you know why we're called the 'lucky' photographers?"* While the girls smiled or answered: "No" . . . he produced the four or five bridal photographs and remarked: *"These girls posed for us less than a year before they were married!"* ZING! Emotionally, this question lead-in hit the unmarried girls right where receptivity was highest. The question approach was in the right relationship to the Listener, Situation, and Time. *In combination with other Rules for Asking Questions, the unmarried women customers completely forgot Money cost as the principal reason for buying!*

5. Have an emotional relationship between your question and what you say.

"Would you like to have more pep?" (Self-Preservation)

"Did you ever see a Christmas card like this one?" (Romance-New Experience)

"Would you like to have a nationally famous daughter?" (Recognition)

"Isn't it awful when a person comes late to appointments and keeps you waiting?" (Self-Preservation)

"A woman with a nose nearly five inches long?" (Romance-New Experience)

"Want to make $50 fast, easily, and legally?" (Money)

"Doesn't it get you peeved when you pay $35 for a radio that your friend buys for $20?" (Money and Recognition)

"Did you ever wish that you were as pretty and talented as a Miss America?" (Recognition)

"Isn't she the sexy one in the low-cut blue bathing suit, Harry?" (Romance)

"How would you like to save as much as fifty cents on a pair of stockings?" (Money)

"Have you heard about this new product that does your dishes

in half the time?" (Romance-New Experience, Self-Preservation)

"How do you manage to keep looking so young?" (Self-Preservation, Recognition)

"Do you always get so many phone calls from eligible young men?" (Romance)

"Want to save time shopping?" asks the supermarket manager. *"We'll deliver at no extra cost!"* (Self-Preservation)

"The contacts you make in our organization can be very profitable for your business, can't they?" (Money)

6. Use a "choice question" when you want definite action or agreement.

Offer a choice of *agreeing* one way or *agreeing* another way:

"When do you prefer delivery, at the beginning of next week or before this week-end?"

"How do you wish to pay—all cash or $10 now and $10 a month?"

"Will you phone me on Monday—or is Thursday evening more convenient?"

Be certain that *either* course of action is acceptable to you before you ask this type of question. Choice is given between one actual course of action and another. It is *not* a choice of doing something or *not* doing it.

Says the charity solicitor: *"Will you contribute one dollar, or would you rather contribute more?"*

It's not a choice of contributing or *not* contributing, but *which* amount will you contribute? An effective variation of this Rule for Asking Questions consists of offering a choice between *something good* and *something awful*, knowing full well that the listener will choose the good.

"Do you want insurance today or a law suit tomorrow?"

"Which will it be, a secure future or no future at all?"

"Isn't it wiser to protect our children now—than to see them crippled later?"

Use of this Rule for "choice questions" requires a little practice, but you will find it surprisingly persuasive!

Memorize and apply the six interlocking Rules for Asking Questions. They will serve you well again and again.

The best way to get people to do what you want is by *persuading them to convince themselves*. Questions help you accomplish this.

Control questions! Spring them at opportune times!

Arm yourself with the defensive question: *"Why?"* This is a difficult question for a listener to shy away from and it can assure you of many Advantages of Questions just when you need them most!

Remember:

The Question you ask can bring you the Answer you want!

Observe the Rules. They make it easier for others to agree with you.

When others agree with you, you will gain confidence, better your initiative, cast off fears, and acquire a much more exhilarating outlook.

Equally important, power-packed Questions with Emotional Appeal will help you command situations in ways you never before thought possible!

Win Arguments and Settle Disputes with Emotional Appeal Technique

The best way to win an argument is to stay out of one.

With deft application of Emotional Appeal Technique, you *can* accomplish this objective!

Alert yourself to eight emotional clouds that hover over your daily living. Realize that they stand ready to sprinkle you with a delightful drizzle or drown you in a dreadful drench.

These "clouds" are Eight Argumentative Subjects.

In every one, attitude is firmly pre-shaped and contains an unquenchable core. The person who argues these subjects has his eyes wide open and his mind almost entirely closed. "Victory" offers no emotional benefit!

The Eight Argumentative Subjects are:

1. Religion
2. Politics
3. Personal Taste
4. Appearance

5. Intelligence
6. Choice of Friends
7. Accomplishments
8. Blood Relations

When any of these subjects arises, follow these suggestions one-two-three and you will "win" more arguments.

First: Find out which side of the argument your listener is taking. *Be sure of every listener!*

Second: Smile and reserve comment *unless you agree!*

Third: Follow the *first* suggestion!

180

When you do not, you will lose respect, embroil yourself in an upset and diminish your powers of Personality and Persuasion.

In the Eight Argumentative Subjects, your attitudes and those of your listeners are extremely prejudicial.

"Reasoning against a prejudice is like fighting against a shadow," said Mildmay. "It exhausts the reasoner without visibly affecting the prejudice!"

As quickly as you can, change the subject with a well-directed question.

Do *not* lead into *another* of the Argumentative Eight. This is like putting on tight shoes when you have a headache; you only remove the pain from your head and put it elsewhere!

Change the subject by asking the *right* question.

You know the Advantage of Questions. Be certain you use the Rules for asking them!

Be an owl.

Owls, they say, are supposed to be wise because they *appear* wise all the time and hoot only occasionally!

Now, let us turn the light of Emotional Appeal Technique upon the arbitrary Eight Argumentative Subjects.

Religion, in terms of the prepotent Fatal Four, is within Self-Preservation and *Recognition;* Politics, Personal Taste, and Appearance are in *Recognition.* So are Intelligence, Choice of Friends and Accomplishments. The subject of Blood Relations is emotionally centered about Self-Preservation and *Recognition.*

Do you notice the common denominator?

Recognition is integrally involved in ALL of the Eight!

Before *you* bite for such emotionally upsetting bait, smilingly ask: *"What do YOU think?"* Or, *"How do YOU feel about this?"* Why?

Because these are controlled questions on subjects wherein your listener's attitudes are emotionally enmeshed with Recognition! Answers will *uncover* your listener's feelings and offer you on-the-spot advice before you express your next thought!

There are many argumentative areas other than the Eight Argumentative Subjects.

Money, for example, is a prime motivator for arguments and one of our biggest desires, worries and fears. By using the Rules for Asking Questions, Money can be much more amicably discussed and compromised than *any* of the Eight. So can argumentative subjects like sex desire and fulfillment.

Getting *into* an argument is a cinch; getting "out" of one is not so easy.

Here is a representative list of Argumentative Subjects and Conversational Traps. These extend far beyond the Eight. They have started innumerable personality clashes, lost friendships, muffed sales, hatreds, divorces, separations—even assaults.

Avoid using similar statements.

Preoccupation-breaking Emotional Appeal is present, but it *offends* the listeners. You can readily identify the reasons from among the Fatal Four Emotional Appeals. (Key: SP—Self-Preservation; Ro—Romance; M—Money; Rec—Recognition)

"You're not the man you used to be!" (SP/Rec)

"I wish you'd learn how to save once in a while!" (M)

"Jane, there's really no use trying to hide your gray hair!" (SP/Rec)

"You're a cheapskate!" (Rec)

"That gift set me back plenty. I thought you would enjoy wearing it!" (Rec/M)

"The wrinkles sure do show on you!" (Rec/SP)

"Can't you let someone else make a dollar?" (M/Rec)

"These ideas are too 'different' to suit me!" (Ro/New Experience)

"I put my money where my mouth is!" (Rec)

"Gosh Pat, you're almost completely bald!" (SP/Rec)

"Why don't you mind your own business!" (Rec)

"Is money so important to you?" (M)

"I should never have married you. Why didn't I think ahead?" (Ro)

"Do you know what it will cost you if you lose this law suit?" (M)

"You're in a rut. You do the same thing, day-in, day-out!" (Ro/New Experience)

"You love your mirror more than you love me!" (Rec)

"Your mother is too fat to wear knitted clothes!" (SP/Rec)

"You'll have nothing good ahead by marrying him!" (Ro/Future Promise/SP)

"Why is it, Dolores, that other girls have lots of boy friends— and you don't even have one?" (Ro/Rec)

"Must you always talk about your operations?" (Rec)

"You'll never be a happy person!" (SP)

"They must have seen you coming. I bought the same thing and paid $10 less!" (M/Rec)

These Conversational Traps have proved to be argumentative dynamite.

Try to steer clear of arguments. They can wind up in heavy cost to you.

Too many arguments? Both your health and disposition may suffer. Then you will *really* have something to complain about.

You can become so glued to your upset that you leave yourself wide open for trouble while hammering a nail, standing on a ladder, walking, driving, talking to your boss—or eating peas with a knife!

How do you handle yourself when you are *hit?*

ONE: *If you have left the person you argued with,* don't bottle up your anger and seethe deep down. *Do something*—even if you privately slap your hands together ten times, not once! Exercise . . . take a brisk walk . . . blow on a tuba . . . write numbers up to two hundred *backwards!* Or, let off "steam" by telling a friend your troubles, knowing full well that he is so Preoccupied with his *own* troubles that he won't really be listening anyway!

Two: *If you are with the person who has just upset you,* why hasten unhappiness with a retaliatory retort? Spare yourself the unnecessary follow-thru. Leave your blood pressure closer to normal. Use *Emotional Appeal Technique!*

Argument is *disagreement.*

The best way to avoid an argument is to AGREE with the speaker!

Say: "You're perfectly right!" . . . and mean it!

The person who yells at you, criticizes you, insults or "digs" you, is doing it for a *personal, emotional* reason. Recognition desires make him want to feel that he is right.

Show he is! *Say* he is!

What? You feel it is *unconscionable* to tell the other person he is right?

Do it anyway!

Unless it has to do with supervisory authority wherein insubordination is involved, the benefits you will emotionally gain will far outweigh your reluctance.

This attitude will retain friendships, improve your outlook and close the door on many of the debilitating diseases that unhappiness can bring.

Try it!

You'll "win" arguments, settle personal disputes and become a far more tactful individual.

The best way to develop tact is by cultivating respect for other people's opinions—even when you disagree with them. They'll return the courtesy—because they're just as emotional as you!

Emotional Appeal Will Make Others Remember, Respect and Like You

O ne of the first "jokes" I remember is about a drunk in a high hat, loosely knotted white scarf and unbuttoned coat who walks around and around a street lamp at midnight.

A curious policeman strides over, twirling his nightstick. "Lose something?" he asks.

"Yeah!" answers the tipsy man. "A ton dollar bill! I . . . I lost it *next block!*"

The policeman scratches his head. "If you lost it next block, why are you looking *here?*"

"Thatsh easy," hiccups the drunk. *"There's more light here!"*

For years, I wondered why it was always so easy for me to remember this old story. But I don't wonder any more.

When I was in the third grade of elementary school, a man came into our classroom and explained the value of a school bank account.

"Save! Save even a few pennies each week," he urged. "Before you know it, you will turn pennies into dollars—just like *magic!*"

A boy sitting next to me started to cry. "How can I save, Mister?" he tearfully sighed. "I don't get *any pennies* to save!"

The man touched his chin, right over a circular, brownish-black mole from which a stubble of black hair sprouted. He turned to our teacher.

"Miss Faulkner," he said, "this little lad reminds me of a story."

It was about a father who decided to test his ten-year-old

son's honesty. "My boy," he told his son, "take the big brown jug and go get me some wine."

The boy picked up the jug and asked for money.

"Oho!" chided his father. "Anyone can buy wine when he has money. It's the smart man who can get it without paying!"

The boy thought a moment, then picked up the jug and left the house. Ten minutes later, he returned.

"Father," he pointed, "please hold out your glass!"

Puzzled, the father held out his glass.

His son removed the cork from the jug and tipped the jughead into the glass. "Drink, father," he smiled.

"Drink? How can I drink?" asked his father. "There's nothing in the glass!"

"Oho!" laughed the boy. "Anyone can drink when he has something to drink. It's the smart man who can drink when there's nothing in the glass!"

I remember these stories and many more anecdotes because they "reached me" with something to remember. I could *see* them and *feel* them because they contained elements of Emotional Appeal that imbedded themselves into my mind.

What were these irresistible elements? Principally the Romantic New Experience and the Visual Preoccupation-breakers-and-holders of Self-Preservation.

The drunk wearing a high hat, loosely knotted white scarf and open coat . . . the lighted street lamp . . . the tipsy fellow walking around and around the lamp . . . the policeman twirling his nightstick . . . the bank man with the brownish-black mole from which a tiny stubble of black hair sprouted . . . the idea of turning pennies into dollars like magic . . . the little boy crying.

Why do I recall that the teacher's name was "Faulkner?" A schoolmate had once told me: "She's the nicest teacher in the school—but she has a nose like a *fork!*"

The savings bank man acting out the story . . . "carrying" the jug . . . "pouring" the wine . . . imitating the father and his son by chucking his head to one side and another as he changed characters.

These stories were clear . . . visual . . . emotionally compelling!

Visual memories and other communicative emotional stimuli affect us more than we sometimes realize. Happy events, sad ones, particular faces, words, actions; sights that produce poignant associative patterns and memory-in-depth.

They filigree our feelings during wakeful moments and perturb our attempts to fall asleep.

These reactions are *with* us or *against* us. We cannot combat them, but, with Emotional Appeal Technique, we *can* begin to identify and control them!

After speaking to a Sales Executives Club audience for about ten minutes, I noticed that the eyes of my listeners were not upon my face.

Some fifty index fingers insistently pointed to my waist and left thigh.

I stopped. "Is something wrong?"

Heads nodded, grins erupted and the pointing became more emphatic.

My jacket had opened and my left shirt tail was hanging down full length!

The unexpected visual effect promptly distracted the attention of my audience. It was necessary to immediately *join* the distraction—not fight it.

I reached for my wallet and extracted a twenty-dollar bill. "See this twenty? I'll give it to the first one among you who tells us the sentence I spoke just before you saw my shirt tail!"

Collectively, the audience knit its brows and tried *very* hard to win the twenty dollars.

Although the sentence had been spoken less than thirty seconds before the offer, not one person remembered what I had said.

My silent shirt-tail had spoken more clearly, more convincingly and with more Emotional Appeal than I!

The audience had "heard" the shirt-tail better than my words because it had greater Preoccupation-breaking ability.

My shirt-tail contained more visual Self-Preservation Emo-

tional Appeal and a potent emotional pat of the Romantic New Experience!

People would rather watch than listen. It's *easier* to pay attention to what you see than what you hear!

There is always a Self-Preservation desire among us to do things the easier, more enjoyable way; it requires less effort!

Listeners had opened their Preoccupied minds to what they saw when they noticed my shirt-tail. Because the preceding sentence lacked Preoccupation-breaking qualities, they remained Preoccupied!

They *believed* that they had heard something—but they didn't actually hear anything that entered their minds and stayed there!

The Self-Preservation preference for the visual is an emotionally tappable portion of every listener . . . even youngsters.

Miss R., a former student, became a teacher. She and a few other teachers were assigned certain South American countries as subjects for a test lesson to be observed by a superior. Her assignment was "Brazil."

She asked her pupils to gather around as she placed a large, white sheet of paper on her cleared desk. With a smile, she raised a one-pound vacuum tin of a popular brand of coffee above her head. "You know what is in this can, don't you?"

Her listeners nodded: "Yes!"

As her pupils intently watched, Miss R. opened the can of coffee and poured it on the paper. "Do you also know that there is more coffee in Brazil than in any other South American country?" She spread the coffee into an outline map of Brazil.

"Here is some of it. How much does this coffee weigh? You're right; it weighs one pound. Can you guess what only one pound of coffee will do for us right now? It will help us study Brazil's geography, history and products. Are you ready to watch and listen? Fine. Here we go!"

With the coffee, her fingertips, and synchronized words and actions of visual Self-Preservation and the New Experience of Romance Emotional Appeal, she traced boundary changes, location of principal cities and other highlights of Brazil. When the session ended, the children wore appreciative smiles.

Miss R.'s observer waited until the children had left the room, then objected to the method of instruction. She admitted that Miss R. had included all the necessary facts, but thought the lesson was ". . . more entertaining than educational!"

During the schooldays that followed, the same pupils received instruction from the other teachers. They were then tested.

Miss R. said that the pupils retained far greater knowledge of Brazil than of any other South American country and that her superior's critical attitude had changed to uninterrupted interest in Emotional Appeal.

By relating her Subject and Audience with a response-motivating Emotional Appeal Communication Technique that utilized unfailing "show" and "say" teamwork, Miss R. had made her pupils *want* to listen.

They *did* listen . . . and *learn!*

Today, in every phase of education, there are too many teachers who do not know how to teach. They "learned" their teaching methods from other teachers who rarely knew how to teach them!

As a result, much of current education is unnecessarily wasteful.

It is one thing to gain knowledge; it is quite another to be able to break Preoccupation of listeners and impart knowledge.

You may multiply this thought by the sum of every job and profession!

When a teacher teaches, how many students are *really* listening? Why can't many *more* be made intellectually receptive *at the same time?*

Over a seventeen-year period, I have asked better than 15,000 of my own students, lecture audiences and clients this question:

"How many of your teachers can you remember?"

Their answer: "*Very few!*"

Essentially, which teachers do we remember? The ones *we* liked or those who tended to like *us!*

Did we *learn* more from the ones we liked? Did we *prefer* their subjects? Were our grades higher in *their* classes?

Emphatically, *yes!*

Education has little meaning unless it teaches teachers and students how to communicate what they learn.

When they say it with Emotional Appeal . . . they succeed!

Even when words alone fail, well-directed approaches containing Romance New Experience and Self-Preservation Visual Appeal can capture interest and sustain it.

B., the father of two children, once told a group of us a fascinating variation of this.

A relative had died in another state and B. and his wife wished to attend the funeral. They arranged to have the wife's mother take care of their two children while they were away.

Their nine-year-old boy presented no problem, but their five-year-old daughter cried and cried. She would accept none of her mother's explanations.

B. made this suggestion to his distraught wife: "Why not use her notebook and draw *pictures* of where we are going, what we'll be doing and how we'll look when we come home? When we're away, her grandmother can show her the pictures whenever she gets lonesome!"

B. and his wife were poor artists, but they managed to make "stick" pictures and descriptions while their little girl watched and asked questions.

When Mr. and Mrs. B. were away, their daughter and her grandmother went over the book more than a dozen times. This placated the child and made their absence and return much more understandable than "talk" alone.

B. assured me that the Emotional Appeal of the notebook and its "stick drawings" will remain a treasured family memory!

Use of visuals in communication makes for more successful communication. The reason? Self-Preservation Emotional Appeal —one of the Fatal Four Motivators in all people.

It is easier to *see* than to hear and easier to *watch* than to listen . . . for adults too.

A nationally-known minister used visual tie-ins in order to heighten remembrance of his sermons.

Once, he started a sermon by showing his congregation a small box. "The most important thing in life cannot be contained in this box no matter how strong the bindings!"

Attention was immediate.

He reached for a preserve jar. "Can this jar or any other—even with the tightest lid—contain this precious something?" He shook his head.

Reaching beneath his robe and turning out his empty right jacket pocket, he moved to the side of his pulpit and added: "No pocket, no hand, no vault can hold it. This mysterious something that *can* be held . . . what is it?"

He paused. "It is the peace of mind that the Lord's presence assures!"

With adroit showmanship, he followed with more Self-Preservation visual projection, emotionally-controlled questions, Romance New Experience and Future Promise and Recognition You-ability. To conclude, he returned to his visuals—the box, the jar and his turned-out pocket as symbols of tangible possessions ". . . far less important than the peace of mind which you can feel without having to touch!"

By their expressive reaction, he *knew* that his congregation had intently listened. When his listeners later said: "Nice sermon, Reverend. . . ." . . . he *knew* that he had really "reached" them.

Reverend R. now regards his choice of Self-Preservation visuals and other power-packed Emotional Appeals as important as his choice of sermon subject!

All human communication is emotionally peppered by the personality of the speaker and the listener. Each has individualized feelings that can overlap more precisely only when speaker truly "reaches" listener.

The Emotional Appeal of our words, actions, and appearances must possess a happy *blend* of rapport elements where listeners, readers or viewers are concerned. All portions—and particularly the visual ones—must be well-aimed and carefully controlled.

With the *right* prepotent Preoccupation-breaking factors, we can truly use Emotional Appeal by *choice* . . . not by some chance. Otherwise, what people *see* about us may result in personal loss instead of gain!

A salesman secured an appointment with an important buyer after waiting nearly three months. He carefully planned his presentation and alerted himself to just about every technical question that the buyer might ask about his products and facilities.

On the day of the appointment, he wore a neat blue suit topped by a matching blue tie with hand-painted, overlarge red exclamation marks.

When the interview was over, he was nonplussed. The buyer had been courteous and attentive but did not drop a hint about placing an order.

After the salesman left, the buyer remembered the tie with the overlarge, red exclamation marks—not the salesman. The buyer had never before seen such a striking tie. It had so captured his attention that he visited men's shops during the next few days searching for one like it!

Ties often speak louder than the men who wear them. Overplunging necklines, overemphasizing makeup and overabbreviated swim suits also accomplish related results.

So do accidentally exposed shirt-tails!

Visual effects should be used to attract, not to distract! Emotionally, visual effects are stronger than vocal ones. Without foresight, they may harm more than they help you.

What you do with your face, body and hands can make others remember you in a "wrong" or "right" way. Gestures may indicate ridicule, anxiety, anticipation, upset, desire, happiness. They can dramatize remorse, satisfaction, enthusiasm, or calm.

Your handshake combines visual and tactile contact. Its meaningfulness must blend into your overall Emotional Appeal.

Words of warmth never sound sincere when accompanied by a cold handshake!

Your gestures are outer expressions of inner feelings and disclose emotional sensitivities.

Gestures are out of mind; they should not be allowed to get out of hand! Keep them under control; they can help make others want to remember, respect and like you.

Attorney E., a student, once told an Emotional Appeal Institute class how attorneys watch for telltale gestures of witnesses.

When a witness turns his head towards the bench or wipes his lips before answering a particular question, this is a strong indication that he wishes he did *not* have to answer. An alert lawyer will instantly grasp this clue and hammer away on the subject that the gesture indicates the witness wants to sidestep.

Many times, Attorney E. told us, gestures by witnesses or clients had given him his first "break" in legal actions!

When speaking to others, gestures and visual effects should be employed to work *for* you.

Control them. Synchronize them with your words and actions. Allow them to s-m-o-o-t-h-l-y and naturally become a part of the outer Y-O-U that others see.

Visual effects, gestures and movements are especially advantageous when you:

> 1. Tell a joke or anecdote.
> 2. Organize a talk.

Want *more* people to remember, respect and like you when you tell a story?

Select a story that you know most others want to hear—not one that you insist on telling!

How do you *know* what kind of story others want to hear?

First, use Emotional Appeal Technique to fit your Subject to your Audience.

Uncover the emotionally important "listening factors" from among the Fatal Four that every person *wants* to hear or *fears* to hear. Those are always the emotionally irresistible motivators in everyone. One, however, will soon reveal itself as the BIG Preoccupation-breaking Emotional Appeal in whatever story or anecdote you are about to tell!

Then, be certain that your communication contains one or more of the following:

1. Visual words.

"*She was writing with a pencil that looked like a frankfurter with a sharp black point!*"

"*Ever see a baby laugh with its mouth wide open and legs kicking up in the air?*"

**2. Words and actions that you can synchronize
   with natural gestures and movements.**

*"Holding a brush in each hand, he kept massaging his scalp
just above his ears—like this!"*
*"Now I am going to tear this dollar bill into four parts. One
. . . two . . . three . . . four!"*

3. The unusual.

Emotionally, a New Experience is always welcome to listeners!
"Your pennies will magically turn into dollars!"
*Buying something without paying for it . . . Drinking out of
a glass with nothing in it. . . . "How come the biggest man in
Texas is only two feet tall?"*

Selecting a story and telling it with Emotional Appeal—the
ability to motivate and make others listen—is now much easier.
Go to it.
See how much better your listeners will *react* when you tell a
story.
With more motivating Emotional Appeal in your words and
actions, it is *easier* to remember, respect and like you in *any*
communication situation!
The people around you are Preoccupied.
Their minds are filled with hopes, attitudes, fears, wishes,
gripes—even with defenses, frustrations and "blank vistas." They
feel that what is on *their* minds is much more important than
what is on *yours.*
Preoccupied minds are "closed" minds. It is necessary to
affirmatively *open* these "closed" minds if you want others to
remember, respect or like you.
How do you achieve this difficult objective?
Emotional Appeal Technique provides Three Components
that will assure your success!

1. Talk to people their way.

Your listener is your reason for speaking.

As an individual, your listener wants to listen only in terms of his emotional needs. To "reach him," you require the *right* Emotional Appeal.

Throughout all of history, it has been so.

In the early 1730's, James Oglethorpe wanted King George of England to free the inmates of debtors' prisons and finance their trip to the New World to found a colony under his leadership. He reasoned that the prisoners could not possibly pay their debts if they remained in prison; he recommended that the King offer these men and women a fresh start in another land; he pleaded that a new colony would be profitable for England.

King George paid little heed. Impatiently, he emphasized that England already had enough colonies. Why add another?

Defensively, Oglethorpe replied: "England does have colonies, your Majesty. None, however, is *named for you*. My plan is to name the new colony 'Georgia'—*in your honor!*"

For the first time, willful King George became receptive. At last, he was "reached." Recognition was the *right* Emotional Appeal.

No one can remember, respect, or like unless Preoccupation is broken by the *right* Emotional Appeal!

King George financed the expedition, freed the prisoners and the rest is history. Oglethorpe and his party founded "Georgia" in 1733.

Did King George *like* Oglethorpe better, *respect* him more, *remember* his request? Of course he did!

Talk to people *their* way.

They will listen—because they *want* to!

2. Observe and uncover particular "listening factors."

Be certain of the Fatal Four Emotional Appeals. Brush up on these Chapters from time to time. They can be your key to *any* communication situation!

Unless you relate your words and actions to one or more of the Fatal Four, you have no reason why anyone will *want* to listen. When your listeners will not listen, they will *not* buy, will *not* agree, will *not* give you the emotional responses so important to your self-respect, happiness and well-being.

Seek out the BIG "listening factor" that fits *your* Subject to *your* Audience. It's *there*—but can you find it?

More often, the answer is in the obvious!

James Oglethorpe communicated Money and other appeals to King George. Did he receive the response he sought? No.

It was obvious that the King *had* Money advantages. Where Oglethorpe was concerned, Romance and Self-Preservation were of little interest and the monarch became impatient.

Then James Oglethorpe said: "My plan is to name the new colony 'Georgia'—*in your honor!*"

Recognition was the *right* "listening factor," so King George *listened* . . . and took action.

When the BIG Emotional Appeal is *not* readily discernible, use Questions to uncover it. As we now know, Questions are emotionally power-packed. Properly aimed, they can command situations while allowing your listener to respond or reveal himself.

According to history, Oglethorpe did *not* use the obvious and he did *not* use questions when his interview was failing. He *accidentally* used Recognition—the right Emotional Appeal—and the King of England responded!

With Emotional Appeal Technique, you need not *wish* for such "accidents" to happen.

The Fatal Four Emotional Appeals of Self-Preservation, Money, Romance, and Recognition *are* the motivating emotional characteristics of the people about you. They are also *yours*.

They contain the BIG "listening factors" that fit *any* Subject to *any* Audience.

Sometimes they are obvious; often, they are not. Observe and uncover them if *you* want to be remembered, respected *and* liked!

3. Use three Emotional Appeals that make everyone listen.

Individuals differ in their apportionment of the Fatal Four. As the years go by, ONE becomes the BIG "listening factor." To persuasively activate others to remember, respect, and like you, this BIG Emotional Appeal should be individually searched out.

Such objective observation takes time. Can some of this time be saved?

Is there a way to use Emotional Appeal Technique on *any* listener . . . in *any* situation . . . *before* uncovering the BIG particularized Emotional Appeal? Yes—there *is*.

Three segments of the Fatal Four Emotional Appeals will make *any* listener "listen"—*every* time!

These are the Three:

A. *Self-Preservation visual elements.* The desire to do things an *easier,* more enjoyable way is an ever-present portion of Self-Preservation. No matter who your listeners are, they would usually rather *see* than hear—because it requires less effort. From a Preoccupation-breaking view, it is more emotionally satisfying. So—use as many well-directed visual elements as you can, when you communicate. They have universal Emotional Appeal!

B. *Romance Future Promise and New Experience.* These are "refreshing" Preoccupation-breakers that make *instantaneous* emotional contact and move listeners along whichever emotional pathway you choose to take them.

Miss A., an English teacher, felt discouraged because of poor response when she taught grammar. She realized that few students enjoyed grammar and that more Emotional Appeal was necessary to inject attention-getting, attention-holding, and remembrance values.

She called upon her initiative and imagination and created two hand-puppets. These she manipulated with her fingers while keeping her elbows beneath her desk. Both had high visual value. They were also so unexpected and unusual in a classroom that they provided a refreshing New Experience for her students.

One was a moustached man with a high hat and tuxedo; the other was a lady wearing an evening gown.

"Meet Mr. and Mrs. Better English," she announced to her fascinated, attentive listeners. "They'll make it far *easier* for you to learn more about grammar!" was her Future Promise. "Are you all ready to watch—and listen?"

With Miss A.'s voice doing the vocal gymnastics, the "lady" corrected the "man's" grammar. The students enjoyed the lessons, paid attention and remembered better . . . and Miss A. became a more persuasive teacher—remembered, respected and liked!

C. *Recognition Emotional Appeal and Questions.* Never underestimate the advantages of well-directed Questions.

Although Questions can be directed into any of the Fatal Four Emotional Appeals in listeners, the Recognition Emotional Appeal of Questions unfailingly activates *everyone* to listen—regardless of individual emotional differences and apportionments.

As mentioned, even such seemingly obvious Recognition Questions as "What is *your* opinion?" or "What do *you* think?" . . . can be of inestimable value in starting another person to respect, remember or like you. By emotionally making others *want* to listen, then leading listeners into the right Emotional Appeal for persuasion, these questions leave no "rough edges" personality-wise. By asking others *their* opinions, they will respect *yours*—and remember and like you.

Notice how Miss A. did it with students who did not look forward to learning grammar? After emotionally capturing attention with the novel "Mr. and Mrs. Better English" puppets, she asked: "Are you ready to watch—and listen?"

Before asking the question, she knew that *all* her students *knew* the answer . . . so the question had powerful Recognition Appeal for every listener!

No matter how we try to invite others to remember, respect and like us, they will do so only upon the basis of their *reaction* to the motivating "listening factors" in our words and actions. With Emotional Appeal Technique, we can begin to *control* these emotional reactions to our communication.

Carry these Three Emotional Components always. Be sure to use them wherever possible.

1. *TALK TO PEOPLE THEIR WAY.*
2. *OBSERVE AND UNCOVER PARTICULAR "LISTEN-ING FACTORS."*
3. *USE THE THREE EMOTIONAL APPEALS THAT MAKE EVERYONE LISTEN:*
   a. Self-Preservation visual elements.
   b. Romance Future Promise and New Experience.
   c. Recognition Emotional Appeal and Questions.

You can now *expect* people to listen to you . . . and *remember, respect,* and *like* you too!

HOW TO ORGANIZE A TALK
WITH EMOTIONAL APPEAL

A student told us about a fat boy who walked through a park, munching on a baloney sandwich.

A chunk of baloney fell to the pavement and a tiny robin ate it.

Instead of remaining silent and content once its belly was filled, the robin began to chirp loudly and continuously.

The noise attracted a cat and the cat promptly pounced upon the robin.

The moral of the story? *"Don't open your mouth when you are full of baloney!"*

The additional lesson is: *"Concentrate upon your listener's emotional needs—not on your own!"*

Here are Four Rules that will organize a talk that others will want to hear. They compel you to concentrate upon your Audience's emotional needs and *prevent* you from opening your mouth when you are "full of baloney."

1. Know what you are talking about.

Emotional Appeal is the reason why people *want* to listen. Often, the *best* Emotional Appeal is built upon *facts.* In certain situations, the *facts* are the prime Preoccupation-breaking portion of your listener.

Visual elements are *facts* too. Facial expressions, motions and mannerisms should be left *out*—if they are not purposefully *in* what you are saying. No matter how carefully you control words —gestures or movements that do not blend in can divert a listener.

Even the way you dress must *synchronize* with what you say and do. If it doesn't, you are inviting *distraction*—not attraction. Distractions, remember, are attention-getters that focus listeners' minds *away* from you.

Know your Audience emotionally—don't guess!

Uncover what your listener wants—not what you want! Tell people what they want to hear—not what you insist upon saying!

Observe first . . . *then* talk. If you don't, you can attract "cats" who may harm you.

A Directress of Nurses was making her daily rounds. She paused at the bedside of a man who had been operated upon the previous day. Without perusing his chart, she reassuringly patted his shoulder.

"Keep your chin up," she urged. "In a couple of days, you won't even know that you had an operation. Matter of fact, I had the same operation only two years ago, so I know what I'm talking about."

The man's face reddened and the flame of embarrassment burned his ears.

He had been *circumcised.*

She thought that he had had a *tonsilectomy!*

Don't guess. Know your Audience and know what you are talking about.

All speaking is "public speaking"—even when you have but *one* listener!

2. Uncover the Emotional Appeals that fit your subject to your audience.

These are the *real* reasons why people will listen. You can *always* find these "listening factors" in the Fatal Four Emotional Appeals.

Does Self-Preservation Appeal initiate *emotional contact* between your Subject and your Audience? Money Appeal? Romance? Recognition?

Think up . . . or write down . . . your listing.

When you do not have at least *one* of the Fatal Four Emotional Appeals as the BIG reason why your Subject fits your Audience, why talk? *You have no reason why any one will listen!*

Emotional Appeals are prepotent Preoccupation-breakers.

In every subject, person, product, or situation, you *can* uncover an Emotional Appeal that will make others *want* to listen. Look for it!

Your ability to uncover these Emotional Appeals can become the most personally profitable project in your life.

Let us put our Technique to work:

Subject? *"Why Auto Brakes Should Be Tested Twice A Year."*
Audience? *Parents.*

What is the Self-Preservation Appeal? *Accidents, injuries, deaths, arrests, prison sentences, tie-ins with children.*

Romance? *Not in this Subject,* except for New Experience or Future Promise interlooks.

Money Appeal? *Yes. Items like loss of income, extra medical or hospital expense, higher insurance rates, damage to property and such.*

Recognition? *Too little to be important here.*

Of the Emotional Appeals in this Subject, our major ones are in Self-Preservation and Money. Of the two, Self-Preservation is the BIG Emotional Appeal!

Now, let us move to Rule Three:

3. Create a powerful Preoccupation-breaker from your biggest Emotional Appeal.

Use it in your *first* sentence, your *first* question, your *first* action—or any combination.

"Do you know that two of us will be dead within the next eight months? Which two? The answer is up to you . . . and whether auto brakes will be tested twice a year! . . ."

Break Preoccupation immediately!

Build your Emotional Appeal *on* facts—not *in* them! When too many statistics come *in*—attention goes *out!*

Visually dramatize the important facts!

Make your listeners perk up with your *first* words and actions. You can *always* do this.

Cover your subject in the shortest time possible! Combine visual elements, Future Promise or New Experience *synchronized* with your words and actions!

"Auto Brakes Must Be Tested Twice A Year!"

Lead *into* it . . . come *back* to it. Make it the *one big idea* that you are getting across.

At the conclusion, you will have listeners who have heard and who agree—because they have been kept *vitally* interested. Moreover, they will remember, respect and like you more!

Get into the happy habit of creating emotionally irresistible attention-getters from your biggest Emotional Appeal. They make it *easier* for you to speak and will serve you well with *any* type of person or group.

Addressing a group interested in plastics, a speaker swiftly captured attention with: "For the first time in the history of this hotel, you will see a martini with an olive on top of the glass— and this will be a martini that you eat! Ready? Here it is!"

One of our students at the Emotional Appeal Institute gave a fascinating lecture on "The U.S. Post Office—Hardworking Friend of Millions."

"Would you like to meet a man who works harder dead—than alive?" she provocatively began. "His picture is on this postage stamp. His name? Abraham Lincoln!" She had created her powerful Preoccupation-breaker from the biggest Emotional Appeal in her Subject!

4. Close with a rememberful remark
that wraps up the conclusion you want.

People who are kept attentive and interested from the beginning, will receive *extra* emotional impact from what they see or hear *last*.

When a talk is spotty, what listeners hear *last* is even more important than what they hear *first*.

In either case, be certain to have a dynamic conclusion that will be remembered.

A not-very-well-known girl named Bassoff ran for Secretary of the General Organization in a Junior High School. Three other candidates sought this elective office.

In addition, there were two other offices in the General Organization and every office had four candidates. Since each candidate had a speaker to electioneer in the assembly-hall prior to the voting, the students had to hear *twelve* speakers try to drum up votes for their respective candidates!

After a while, the "voters" became impatient, uneasy and confused.

Then Bassoff's speaker walked to the platform.

She showed them three visual elements—a fish, a tuning fork and a sign with Bassoff's name on it.

When she ended her two-minute talk, she synchronized these elements with her closing words in a poignant and emphatic manner.

"In a few minutes, you will go to your classrooms to vote. When you do, remember B-A-S-S for FISH!" . . . and she showed them the fish . . . *"B-A-S-S-O for SINGING!"* . . . and she banged the tuning fork . . . *"and B-A-S-S-O-F-F for SECRETARY OF THE GENERAL ORGANIZATION!"* With this, she raised the sign with Bassoff's name and sat down.

Bassoff won the election by a landslide!

Ready to re-check the four rules that organize a personal discussion or group talk with Emotional Appeal?

1. *Know what you are talking about.*

2. *Uncover the Emotional Appeals that best fit your subject to your audience.*

3. *Create a powerful Preoccupation-breaker from your biggest Emotional Appeal.*

4. *Close with a rememberful remark that wraps up the conclusion you want!*

Apply these four rules.

Notice how they will improve your ability to add more Emotional Appeal to *whatever* you want to say!

Use Emotional Appeal Technique
To Assure More Satisfactory
Marriage Relationships

Evening. Mr. and Mrs. Smith are seated in their living room.

"This item in the newspaper sure is a funny one," says Mr. Smith. "A little woman, less than five feet tall, beat up her husband, a wrestler weighing more than two hundred and fifty pounds!"

"He must have given her a good reason to do it!" nods Mrs. Smith, looking up from her book. "What did he do?"

"He hid a box of ladies' stockings in his dresser drawer. His wife found it and accused him of running around with other women!"

"What did he say about that?"

"He said that he brought the stockings home for her birthday," chuckles Mr. Smith. "Her birthday isn't until late next month, so she refused to believe him."

"Would you?" asks Mrs. Smith.

"Of course! Perhaps the fellow was afraid that he might forget her birthday." He laughs. "Maybe his wife isn't like mine!"

"What does that mean?"

"Honey, you just won't let me forget! You start reminding me about your birthday six weeks ahead and continue reminding me right up to the last minute!"

"You have a nerve to say that!" bristlingly responds Mrs. Smith.

"Nerve? It's true, Honey!"

"Don't you 'Honey' me!" she testily retorts. "I suppose it's all right for me to save and scrimp for half a year just to buy *you* a birthday present. Why, if I didn't remind you, I'd never get a present and you know it!"

"But—"

"Don't deny it. Before we were married, you used to find plenty of reasons to buy me presents!"

"Well, now it's not exactly the same as when you were single!" he retorts.

"I—I wish I were. Now I feel like a prisoner!"

"You . . . you mean that you're disappointed in me?"

"I certainly am. My mother always told me that you'd never amount to anything!"

"Don't bring your mother into this," he sighs in a tone that underscores mounting impatience. "You know that she doesn't like me."

"Why should she? You insulted her in front of her friends when you said that she was too fat to wear tiny earrings!"

"Insulted her? Why, I only. . . ." Mr. Smith stands up, turns his back and tightens his lips. "I thought that we were all over that matter, but you keep bringing it up again and again. There's no reason for you to act like a . . . like a *witch!*"

"A *witch?*" Mrs. Smith's eyes fire up with the blue flame of an acetylene blow torch.

"That's right! I start to tell you about this little woman who beat up her wrestler-husband and you twist the whole thing into an argument!"

"*I* twist it?"

The battle grows hotter and louder.

Dr. and Mrs. Clark, their next-door neighbors, knowingly glance at each other.

"The Smiths are at it again," remarks Mrs. Clark. They're such an *emotional* couple."

"They certainly are," agrees Dr. Clark. "I'd better close the window on their side. I need a clear mind when I go over these bills."

"Please don't close the window," pleads Mrs. Clark. "Let's find out what they're arguing about this time!"

"Absolutely not!" emphatically declares Dr. Clark. "I want to close the window and I'm going to do just that. There's too much draft in here anyway—and I can't afford to pick up another cold!"

"Can't you leave the window open for just a little while?"

"No! You only want to listen in so that you'll have something to gossip about!" Dr. Clark lowers the window. "Isn't it time that you learned to grow up and mind your own business?"

Mrs. Clark swishes her hands to her hips. "That's a nasty thing to say! I want to listen because it gives me a little diversion. It's too bad *you* don't think of giving me some. I'm bored stiff—doing the same thing day-in and day-out. The Smiths may be an emotional couple, but they go places and do things. Mr. Smith isn't the stingy miser that you are!"

"Miser?" Dr. Clark leaps to his feet. "Look at these bills! You have twice as much as any woman on this block! You have your own car and—"

"I got it because your patient couldn't pay cash for what he owed. You've never yet given me anything that didn't have some sort of a string attached or wasn't the result of a cheap trick!"

"That's a lie—and I don't like liars!" he bellows, amid reverberating rumbles of rage.

Mrs. Clark slithers forward and her fingertips bite into the arms of her chair. "A liar? Me? Why, you miserable imitation of a husband, you haven't fulfilled anything in our marriage except the promise of filling your fat pocketbook! You——!"

The argument resounds into a thunderous recurring bass-drumbeat.

Marge and Max, the newlyweds who recently moved into the upstairs of the two-family house on the other side of the Clarks, shake their heads.

"They're going at it hot and heavy, Sweetie," says Max, in a tone twenty years older than his twenty-six years. "It's too bad that Dr. and Mrs. Clark are such *emotional* people!"

"*Who isn't?*" wonders Marge, casting a sidelong glance at her husband.

Marge is so right. The Smiths aren't "such an *emotional* couple," nor are Dr. and Mrs. Clark "*emotional* people."

Every human being is emotional!

No matter *what* we say, we direct words and actions at Someone. That Someone is going to react because of the Emotional Appeal in these words and actions or the lack of it.

This reaction may be a smile or a frown, desire, fear or dislike . . . accord or argument.

In marriage, there are innumerable opportunities to enlist the objective observation of Emotional Appeal Technique for happier relations. Here, the relationship is more intimate; it is therefore *easier* to uncover inner feelings by observing and identifying outer expressions.

Love isn't blind; it's nearsighted.

Today, the odds against reciprocally happy marriages are great. Almost every other marriage is darkened by the light-switch of unhappiness. In some cities, more marriages are breaking up than "breaking in."

Too many women select permanent waves more carefully than they select "permanent" husbands; too many men choose "sure things" at a racetrack more analytically than they select wives.

Once people talked about marriages being "made in heaven;" now, half the married people live in hell trying to prove it! When the tantalizing tingle of sex diminishes, are there too few emotional bonds to keep some couples *friendly* with one another?

Many desperately unhappy husbands and wives are more fearful of the wagging tongue of convention than the gnawing erosion of mutual disrespect. Nearly a third of marriages wind up in divorce. It is almost impossible to estimate how many more would also end this way except for social and religious reasons.

Along come the second-guessers. They allocate the reasons for marriage failure into sex, money, relatives, temper or other inclusions. These are only filigree phases of the BIGGEST over-all reason for marriage failure . . . communication.

The principal reason why marriages fail is that the husband and the wife do NOT know how to speak to one another! Without properly-directed Emotional Appeal, no marriage will succeed!

People do not want to think; they want to *feel*. When you can emotionally sway the other person's *feelings* you can bring more mutual success into your communication. When you hurt someone's feelings, you bring more failure.

In marriage too, Preoccupation implants itself as the invisible barrier between husband and wife . . . between speaker and listener. When you break this Preoccupation with the right response-awakening Emotional Appeal, you can succeed in securing a far more rewarding marriage relationship.

When you use the wrong Emotional Appeal on your mate and repeat the same error too often, you need not seek trouble in marriage; trouble will find *you!*

Pat and Lorraine have been married for three years. Lorraine has worked for the first two years, but Pat wants her to practice up on her one "weakness"—housekeeping.

Although she misses her job as a department store buyer, she resolves to "unselfishly" placate Pat, a public accountant. Even though she does not relish the work, she attends home-making classes, collects recipes and makes tremendous advances in her many housekeeping chores. Of these, she takes particular pride in her "natural" cooking ability.

One evening, Pat comes home after a joust with a client.

Lorraine, spic-span-and-lovely in her apron, greets him with a welcoming smile and a kiss. "Forget all about the bad, Pat!" she admonishes. "Tonight we'll have your extra-special favorite for dinner—my own recipe for *Irish stew!*"

Pat's eyes brighten. "Say, that's wonderful. Irish stew is my favorite dish—and you know it!"

Moments later, he inhales the savory aroma of the stew as she serves him.

She seats herself on the other side of the table and watches him take his first bite. "Well, Pat?" she queries expectantly. "How is the Irish stew?"

Pat chews thoughtfully for a few moments, then says: "It's mighty good, Lorraine—*but not like my mother used to make!*"

POW!

Lorraine leaps up. An argument starts . . . and goes on and on . . . and on.

That night, they sleep back to back. For days, they do not speak to one another!

The next Tuesday, Pat phones home at noon. He apologizes. "It was all my fault, Lorraine. I'm sorry. I should never have said what I said to you!"

She accepts the apology, but there's more.

"Lorraine," he says, "let's not have dinner home tonight. Why not take a little rest and have a change? Tell you what! Suppose I meet you at six o'clock at the Restaurant Royale. They have a big menu with plenty of variety. What do you say?"

"Why, Pat, that's a wonderful idea. It'll be a pleasure not to have to shop and cook dinner!" she trills.

At 6:05, they are seated at a table for two. An impeccably attired waiter attends them. Pat carefully peruses the four-page menu as Lorraine snuggles close.

She orders filet mignon.

With a huge number of entrees to choose from, what does *he* order?

You guessed it . . . *"Irish stew!"*

After they are served, the waiter lifts the cover of the casserole off the stew and Pat exhuberantly inhales.

"M-m-m-n!" he m-m-m's as Lorraine suspiciously stares at him.

"Tell me, Pat. How is the Irish stew?" she purrs.

"Delicious!" he approvingly nods. *"Just like my mother used to make!"*

BOOM!

Lorraine jumps to her feet . . . spouts some angry words . . . bangs her napkin on the table . . . and stalks out!

Alert yourself! Once you discover the other person's emotional "bad spots" do not purposefully return to them. When you do, you invite trouble.

How much better it is to seek out the other person's "inner feelings" through use of Emotional Appeal Technique. This way, you can set up words and actions to promote a harmonious relationship—not a discordant one.

In marriage, "little things" often lead to big trouble. Emotional upsets can start at the table, follow into the bedroom and cause an accident or serious error on the job!

The more intimately you communicate with a person, the more respect you must offer his feelings.

Uncover your marital partner's "bad spots." Learn yours!

Brush up on your understanding of the Fatal Four Emotional Appeals that make up your mate's Viewpoint. Realize that, as in your own case, fears and desires are in each.

There are always emotional motives behind words and actions. Identify them! This way you can put Emotional Appeal Technique to work *for* you!

With Emotional Appeal Technique, you need not merely react to words and actions; you can look beyond them.

When we can begin to *identify* motivations, we can better *understand* others. Within the framework of the same Fatal Four Preoccupation-breaking, Preoccupation-holding Emotional Appeals, we can better understand ourselves.

In marriage and every human relationship, this is the reciprocal pavement for a more harmonious path!

Human beings are emotional; from fears and desires within the Fatal Four, they set up a protective camouflage for their words and actions. As a result, there are usually two reasons why people do and say *anything*:

1. The reason they give you.
2. The *real* reason.

The *real* reason is frequently the deep-down *emotional* reason that relates to an individual's apportionment of the Fatal Four motivating Emotional Appeals.

In marriage, communication relationships are so intimate that a remotely-fused stimulus may erupt into a reverberating, close-range emotional reaction. Because Emotional Appeal is the motivating and "listening factor" in communication, it may mean "good" to some and "evil" to others—depending upon the innate sense of "right" and "wrong" in each!

This is why:

> • A wife says: "You can't please everyone—especially if she's your husband's mother!"
> • Men will always fall in love with women who know how to listen better than they look.

- The commonest sin in marriage is a nagging wife.
- A calculating bride is one who figures a way to make three out of two as quickly as possible.
- When the divorce is a quiet one, Money often speaks louder than words.
- The girl who is "swept off her feet" in courtship hates to push a broom in marriage.
- Some wives are so busy with outside activities that they neglect the inside needs of their husbands.
- Time never stands still when a man marries a woman much older—or much younger—than he is.
- Many wives criticize their husbands before strangers.
- The fellow who insists upon an "ideal" for an overlong courtship won't close a "we-deal" for marriage.
- Millions of wives watch late TV as an excuse for not going to bed.
- The wife who lets others "talk her into" unnecessary purchases will not allow her husband to talk her out of returning them.
- The child whose feelings are respected at home will respect other people's feelings on the outside.
- The wife who feigns illness to attract her husband's interest really *does* need doctoring.
- A marriage is never a happy one when each of the partners is "too hard to please!"
- The loneliest women are those whose husbands appreciate little and say less.
- The wife who makes important family decisions without consulting her husband will not be consulted when he decides to stray.
- When a very tall man marries a very short woman he has a very long reason.
- The husband who is ashamed to be seen in public with his wife is hiding something under his hat.
- When a wife becomes pregnant, some husbands prepare to pass out cigars; others just "pass out!"
- Few marriages can weather the storms of constant quarreling.

• The married man who boasts about his material possessions does not possess self-confidence.

• A husband or wife who seeks "understanding" at bars and cocktail parties requires more understanding at home.

• The couple that does not know where to turn when sex wears off will soon be uncoupled.

• Good looks may attract a man, but it takes better words and actions to hold him.

• A "frigid woman" is the unhappy happenstance of cold communication.

• The married twosome that does not go out together will seek personal satisfactions separately.

• A wife who concentrates too much attention on her children and too little on her husband does not know how to concentrate.

• A wife who must be promised rewards for favors doesn't really love her husband.

• The man who constantly pampers his wife only helps her become domineering, dictatorial . . . and miserable.

• A "winning wife" is one who lets her husband win most of the arguments.

• The man of good judgement does not blame his wife for the bad behavior of his children.

• A wife who knows how to ask questions can always impress her husband with her ability to handle money.

• Too many wives admit: "I can get along with my husband for only a short time; then he gets tired of listening!"

• A wife wants to feel that her husband is kindly, decisive and protective; the suggestion of a "50-50 marriage" adds up to 100 per cent bunk!

• The difference between a "picker" and a pucker is a husband who is late for dinner.

In parent-child relationships too, the need for well-directed words and actions with Emotional Appeal is expressively apparent. Children, like adults, are emotionally encased in a Preoccupation coverall. And, of course, there are always individualized emotional differences.

Parents claim that one of the world's most difficult accomplishments is that of getting a child to listen. In order for a child—or anyone—to listen, Preoccupation must be pierced with the *right* Emotional Appeal for the listener.

Often the right Emotional Appeal is so obvious that it is overlooked!

One of my students was a nurse who had a six-year-old daughter by a former marriage. When she remarried and a new girl-baby arrived, her older child became excessively jealous.

The little girl tried many ways of focussing attention upon herself. She became destructive, late for meals and tried to worry her mother about her whereabouts. Spankings did little good; deprivation of enjoyments and offers of rewards for improved behavior accomplished even less.

Very peeved, she said to her mother: "You better tell me, Mommy. Which of us is the girl you love the *most?*"

The mother might have caused a deep emotional scar by giving the wrong answer. Instead, she smiled and opened her arms. Her reply was: "*You're* the girl I love the most. Your tiny sister is just my favorite *baby!*"

The child's words and actions had *offered* the key to her closed mind and *indicated* the Recognition response she then emotionally needed. "*You better tell me, Mommy. Which of us is the girl you love the most?*"

Alert for a break-through, the mother captured the clue and told the child what she emotionally desired. Thereafter, the "girl" and the "baby sister" became "friends" for the first time!

Here, the Self-Preservation approach via threats. spankings and deprivation of enjoyments had not "reached" the child; nor had the Money Appeal of reward. The right Emotional Appeal had to be in either some phase of Romance or Recognition. This mother found that her child's BIG "listening factor" in the situation was in Recognition.

Even at the age of six, children begin to reveal strengths and weaknesses among their Fatal Four Emotional Appeals. Be on the lookout for them if you want a child to respect you more and listen better. As it is, a youngster requires adequate time and good emotional environment to bring a healthy personality forth.

A child is an emotional being; he possesses a particular apportioning of the positives and negatives in Self-Preservation, Money, Romance and Recognition just as his parents do. As time passes, his individuality emerges more definitely—just as his parents' emotional highlights emerged before he came along.

Parents should uncover the BIG Emotional Appeal in their child's life as soon as it becomes repeatedly apparent. Is it mainly a Money desire for reward? Aspects of the Self-Preservation definition? Phases of Romance Recognition? Response to certain subjects, words, actions and situations will make this more and more evident. Use Emotional Appeal Technique to interpret what you see and hear.

What a person *wants* to hear or *fears* to hear will always be the BIG Preoccupation-breaking reason why he wants to attentively listen. With Emotional Appeal Technique, you can use your knowledge of the Fatal Four Emotional Appeals as your guide to uncovering and identifying it. Thereafter, you can communicate more successfully.

By doing so, you will help yourself handle children, teen-agers and adults firmly, fairly, respectfully and lovingly. Even when such "difficult" subjects as sex, personal happiness, money, pride, in-laws and property arise, you will know the "listening factor" that can make proper emotional contact with the individual involved.

As the years roll on, your awareness of the dominating Emotional Appeal that motivates and makes you and others react will assure happier and more persuasive relationships.

In your wish to get married, stay married and be happy-though-married, your ability to control the emotional effect of your words and actions is your greatest personal power.

Satisfying sex relations, for example, come about only when the Emotional Appeal in one partner's *words* and actions are satisfying to the other! Sex reactions in marriage are emotional reactions to communication. Again, the difference between *trying* to communicate and communicating *successfully* is the choice of the RIGHT Emotional Appeal!

Most couples are mismated emotionally—not physically. With working knowledge of Emotional Appeal Technique, they can both begin to enjoy the benefits of more completely satisfying sex relations!

Mrs. E., a student, was a free-lance writer. She had been married nine years and was the mother of two children. Although she had frequent marital relations, she had not truly enjoyed them. In all her years of marriage, she had never had a climax and was certain that she could not achieve one.

Sex relations, she felt, were part of her wifely duties and ". . . keep my husband from straying!"

Of late, however, her long-time lack of fulfillment had led her to invent one excuse after another in an effort to avoid sex relations. She sorrowfully admitted that her refusal to cooperate had begun to make her husband violently quarrelsome and seriously threaten to break up the marriage.

It was rapidly established that Mrs. E. did not approach sex relations with secret fears or hesitancies and she had no physical abnormalities. Like many married women, she claimed that she had a fair amount of "knowledge" and seemed to have a "normal" craving for complete enjoyment of her marital intimacies.

Her enjoyment, however, had been so repeatedly inadequate that her expectations had become ". . . as routine as dusting the furniture—and I hate dusting the furniture!"

Mrs. E. had first spoken to me about her problem after the second session of a 13-session Course in Emotional Appeal Technique. By the end of the Course, she would have ordinarily known much of the answer. Now, however, time was of the essence and her anxiety was obvious.

We spent two full-hour consultations together. She made careful, painstaking notes and agreed to follow instructions to the letter. Then, upon my request, she tore up her notes and dropped them into my wastebasket.

In her daily communication with her husband, Mrs. E. began to apply Emotional Appeal Technique. She schooled herself in the Advantages of Questions and the Rules for Asking Questions. She alerted herself to her husband's communicate individualities, opinions and needs and made her own desires *secondary* to his. She smiled more, used more femininity, offered more "come hither" glances.

As was expected, her husband became suspicious . . . and attentive. Here, indeed, was a Romantic New Experience for him!

It required a few days for her unaccustomed warmth to "reach" him, but it did.

As his harsh attitude smoothed its edges, his desire for her increased.

With his passion stimulated, he reached towards her and received another delightful New Experience. She did *not* passively surrender, make an excuse or do a "let's get it over with" act. Instead, she *communicated* an appreciative reaction to his every caress!

Her actions and expressions let him believe that she was receiving wonderful satisfactions from his love-making . . . *even though she wasn't!*

She was giving him some of the Recognition that every person needs in communication—and sex relations are communication relations too!

By making *his* fulfillment more important than her own, he soon began to pay more attention to her needs. As a result of her Recognition response to his loveplay, he became more imaginative and original in arousing her desire; this eliminated much of the "routine" and "monotony" she had previously complained about!

Some weeks later, Mrs. E. blushingly told me that her sex life was closer to perfect than it had ever been. Her husband had become kinder and more considerate of her in many ways . . . and she had had her first orgasm!

In mutually rewarding marital relations, communicative emotional insight is a required parallel to passion. To gain such emotional insight, you must use Emotional Appeal.

Sex desire is in Romance. Sex satisfaction is a Self-Preservation need. To achieve the most mutually fulfilling climax, the art of love will gain its *pinnacle* of physical and emotional delight when words and actions bespeak Recognition of your marital mate's communication.

This is another form of unfailing Emotional Appeal in which Recognition requires both partners to *remove* their inhibitions, *express* their satisfactions . . . and *remember* the importance of timing!

Marriage is a state of mind self-enclosed by feelings. To successfully enter this mind, you must penetrate its protective Preoccupation with on-target Emotional Appeal in words or actions.

To help yourself to happiness in Marriage, here are ten rules you may rely on:

1. Before marriage and after, pinpoint your mate's B-I-G Emotional Appeal as quickly as possible.

This is the most gratifying way people can "reach" each other on both *important* and *unimportant* issues. If you can't "reach" a person *before* marriage, it will be difficult to "reach" that person *after*. Avoid unhappiness. Use Emotional Appeal Technique! Pinpoint your listener's BIG motivating and "listening" characteristics! Mutual accord is still the foundation for happier human relationships!

2. Place your mate's emotional needs before your own.

Think and act upon your mate's desires and comforts Make yours secondary. By-pass pampering. In marriage and out, *give* if you expect to *receive*. With amicable persistence, both of you will soon be *sharing!*

3. Let a husband feel that he is the boss.

He will become more decisive, kindly and protective. Show that you agree with his decisions, particularly when others are around. Women who "wear the pants" usually bulge at the seams—then burst!

4. To persuade, ask . . . don't tell!

People are more persuasive and attractive when quietly questioning than screamingly ordering others. Question marks, remember, have far greater Emotional Appeal than exclamation marks!

5. Listen! Listen! Listen!

Whenever possible, look *deeply* into the eyes of the speaker. Show that you are truly interested in your marital mate's remarks, opinions or problems. Rid yourself of ". . . that Preoccupied far-away stare!" More married men go to barbers because they are "nice fellows" than because they give good haircuts. It seems that they "listen better" than many wives do!

6. Readily offer deserving praise.

Sincere praise has powerful Emotional Appeal. Praise actions, taste, appearance or accomplishments. Deserving praise makes heartwarming emotional contact, even when such praise is for the way the car was cleaned or the dinner was served!

7. Put more "intimate caress" into your eyes, expression and actions.

Offer the "look" that says you *want* your mate . . . alone. A smile, gift, special dish, even a well-timed wink, offers a delightful and intimate Emotional Appeal!

8. Play "opposites" when your mate is angry.

When your mate's voice is raised in anger, keep yours low. Make no retort unless a reply is essential. Then, keep your voice down and speak in a sincere voice tone. Most arguments *can* be avoided; those that are not should *never* be allowed to leave unhealed emotional scars. Stay away from subjects that have repeatedly shown themselves to be "sore spots" to your mate.

9. Do not try to seem younger than you are.

Your attempts to accomplish this end will be more obvious to your mate than to almost any other person. The Emotional Appeal in well-directed words and actions . . . your ability to motivate and make your mate *want* to listen and pay more attention to you will make you more attractive. Age means little when you have a lot of the *right* Emotional Appeal!

10. Avoid sameness and monotony.

Bring more Romantic Emotional Appeal and New Experiences into your daily living. Variety adds reawakening zest to marital relationships, even intimate ones! The same dish, served too often, loses its flavor. Avoid sameness and monotony in appearance, subjects, actions and situations!

Before and during marriage, Emotional Appeal Technique will not only help you know yourself, but *believe* in yourself as a human being in relationship to the person who is your mate, listener, relative or child.

Emotionally, there is a good motivating portion of you wrapped up in somebody else. This is why happier relations—even between husband and wife—*can* be achieved.

Marriage is a *human* relationship.

With Emotional Appeal Technique at your command, it need *never* be as "inhuman" as so many married people claim it to be!

Profit by Bringing Emotional
Appeal into Your Job or Business

"How's your job, Gert?"

"Job? Oh, I quit last week. Couldn't stand my supervisor!"

"But . . . Gert! You were with that company for a long time, weren't you?"

"Nearly seven years!"

"What happened?"

"Oh, that supervisor! I couldn't even concentrate when she was around. Would *you* like to be bawled out regularly in front of the people you know? And by whom? By a woman who never smiles, loves to criticize and doesn't even say 'Thank you' when you help her with rush jobs on your own time!"

Isn't it shameful that "personality clashes" cause trained, qualified employees to be fired or quit their jobs?

Every working day, thousands of needless personality clashes stimulate personnel turnover. Aggregate money losses to the businesses and employees run into the multi-millions. And no one has yet discovered the "price tag" on emotional upsets to the minds, bodies and families of the people involved.

Miss Sadie Brown, head of Collegiate Business Institute, one of New York's oldest and largest, told me: "When graduates return to our employment service seeking new positions, their reasons for leaving or losing jobs are usually: 'I couldn't get along with some of the people I worked with' . . . 'The manager was impossible!' . . . 'My boss didn't have any respect for my feelings!' Business needs much more Emotional Appeal Technique training for employees and executives. Untold numbers of employers are losing a great deal of money and experienced employees because of unnecessary personality clashes!"

It takes time, overhead and energy to break in "new" help, no matter how large or small a business. Most often, one to five months are needed to make a new employee productive enough to actually earn the wage he or she receives.

In the United States, where the word s-a-l-e-s circles the bulls-eye on the economic target, it requires a huge *extra* gross income to offset the multi-million-dollar "unseen" net loss caused by preventable personality clashes.

Sometimes the clash does not result in an employee quitting or being fired. Instead, it paints an "I don't give a damn!" or "Grr! Would I like to get even!" kind of Preoccupation. And, what an all-around loss *this* can be!

Have you ever met up with this attitude in a department store salesperson . . . a telephone operator . . . a receptionist? Perhaps you have been offended by a bank teller, clerk or beautician?

Do you recall your reaction?

Rather than face the unpleasant possibility of meeting up with the offending person again, you take your business elsewhere!

Today, there are more than 20,000 occupations containing millions who picture themselves as "right" people in the "wrong" jobs, jobs that offer neither stimulation nor satisfaction, jobs that nurture a "wish it would be time to go home" outlook, jobs in "communication businesses" like advertising, sales, marketing, public and human relations, art and display—where people do not know how to communicate with each other!

Too many executives and employees feel: "The job isn't *right* for me, but what can I do?" . . . "It's the same thing over and over again—day after day!" . . . "It's bad enough that Mr. C. aggravates me during working hours. Must my feelings about him also spoil my evening at home?"

Education for a job or profession is meaningless unless it teaches how to *communicate* what you learn! To successfully communicate, you must "reach" others *emotionally!*

Better empathic behavior is vitally needed in today's business, personal, professional and job communication. Both the speaker and the listener have "feelings." With Emotional Appeal Technique these can be uncovered, properly activated and objectively controlled in order to ensure more mutually satisfactory response.

People are rarely dismissed because they do not "know" their jobs. Research studies have repeatedly revealed that as much as 85 per cent of a person's success results from a "nice personality" and only about 15 per cent from specialized skills or training.

In four out of five situations, the real reason why employees are unhappy, quit or are fired is a *personality* reason—their inability to "get along" with others.

Personality is a reaction to the Emotional Appeal of someone's words or actions. If we like the motivating Emotional Appeal, we like the personality. When we dislike the Emotional Appeal, we *dislike* the person.

Reactions to words and actions are *emotional* reactions that can delight, disturb or slashingly remain in our Preoccupation.

Job relationships are communication relationships. When communication is better, jobs are more enjoyable. On jobs, people interact with the attitudes of others. Some are heartwarming or inspiring; others are boring or upsetting.

Often, a personality clash is the "bad day" at work that permeates Preoccupation and becomes a worse evening at home.

De G. was a student of mine who drove a truck with a construction gang. The work was rough, according to De G., but it became "unbearable" when a tough construction foreman named Desmond was placed in charge. In four work days, said De G., Desmond clashed with almost every man under him.

The men so hated Desmond that they snidely referred to him as "Desperate" Desmond and wished he could "accidentally fall off a roof!"

De G. was particularly upset. He became so tense that he would return from his day's work with a "chip on his shoulder" —ever-ready to argue with his wife and yell at his two children. He did not dare quit or lose his job because of family responsibilities, so he bristled with overbearing unhappiness that even disturbed his sleep.

He asked me whether there was some way that Emotional

Appeal Technique could be employed to . . . "stop Desperate Desmond from picking on me!"

Although it was early in the Course, I suggested that De G. state his problem to the class. Thus, we could collectively pinpoint the emotionally persuasive words and actions that would "reach" Desperate Desmond—and "save face" for De G. where the other men were concerned.

Four students, Dr. L. a psychologist, E. a TV producer, K. a secretary and F. a salesman, sparked the approach that "Desperate" Desmond wanted to "look good" to his superiors. Others felt there was little doubt that his responsibility was great and he was under a daily "pressure" to complete the construction work on time. Like many supervisors, he knew little about particularizing human communication and was not "leading" his men—but "driving" them!

De G., under questioning, admitted that Desmond was actually quite efficient and did have a big responsibility because of a time element for completion that was usually included in construction contracts. He also revealed that he and some of the other men had formed a "defensive clique" that did not make Desmond's lot any easier.

Based upon the information we elicited from De G., the class employed Emotional Appeal Technique and delved into the Fatal Four Preoccupation-breaking Emotional Appeals that would make "Desperate" Desmond want to listen. There was little emotional contact in Self-Preservation, Money, or Romance Appeal. The *big* Appeal had to be in Recognition.

From Recognition Emotional Appeal, the students developed a basic sentence and action that De G. agreed to use on his foreman the very next day.

He was to go over to Desmond after a phase of the work had been completed, look directly into the foreman's eyes and *honestly* say: *"You may be an awfully tough man to work for, but you sure know how to get the work out!"*

Then he was to smile!

De G. thanked the class for its cooperation and promised to let us know what happened.

A week later, we had our next class session at the Emotional

Appeal Institute. A grinning De G. was surrounded by curious students the moment he came in. Wisely, he withheld his remarks until all were seated in the classroom.

He told us that he had done *exactly* what he was supposed to do.

"I walked over to Mr. Desmond and said: *'You may be an awfully tough man to work for, Mr. Desmond, but you sure do know how to get the work out!'* Then I smiled.

"He looked into my eyes, saw I meant it and *he smiled too!* Then he said 'Thanks!' "

"When I walked back to my truck, *for the first time* I thought that maybe 'Desperate' Desmond wasn't such a bad guy at all. Maybe he was just a man who had a difficult job and was doing it the best way he knew how!"

De G. rubbed his chin thoughtfully. "You know something?" he continued. "Sometimes I think that I should never have used Emotional Appeal on Desmond! Since we got to like one another, I've been working harder than ever to please him because I'd hate to have him lose his new respect for me!

"Little by little," he added, "the other men are beginning to go along with my feelings about a supervisor-employee relationship being a two-way road with a lot of personal feelings in the concrete. At the end of the working day I'm dog-tired, but I don't fill my family life with so much hatred for Desmond or my job. And," he concluded, "it's wonderful to get a good night's sleep again!"

There is little doubt that improved supervisory attitudes can offer a big contribution towards increased happiness and efficiency of employees—but good management without well-directed Emotional Appeal is like a moon without a sky.

For people to "get along" better, they require more understanding and training in controlling their communicative Emotional Appeal, the ability to motivate and make others *want* to listen.

In seeking better job and business relationships, management must learn to emotionally translate attitudes into action. Otherwise, the door remains open for personality clashes that can harm the supervisor, the employee and the business itself.

You can always profit by bringing the advantages of Emotional Appeal Technique into your job or business communication. Here are Three Important Ideas that will help you:

1. Avoid personality clashes.

To create a personality clash, two or more personalities must communicate. The speaker's words or actions either have the *right* Emotional Appeal . . . the *wrong* Emotional Appeal . . . or *no* Preoccupation-breaking effect.

When we *like* the Emotional Appeal, we *like* the speaker and tend to enjoy doing what the speaker requests. When we *dislike* the Emotional Appeal, we dislike the speaker and emotionally rebel—even though we do what the "voice of authority" demands. When we "hear but do not listen" . . . the speaker might just as well *not* have spoken at all!

If, over a period of time, a person—even a job superior—repeatedly slashes an emotional "bad spot," our inner feelings may become so festered that a clash becomes imminent or actual. And most personality clashes in work contact have seemingly unimportant origins!

Vincent was an office manager. A husky six footer, he had worked in the New York office of a national distributor for nearly eight years.

One of the people he supervised was R., a serious-minded man only 5′ 3″ tall.

Despite R.'s discomfiture and frequent, courteous requests to "please cut it out!", Vincent repeatedly referred to R. as "Mr. Shrimp" . . . "Ankle-High" . . . "Shorty" . . . "Infinitesimal" . . . "Half-a-Man" and such. Variations of this theme continued almost every working day in the presence of other office personnel.

R. resented Vincent's attempts at being "funny." Like many short people, he had been emotionally buffeted about height since childhood—and he was now in his middle thirties. A quiet fellow, he seethed inwardly, said nothing and tried to concentrate on his work. Preoccupied by his upset, he made errors and omissions that office manager Vincent discovered and publicly criticized.

On a number of occasions, the executive-in-charge overheard and cautioned his office manager to stop the name-calling.

"It's only a joke," Vincent would assure him. "A little humor is good for office morale. Don't worry. I can handle R.!"

A few days would pass. Then, Vincent would pick up where he had left off and call R. "Inchworm" . . . "Minute" . . . "Next-to-Nothing-High" and so forth—always at a time when others in the office could hear.

One afternoon, R. decided that he could no longer "take" this emotional slashing. He waited until the other employees had left for the day and again asked Vincent to stop the cutting remarks.

When Vincent smirked a taunting refusal, R. slammed his clenched fist into the office manager's face. Vincent fell over backwards and a black eye took swift shape.

Beset with rage, Vincent vowed to have R. dismissed the next day.

When he made this recommendation to the executive-in-charge, he was promptly rebuffed.

"Sorry, Vincent," announced the executive firmly. "R. will stay and *you* will go. You prompted this trouble and you're not the supervisor we had hoped you could be!" Then he drew himself up to his full height. "Now that you're no longer working here, you may want to take a better look at *me*. See?"

While the still-stunned Vincent stared, the executive said: "I'm slightly *shorter* than R., but you've been so Preoccupied with ridiculing R.'s height that you've never really noticed *mine!*"

The executive, one of my students, told me the story.

A personality clash can cause an upset that takes a terrible toll in unhappiness, job or income loss, ill health, as well as worsened personal, family and work relationships. Why become a victim?

Whether you are an Employee, Supervisor, Executive, or Professional, you *can* become upset. Most upsets, however, *can* be avoided.

Latch on to the Emotional Appeal of Questions in Chapter Nine. Familiarize yourself with the Emotional Appeal Technique for Handling Upsets in Chapter Ten. Make these personal powers a rewarding portion of your personality. Keep them at your emotional fingertips in *all* work relationships.

Avoid personality clashes.

They can cause you to lose respect, reduce your chances for advancement and minimize both your supervisory and persuasive abilities!

2. Emotionally identify the people with whom you work.

Employees are people; so are supervisors, executives, customers and clients.

As individuals, they possess the Preoccupation-breaking, Preoccupation-holding Fatal Four Emotional Appeals. In order to gain more job enjoyment, increase production and avoid personality clashes, people must emotionally identify themselves and those around them as *individuals!*

While "appreciation" . . . a "pleasant disposition" and other oft-repeated phases of job and business contact may be much-needed, they are generalities. Difficulties that arise from personality clashes are rooted in the emotional *particularities*—the "feelings"—of people!

Often a gentle, private criticism of a Recognition Cow can cause a much bigger reaction than a public bawling out of a person whose *big* Emotional Appeal is Romance. Why? Because a Recognition man or woman is far more *sensitive* to criticism!

To "get somewhere" on a job, it is *never* necessary to "butter up" or become a "Yes-man." Want to prove it? Just try "buttering" *any* man or woman whose responsively *big* Emotional Appeal is Self-Preservation, Money, or Romance.

The "butter" will melt in the lap of your embarrassment!

Realize, too, that even a Recognition Cow is usually quick to recognize insincerity!

Every individual—employee, professional, supervisor, or executive—is susceptible to all of the Fatal Four prepotent Emotional Appeals in lesser or larger personal apportionment. One, however, stands out.

Which one is it?

Are you trying to "reach" a person whose *big* "listening factor

in a Subject is Self-Preservation? Are you talking to a Romance
Cow? A Money Cow? What about Recognition? Is *this* the
dominating Emotional Appeal in the man or woman you are
trying to communicate with?

Find out!

Your chances to be singled out for a promotion or raise can
depend upon it! Your ability to more successfully supervise
others or create a happier relationship between yourself and your
boss *will* depend upon it!

L., one of my students, worked for a large retail furniture
store for nearly five years. His boss, Mr. B., was a worrisome
man who had a larger assortment of rainwear, protective clothing, and vitamins than most families have relatives.

According to L., he and the other store employees used to
jest with one another about Mr. B.'s fear of ill health. Never,
until L. participated in the Emotional Appeal Course, did he
realize that such attitudes and actions were pointing to the fact
that Mr. B.'s *big* Emotional Appeal was Self-Preservation.

Once he had emotionally identified Mr. B., L. found it easier
to "reach" him. L. used every tactful opportunity to offer assist-
ance when challenging and difficult jobs arose.

"You have plenty to worry about, Mr. B.," L. would say.
"Maybe some extra help now and then will help lighten your
load!"

Little by little, L. began to enjoy more job satisfaction than
he had ever known. He improved his initiative, made more
decisions and began to develop more creative imagination in
communication with others *and* Mr. B.

It wasn't long before Mr. B. began to take notice. He liked
L.'s desire to assist . . . he had opportunity to observe L.'s
ability to see things through . . . and he was pleased to discover
that L. had good executive potentialities.

Self-Preservation Mr. B. was happy to have an experienced
man about who was interested and resolute enough to "relieve
me of a lot of unnecessary headaches!"

L. got a substantial raise, a nice-sounding title and a position
with supervisory responsibility. He had emotionally identified a
person he worked with—his boss—as a Self-Preservation Cow!

And he, his employer and his outlook benefited!

Nobody ever wins a job, promotion or a raise without getting somebody to want to listen. People will always listen when their Preoccupation is broken and their attention centered. The repeatedly *right* Emotional Appeal in your words and actions can open *any* "closed" mind.

In job, business and professional relationships, there are countless opportunities to uncover the *big* Emotional Appeal that makes a certain person want to listen. To a Money Cow supervisor, even the fact that you are economical and avoid waste of time, ink, or electricity can become a "listening factor" that creates interest in you.

To a Recognition Cow, a well-deserved compliment, a reassuring word or a bit of appreciation can start a competitively advantageous remembrance chain for opportunity, sale or favor. To a Romance Cow, Sex attraction, a Future Promise that can be fulfilled or a Desire for New Experiences can promptly increase your popularity, persuasive ability, and individuality.

You—and the nicest people you know—are always responsive to communication that properly taps the *big* listening factor that unfurls inner feeling.

Put your ideas across! Help yourself, from time to time, by brushing up on the Chapters in this book that help you identify the Fatal Four Emotional Appeals . . . one by one. Objectively observe the words, actions, appearance, attitudes and communicative indicators of those about you.

Emotionally identify the people with whom you work.

You'll "reach" them . . . even at decision-making level!

3. Take notes and act upon them.

Those who speak to you and those to whom *you* speak are Preoccupied. So are you.

While use of Emotional Appeal Technique can unfailingly help you break the Preoccupation of others, the person who speaks to you may *not* have enough Emotional Appeal to break *your* Preoccupation and make *you* listen. As a result, you may not *really* hear, even though you *seem* to be listening!

Why attempt to be a memory expert? It's much easier and more advantageous to *take notes*.

    a. Have a pen or pencil and notebook handy.
    b. Write down instructions and job-or-business ideas and *act* upon them.
    c. Complete one thing before you start the next.

You'll save time, avoid errors and upsets . . . even *look* efficient.

If your boss or supervisor has an eye for efficiency, your attitudes and actions will make you a standout . . . the first step towards being *singled out* for an opportunity.

Take notes and *act* upon them.

You will add more variety to your work, become more self-reliant, initiate greater executive ability and have more rememberful Emotional Appeal to people you want to "reach."

Blend these Three Important Ideas into your job or business:

1. *Avoid personality clashes.*
2. *Emotionally identify the people with whom you work.*
3. *Take notes and act upon them.*

Whatever *your* occupation, they can help you

1. Get more job enjoyment.
2. Improve your persuasive power.
3. Supervise others more successfully.
4. Develop your initiative and creative imagination.
5. Stimulate superiors to single you out for promotion.

You *must* communicate—even in sales and professional relationships. Again, the predetermined Emotional Appeal in your words and actions is your most direct route to personal success and happiness.

Dr. V. was a contact lens specialist. Many people in show business were his patients. To them, appearance was an emotionally important reason for wearing contact lenses and Recognition was far more vital than cost or other emotional factors.

Most of Dr. V.'s patients, however, were *not* in show business. They came from more usual walks of life or had been recommended by eye doctors. Often, Dr. V. had difficulty in persuading

such patients that contact lenses might offer advantages over
the eyeglasses that they had become so accustomed to wearing.

It is not easy to change a habit, but you *can* do it . . . with
the right Emotional Appeal.

Dr. V. asked "first-time" patients to read certain lines on the
eye chart *with glasses*. While a patient continued to look directly
at the chart, Dr. V. removed the patient's eyeglasses and said:
*"How would you like to see those lines perfectly—even when
your glasses are off?"*

The patient, of course, wanted this very much.

"You can," reassuringly stated Dr. V., *"when you wear contact
lenses!* See how easy it is to put them on?"

Dr. V.'s two sentences and one action prompted his listeners
to cast off eyeglasses in favor of contact lenses! His question:
*"How would you like to see those lines perfectly—even when
your glasses are off?"* . . . was a Romantic Future Promise,
worded in such a way that it got the answer he wanted. It led
directly into the *right* Emotional Appeal—the Self-Preservation
desire to enjoy better vision!

People who listen *can* be persuaded. Listening, however, has
little to do with hearing ability; it has much to do with motivating
Emotional Appeal.

Warren, one of my students, owned a sales agency for a
famous line of hearing aids. He told me that, despite the advances
in hearing aid manufacture, many individuals who need hearing
aids do not want to buy them.

Why?

People who have never worn a hearing aid fear that, by wearing one, others will think them *deaf!*

As a result, Warren had lost many customers whose minds
he had not been able to change about this fear.

When you cannot *change* a mind, it is because you may not
have *entered* it . . . with the *right* Emotional Appeal!

Confident in his new knowledge of Emotional Appeal Technique, Warren developed more initiative as a result of better
understanding his customers' feelings. He added some creative
imagination and came up with a sure-fire way to break past this
Preoccupation.

First, he would test the hearing of a person who had never previously worn a hearing aid.

"I have some good news for you," Warren would announce, in a tone that his listener could hear.

"Good news?"

"Yes. You are *not* deaf!"

"I'm *not?*"

"No, you're not. *Deaf people do not wear hearing aids!*"

His customer sighed in relief and became immediately receptive to the selection of a much-needed hearing aid!

Warren's statement: *"Deaf people do not wear hearing aids"* emotionally allayed the fear of being thought of as "deaf." It opened customers' minds to the *advantages* of wearing a hearing aid.

In fitting his words and actions to his listener's feelings, Warren used a Recognition approach to a Self-Preservation desire—the desire to enjoy more by hearing better!

Z., an executive, was a student who had been long harassed by junior executives who bothered him with decisions that they should have made themselves. To solve this problem, and do much for his own Self-Preservation and peace of mind, he created a Recognition Emotional Appeal that he claimed was infallible.

When a junior executive came to him with a departmental problem, Z. would save a great deal of time by saying: *"You handle it the way you think best—and that's good enough for me!"*

Z. told me that the Emotional Appeal in *"You handle it the way you think best—and that's good enough for me"* was so persuasive that it made the junior executive work harder in order to *show* that his way of handling the problem *was* the best way!

In every human relationship, we interact with other people's attitudes in action. Even when seeking a job or trying to better ourselves with a present employer, the interviewer whom we can make *happier* by our presence will do *more* for us!

Do you know that the most important word on a job application is by-passed by almost every applicant? It's the word: "Remarks" . . . or "Comment."

Whose remarks? *Whose* comment?

The job interviewer's!

Most jobs are awarded on the basis of the applicant's personality—not his or her experience alone. When the interviewer likes the Emotional Appeal in the job applicant's words and actions, his "Remarks" or "Comment" often become: "X does not have all the experience we might hope for, but he is alert and intelligent. He seems to have a nice personality and may work out quite well!"

The job interviewer, whether boss or employee, is a human being with feelings and emotions . . . and he is Preoccupied.

Competition to get a job is a competition to enter a Preoccupied mind. Break this Preoccupation with the right Emotional Appeal and you can "control" an interview and create a competitive advantage for yourself!

Ethel, one of my students, was thin, quiet and reserved. Unlike many women, she wasted few words. This "weakness" offered a "cold" first impression.

Before starting her course, she had lost a long-time job with a large company as the result of a personality clash with a superior. Highly selective, she wanted a position that blended with her interests and experience—but she had been unemployed for nearly five months.

Using her new knowledge of Preoccupation and Emotional Appeal, she organized her job-hunting efforts, wrote attention-arresting letters and secured four interview appointments.

One was of special interest to her. She knew that competition for the job was certain to be keen, so she carefully prepared a Preoccupation-breaking approach.

At her first opportunity, she asked the interviewer: *"Have you heard that women talk a lot?"*

The interviewer reminiscently nodded.

Ethel's smile greeted his. "Not this one!" While the interviewer intently watched, she rapidly wrote on a pad that bore her name, address and phone number: *"My nickname is 'Mind-Your-Own-Business Ethel.'"*

"Will you please remember me this way?" she asked, handing him the paper, after tearing it off the pad.

Chuckling, the interviewer replied: "Gladly!"

"Do you know why I make this request?"

"No, I don't!"

"Because, if you give me the job and some of *your* business to mind, you'll see that 'Mind-Your-Own-Business Ethel' really attends to her work!"

"Mind-Your-Own-Business Ethel" provided a refreshing and rememberful Romantic New Experience to the job-applicant-jaded interviewer. It highlighted her name and qualifications.

She satisfied his need *emotionally* . . . and got the job!

Ethel had turned her obvious "weakness" into a strength!

In job interviews, knowledge of Emotional Appeal Technique is your most persuasive weapon when you remember these Five Potent Pointers:

1. Competition to get a job is a competition to enter a preoccupied mind.

The mind is that of your interviewer.

Aside from any other preparation, be certain to equip yourself with an attention-getting, Preoccupation-holding New Experience. Before *any* interview, review the meaningfulness of the New Experience in the Romance chapter and throughout this book. Someday, perhaps *tomorrow*, it can be of lifetime value to you in getting that "job with a future!"

If you have an obvious physical defect or weakness, turn it into a strength! Tie it into a rememberful *individuality* that offers a New Experience to your interviewer. Quiet, reserved Ethel did it by spotlighting *how an employer could benefit* because "Mind-your-own-business-Ethel really attends to her work!" . . . Another student, a pretty brunette, had an easily discernible lisp that had long discouraged her in job hunting. She secured an excellent executive sales position with a major New York hotel when she told her interviewer: "I'm the only sales executive in the hotel business who sells successfully—*with a lisp!*"

With a Romantic New Experience, a competitive advantage can be *yours*, because the New Experience can concentrate an interviewer's mind *off* others . . . and on you!

2. Make the job interview a romantic new experience for yourself.

Just as your Preoccupied job interviewer emotionally welcomes a refreshing change of pace that takes him "away from it all" for a few moments—you do too!

Look *forward* to a job interview.

Think of it as a personal challenge! Face your interviewer with confident assurance!

Smile! Realize that you can quickly capture control of the situation with Emotional Appeal Technique and a little creative imagination—even if you meet up with the most Preoccupied grump who ever handled an interview!

When you give your job interviewer *and* yourself a New Experience, you double the impact of your outlook, your personality . . . and your chances!

3. Start the interviewer talking your way— as soon as you can.

Don't take a passive, defensive role.

Get into the act and interview the interviewer! With the right Emotional Appeal, he'll love you for it!

At your first opportunity, ask a question. Get an answer that leads you into another question.

Understand the Advantages and interlocking Rules for Asking Questions. Use them!

See how "Mind-Your-Own-Business Ethel" *questioned* the interviewer and *kept control* of the situation? Note how her questions *got her into* the interviewer's Preoccupied mind . . . *planted* her seeds of Emotional Appeal . . . and *led him* towards the conclusion she wanted?

Hers were the questions and the actions; his were the *answers*. At a job interview, *you* need answers as much as the interviewer does!

You *can* get the *right* answers when you know how to ask the *right* questions.

Spark your interviewer into doing as much of the talking as possible. When your words and actions emotionally "reach him" he'll like you more, remember you better and start talking *your way*.

4. Keep your interviewer attentive.

Have visual elements in what you say and do. They assure the advantage of Self-Preservation Emotional Appeal.

Interviewers—like people in general—would rather see than hear. It's easier! Use words that are visual; synchronize them with actions.

Early in the interview, "Mind-Your-Own-Business Ethel" *brought out the pad* that bore her name, address and phone number—a visual element. Then *she wrote:* "My nickname is Mind-Your-Own-Business Ethel"—another visual element. She then *handed it* to her interviewer . . . more visual.

These little visuals kept the interviewer attentive to what she was saying and doing; they also offered a natural follow-through for her attention-getting, Preoccupation-breaking Questions.

5. Stop! Look! Listen to your interviewer!

Use your eyes and your ears. Get your listener to *really* listen!

With Emotional Appeal Technique, you approach any new communication situation or interview with the certainty of the Romance New Experience . . . the fact of Self-Preservation visual Appeal . . . the Recognition Appeal of Questions . . . all *with* you.

Now, help yourself even *more*.

What do you *emotionally* see when you look at your interviewer's appearance, desk, actions, personal mannerisms? Does he "give himself away" by an unexpected expression, opinion or chance remark? Is he an interrupter?

Know the Fatal Four identifications!

Is there identifying indication that your listener is a Money Cow? A Romance Cow? Is your "look" and "listen" suggestive of Self-Preservation or Recognition as the *big* Emotional Appeal? Stop!

Start a follow-up. End your reply to a question *he* asks with a question or two of your own. Do his remarks tend to blend with your original impression of his dominating Emotional Appeal?

If they *don't,* and time is of the essence, stick with the ever-present communicative advantages of the Romantic New Experience, the Self-Preservation visual elements and, so very important, the Recognition Emotional Appeal of well-directed Questions.

If they *do,* go all out! Concentrate on your word-and-action expression of the *big* response-stimulating *Emotional Appeal* that you have uncovered. Make it your last Preoccupation-breaker and your most powerful Preoccupation-holder!

Remember William, who was interviewed for that job as Assistant to the President of a medium-sized corporation? The President claimed that he ". . . did not need an Assistant." He told William: "I'm in good health. I built this company . . . and only my wife thinks that I shouldn't handle things myself. Matter of fact, I don't care if I have to work seventeen hours a day every day."

At last, William was offered the clue to the President's *big* listening factor. The President evidently had Money; little Romance or Recognition desire was apparent. The *big* remaining Appeal, then, had to be Self-Preservation.

William asked: "Do you know that over 60 per cent of the wealth of the United States is in the hands of widows?"

The President was emotionally "reached" . . . and William became his Assistant!

Whether you are at a job interview, a social, personal or sales interview, train yourself to stop, look, and listen to your listener. Alert yourself—and he'll often *hand* you the emotional key to his Preoccupation.

Everyone—even an interviewer—has a dominating Emotional Appeal.

Stop! Look and listen for it!

Remember, the Five Potent Pointers are:

1. *Competition to get a job is a competition to enter a Pre-occupied mind.*
2. *Make the job interview a romantic new experience for yourself.*
3. *Start the interviewer talking your way—as soon as you can.*
4. *Keep your interviewer attentive.*
5. *Stop! Look! Listen to your interviewer.*

The more you practice and review these Five Potent Pointers for a Job Interview, the better you will realize how persuasive they can be.

An interview, whether to *get* a job or *advance* on a present one, contains at least two Preoccupied people. Both the speaker *and* the listener have attitudes and defenses that emotionally block a persuasive break-through.

Emotional Appeal—your ability to motivate and get others to *want* to listen—can pierce this barrier, establish a competitive advantage and bring more respect and better understanding into your job and business.

Here, indeed, is the "knack" of winning jobs, promotions, and raises. Here, in fact, is the mutually rewarding approach to sales, supervisory and inter-employee situations.

Here, in action, is Emotional Appeal Technique—the "secret" of more successfully "getting along" with others!

Enjoy Extra Benefits by Adding Emotional Appeal to Your Voice

When your voice tone fits a surrounding situation and your communication properly taps a listener's emotional attitude, you can make others *want* to listen!

Say: "Tell me—this minute!"

Roll your lips over this sentence once or twice.

Now, vary the way you speak it. Say: "Tell me—this minute!" . . . *fearfully*. Say it . . . *hesitantly*. Say it . . . *angrily*. Say it . . . *matter-of-fact-like*. Say it *sneeringly*. Say it . . . *murderously*. Say it *hopefully*.

"Tell me—this minute!"

Pretend that you are saying it each way, from the front of a small auditorium, from a stage in a large theatre with a balcony, to a group of three people six feet away from you, to a person taller than you, three feet away.

Whisper: "Tell me—this minute!" to the one you want to kiss, as he or she stands only three inches away from your lips!

Notice how smoothly and dramatically your voice is beginning to *tonally* fit many varied situations?

Now, *twice* speak the words: "Oh, Jack. Please don't kiss me!"

Add some creative imagination:

You're a girl. It's his first attempt to kiss you. You *really* want to be kissed. You're alone, together.

Pronounce the sentence, over and over, each time removing the last word.

"Oh, Jack. Please don't kiss me!"

"Oh, Jack. Please don't kiss . . . !"

"Oh, Jack. Please don't . . . !"

"Oh, Jack. Please . . . !"

"Oh, Jack!"

"Oh . . . !"

Have you kept a firm grasp on every word? Have you adequately varied your voice tones and sharpened your delivery?

Your voice now seems to have more Control, Color and Clarity —doesn't it? Remember these "3 C's." They will surely help you add Emotional Appeal to your voice.

Your voice is a musical instrument. When played, it may give pain or pleasure to your listeners.

Kreisler, Heifetz, and Stern are thought of as great violinists, but Jimmy-next-door who starts-practicing-just-when-you-want-to-sleep is a violinist too. The big difference is that Jimmy's violin-playing sounds like six cats wailing on the back fence!

A good musician *controls* his instrument; a good speaker *controls* his voice. Each must be clearly heard with individually interpretive mood and color.

Voice tone should synchronize with the Preoccupation-breaking, response-awakening Emotional Appeal in your words and actions. A blaring voice will not support a tender love scene; a soft voice will not identify a fight announcer!

Voice tones are pleasant and believable when they are palatably fashioned to fit your listener's needs.

Most speaking voices are not naturally beautiful; they are frequently too high or too low. In radio and telephone communication, such tonal particularities may be embarrassingly highlighted.

It's breakfast-time and you're completing your shave.

The phone rings and your wife hastens to lower the flame on which she is scrambling eggs.

She hurries to the phone. "Hello!" she says.

"Hello, Mary," replies a high-pitched voice. "May I speak to Mike?"

"Hello, Elsie. Just a minute!" She dashes back to the eggs.

"It's Elsie!" she calls out to you. "Will you speak to her while I make sure the eggs aren't ruined?"

You pick up the phone and say: "Hello, Elsie, I . . . !" Instantly, you are embarrassed. You stop talking—but there is far more embarrassment on the other end of the line.

As your wife returns to the phone, you grimly grunt: "It isn't Elsie. It's her husband—*John!* Too bad he has such a high voice!"

Want to add more Emotional Appeal to *your* voice—*regardless of its present tonal quality?*

You will when you translate three ideas into *action:*

1. Visualize yourself as a LISTENER—not as a speaker.
2. Inject the Three C's—Control, Color, and Clarity.
3. "Build" your own "Voice Control Box!"

Control is the encompassing "C." When you control your voice, it will never "run away."

If your voice is too high, too low or "not good enough," you can "build" a "Voice Control Box" that will show you how to improve your voice tone and range *in less than five minutes.*

With five weeks of adherence to the Voice Control Box principle in ordinary daily conversation, you can *permanently* change your voice for the better!

The Voice Control Box contains eight steps—four below the Middle Tone and four above it:

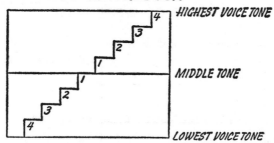

THE VOICE CONTROL BOX

HIGHEST VOICE TONE

MIDDLE TONE

LOWEST VOICE TONE

All of us have high, low, and middle tones when we speak. Yet, almost every spoken sentence contains a core of *Middle Tones.*

For example, speak aloud the sentence: "Say it with Emotional Appeal . . . and succeed!"

Try it again.

"*Say it with Emotional Appeal . . . and succeed!*"

Fine. *This is your Middle Tone.* Hold it!

Now, speak the same sentence *four* times. Each time you do, drop your Voice Tone *one step lower* until you reach the Lowest Voice Tone in *your* Voice Control Box.

Next, repeat "Say it with Emotional Appeal . . . and succeed!" in your Lowest Voice Tone—no matter how it sounds. Step your way back *up* to your Middle Tone . . . one step at a time.

When you reach your Middle Tone, repeat the sentence.

Then, say: "Say it with Emotional Appeal . . . and succeed!" step-by-step *on each of the four tonal steps upward,* until you reach your Highest Voice Tone—no matter how this sounds!

When you do not have enough *upward* range from Middle Tone to Highest Voice Tone, *your Middle Tone is too high— and so is your voice!* If you do not have enough *downward* range from Middle Tone to Lowest Voice Tone, *your Middle Tone is too low—and so is your voice!*

Millions of people need *better* speaking voices. If *you* are one, you know it. With the Voice Control Box, and a little practice, *you* can have a better voice for others to listen to!

Here is how:

"VOICE CONTROL BOX"

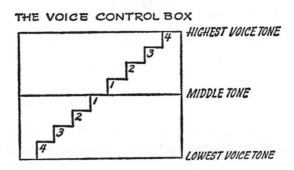

THE VOICE CONTROL BOX

HIGHEST VOICE TONE

MIDDLE TONE

LOWEST VOICE TONE

Voice too low? Raise your voice and gain a much wider tonal range by establishing a higher Middle Tone! The Voice Control

Box and ordinary daily conversational follow-through will help you do it!

Voice too High? Develop a lower Middle Tone. Speak more s-l-o-w-l-y. With persistence, you will have a better-sounding, better-controlled range of voice. You will achieve needed depth and you will reach a *truer* Lowest Voice Tone!

Use of the Voice Control Box will improve your speaking voice quickly and easily.

With your Middle Voice Tone now better known to you, you will encounter no difficulty in controlling whispers and quiet expressions as well as emphatic higher-range Voice Tones. You will add better *sound* to better *sight* when others see and hear you say it . . . with Emotional Appeal! Try it with *any* sentence —even this one!

Hundreds of my students have successfully used this Voice Control Box method to permanently improve their listenability. So can you.

With the first "C"—Control—we can more completely *possess* the words we speak.

Now, we are ready to add the second "C"—Color—to our voices.

Shade your voice like a skillful painter shades a sky or ocean. Dab tints of the same color. Splash *different* colors into the voice picture if it will sound better to your listeners!

Put more s-m-i-l-e into your voice. It will add smile to your disposition and outlook.

S-m-i-l-e the word *"Hello!"*

Say *"Hello!"* again.

Now, smile "Hello!" three *different* ways.

"Hello . . ."

"HELLO! . . ."

"H-e-l-l-o-oo!"

Notice how much more Color you have blended into your voice?

Remember . . . all speaking is "public speaking" unless you speak to yourself! Add Color to your voice and you add a more satisfying listenability that heightens your Emotional Appeal. It's the way your voice sounds to *others* that counts!

The more monotonous your voice, the quicker you admit your listeners to slumberland. Your listeners are Preoccupied enough *before* you speak; why keep them Preoccupied *after* you start?

Monotony never breaks Preoccupation; it only deepens it. Don't be a Johnny-one-note. Why imitate a hypnotist who induces sleep by steadily sprinkling monotony?

Get *variety* and *mood* into the voice tones you use to dramatize your words and actions.

"What a nice day!"

Is it—or *isn't* it?

Say *"What a nice day!"* . . . BOTH ways. Quite a difference when your voice interprets these two different situations, isn't there?

We know that our listeners want more New Experiences. Give them plenty of Preoccupation-breaking Emotional Appeal. Be certain that there is good change-of-pace and adequate Color in your voice.

Always think of yourself as a listener—not as a speaker. If you don't, you may acquire the reputation an erudite college professor had among his students.

Said one student to his classmate: "Shall we cut philosophy today?"

"Can't!" replied the other. *"I need the sleep!"*

Now we have a better understanding of Control and Color, the first two of The Three C's that add Emotional Appeal to your voice.

The third "C" is Clarity.

Clarity involves *complete* understanding by your listeners of whatever your voice, appearance and gestures are trying to transmit.

A lanky candidate for election once punctuated his talk by flailing his long arms above his head much faster than his mouth was moving. He noticed that a well-dressed gentleman in the front row watched every motion intently. Encouraged by this responsiveness, he continued the arm motions through his speech.

Afterwards, he approached the attentive listener.

"You seemed very interested in my talk. Did you enjoy it?"

"I don't hear so well, Mister, so I'm not sure that I was able to understand all you were saying," was the reply. "For instance, what does your election have to do with *windmills?*"

With Clarity, you convey the *right* impression!

Use crisp, clear voice tones. Let your words and actions form a sharply-defined, clearly focussed, well-integrated unit.

Here is an exercise that thousands of Emotional Appeal students have used, enjoyed and continued to practice. It will *synchronize* words and actions and assure that what you are saying is unmistakably clear to your listeners.

Say the words: *"No matter where you may come from—whether from the North, the South, the East or the West—there's just one thing you must remember . . . and here it is!"*

Repeat these words a few times so they'll stay with you.

Next, let us combine these words with Preoccupation-breaking, *interlocking* actions.

When you say: *"No matter where you may come from,"* make a broad, sweeping gesture with one of your hands—from left to right, or right to left.

"Whether from the North," and you point UPWARD; *"the South,"* and your motion is DOWNWARD; *"the East,"* and your gesture goes RIGHT; *"or the West,"* and your indication is towards the LEFT.

"—There's just one thing you must remember." Raise ONE index finger and keep it raised until the end of this thought.

"And here it is!" Now, furl the finger into a fist and bang this fist into the palm of your other hand in a one-two-three timing with ". . . here . . . it . . . is!"

Again, let your words and actions form the *sharply-defined, clearly-focussed, well-integrated* unit of YOU that your listeners will enjoy seeing, hearing and remembering.

No matter where you may come from—whether from the North, the South, the East or the West—there's just one thing you must remember, and here it is!

Want to give your Emotional Appeal an *extra* lift? Practice this little exercise before a personal, social, job, business or speaking engagement. It will increase your confidence, flex your voice muscles and give you more poise when you face your listeners.

One of my students, a stunning actress and TV personality, told me: "Even a visualization of the North-South-East-West words and actions limbers me up for what may come—like a dancer who practices kicks or pirouettes before facing her audience!'"

The exercise, you will notice, subtly emphasizes Control and Color while building a more powerful pivot for the Clarity of your words and actions.

Make Clarity the foundation for your *understandability* to others.

Emmett Kelly, the famous clown, could say: "If you're a Joey in Big Bertha's alley, you can do the Silly Kid on the bulls—and life's like being on the Big Lot."

Experienced circus people might understand that this "circus talk" means: "If you're a clown with Barnum & Bailey, you can do your act on the elephant—and it's like Heaven on Earth."

Would you?

Your listeners should not need super-sharp ears, nor require super-intelligence, to understand what your words and actions mean!

Is there a way for you to know whether your voice is loud enough or soft enough when you speak to a fair-size audience *without* a public address system? There is.

Speak to the person furthest away from you; this way, all those in between will hear you.

This hint is equally important for guiding your voice tones when you speak to a person close by . . . or some distance away.

Speak to the listener furthest away from you—no matter how near that person may be!

In any situation, voice tones are emotional delineators of personal feelings. When someone you know introduces you and says, "Dot, I'd like you to meet Kenneth," his voice's Control, Color, and Clarity will *instantly* inform Dot whether it's a pleasure to introduce you—or a pain.

Whatever message your voice carries, be certain that it is

adequately wrapped in the right motivating Emotional Appeal for your listener and the Three C's of Control, Color, and Clarity.

An anecdote was related about a lecturer who droned a speech for nearly an hour. His listeners began to impatiently squirm and chatter. The speaker, however, carried on with a voice that sounded like the wheels of a slow-moving railroad coach steadily rolling over a hundred miles of straight track.

To quiet the audience, the banquet chairman banged his gavel seven or eight times. Unexpectedly, the handle flew off and sharply struck a man in the audience on top of the head.

The banquet room hushed and the horror-stricken chairman was about to offer an apology.

Before he could start, the injured man wet his lips, shook his head and pleaded: "Hit me again, Charlie. *I can still hear him!*"

Listeners will never feel that way about you if you remember to visualize yourself as a Listener—not as a speaker. To enjoy extra benefits and add more Emotional Appeal to your voice, rehearse the Voice Control Box exercises with any sentence in this book that you particularly like. And, bring the 3 C's into your daily conversation.

It's *how* you say *what* you say that makes your listeners feel that YOU have Emotional Appeal.

With Control, Color, and Clarity in your voice, you can project Preoccupation-breaking words, actions, and facial expressions that keep any audience *vitally* and *pleasantly* interested!

Better Your Personality and Persuasion by Increasing Your Emotional Appeal

Talent, skill, and personal appearance are often meaningless without "personality."

This fact often evidences itself in our everyday living.

There are certain people whom we like, and others whom we do not. For those we like, we'll spend extra money, time and effort; for those we don't, we *won't!*

Have you ever waited in a crowded store, for example, just to have a *particular* sales-person serve you?

Why do so many men await a *certain* barber—while others stand idly by? Why do most women select a *favorite* beautician? Why do you *cheerfully* anticipate a visit from some people and *abhor* the coming of others—whether they come into your life via radio, TV, on recordings, in writing or in person?

The answers lie in "personality" and its *personal* meaning to you. The person's words and actions please you or displease you . . . *emotionally.*

Now, with Emotional Appeal Technique, a better and more persuasive personality can be acquired and effectively projected—because *your* personality is actually *another* person's reaction to the response-compelling Emotional Appeal in your words and actions!

With *better* Emotional Appeal, you will have a *better* personality; with *better* personality, you gain *more* persuasive power.

The powers of Personality and Persuasion are the two greatest assets an individual may possess. They can help us attain most of the objectives for which we strive . . . even better health and outlook.

Such attainment, however, lies in an ability to understand and control our own reactions and the emotional reactions that our words and actions cause upon those with whom we come in contact. Emotional Appeal Technique makes it possible for us to *gain* this control!

Here are Twelve Ways to better your Personality and Persuasion by increasing your Emotional Appeal:

1. Ask questions.

Find out the other person's opinion before blurting out your own. If it is very definite and relates to one of the Argumentative Subjects mentioned in Chapter Ten . . . steer clear.

Know the Rules for Asking Questions and the Advantages of using them. *Right* Questions can bring you *right* answers that keep you in "command" of people and situations—whether in personal, job, marriage, sales or social relationships.

2. Tell people what they want to hear.

Talk to others *their* way and they will *want* to listen. When they listen, they can remember, respect, like you . . . and act upon your suggestions.

People rarely like to *think*—they f-e-e-l. Such "feelings" are emotional reactions to subjects, individuals and situations. They are the Preoccupation-holding elongations of the fact that emotions and thought are inseparable.

Every thought and action process has an emotional basis and tonal implication.

For communication to be more successful, there must be empathy between speaker and listener; for you to better your Personality and Persuasion, your words and actions must more pointedly "reach" your listener by "touching" his or her "feelings!"

Despite individual differences, these feelings are "listening factors" related to the Fatal Four Prepotent Emotional Appeals of Self-Preservation, Money, Romance, and Recognition.

One of these is always the BIG "listening factor" in a person or a subject. In all communication relationships, including marriage, it can be activated "for better" . . . or "for worse!"

N., an engineer, surprised his heavy-set wife with a mink coat on their 15th anniversary. When Mrs. N. saw the beautiful coat, her eyes brightened and widened with joy.

Rapturously elated, she slipped it on.

"Darling!" she enthused. "I never dreamed that I'd ever have such a gorgeous mink. This is the most wonderful gift!" She gave N. three resounding kisses and hurried over to a full-length mirror.

N. glowed too. "I'm so happy you like it," he said.

"Like it? I love it!" She wrapped it tightly about her waist and whirled around. "Just wait until the girls see me in this magnificent coat. It makes me look so luxurious—and so much thinner!"

"That's what the people in the store said it would do, Honey, when I told them how fat you are," began N.—but he never finished.

"You told them how *fat* I am?" shrieked Mrs. N. in horror. "Since when—!"

By the time her upset had subsided, she insisted that she could "never enjoy wearing this coat—even if it *is* mink!" And, what should have been a happy anniversary was ruined.

Imagine! A man buys his wife a coat that costs him thousands of dollars and she's *happy*; then he says a few words that cost him nothing . . . and she becomes *irate*.

Beware of an upset to the *big* Emotional Appeal in a listener. It can turn joy into sorrow in an instant!

Cultivate the habit of telling people what they *want* to hear. It will develop your objective observation, increase your persuasive power and make you more cognizant of the feelings of others.

When people are not talking, they are Preoccupied with blank vistas or inner feelings and "listening to themselves." With the *right* Emotional Appeal, you will pierce this Preoccupation barrier—and they will listen to *you!*

There is always a persuasive Emotional Appeal that can be uncovered and that blends with what a person *wants* to hear—or *fears* to. It is either in Self-Preservation as we now know this motivating and "listening factor" in everyone—or in Money, Romance or Recognition.

Look for it!

When Connie Mack managed the Philadelphia Athletics, Max Bishop was one of his star sluggers. During one season, Bishop repeatedly overate and gained so much weight that he began to slow up on the basepaths.

Mack tried many ways to convince Bishop not to pack in so much fattening food. He warned, threatened and pleaded—to no avail.

One afternoon, heavy-hitting Max slammed a sure three-bagger but was easily tagged out before reaching third base. Boos were heard as Max jogged back to the dug-out.

Connie Mack walked towards him and, in a tone the other players could hear, said: "Max, the next time you hit a triple, don't forget to *stop* at second base!"

Max Bishop winced—and began to stop overeating! His manager had "reached him" at last!

Don't tell people what *you* want to tell them.

Tell them what *they* want to hear . . . *emotionally!*

3. Remove the "I" pronoun wherever possible.

Your listener is more important than you.

When you speak the pronoun "I"—you self-center yourself when you communicate! This is poor Emotional Appeal.

Use words like "we—you—us—our—your problem and mine—both of us." This approach makes your listener more a *part* of you. It creates prompt communicative rapport and is excellent Emotional Appeal.

The most persuasive uses for "I" are with expressions like: "I suggest . . ." or "I recommend . . ." or "I believe . . ."

"I" is miserly.

"You" and its family are warm, friendly, generous . . . replete with persuasive emotional contact.

Remove the "I" pronoun wherever possible. Your listener is the reason why you are speaking!

4. Jibe at yourself—not at your audience.

If someone has to be the "fall guy" for a gag or friendly jibe, let it be *you!*

"A dumbell? I'll say I was. Spent six of the best years of my life in the sixth grade!" Your listeners will enjoy this—because you've made them feel *smarter* than you.

People love the speaker who emphatically admits he is wrong or who says he's "not very bright."

A woman student said she inadvertently told a "confirmed bachelor" that she was "not very bright." She asked him how *he* would handle a situation—and it was the beginning of his romantic interest in her! Emotionally, she made him feel *brighter* and *much more important.* Desire for Recognition happened to be his *big* Emotional Appeal. This was the biggest undergirding of his Preoccupation!

If it is impossible for you to resist making an uncomplimentary remark, the Rule still applies. "Sam, you're a sap," you say, "but I guess I'm one too!"

Sam will get the point—but he will *not* think less of you for your uncharitable opinion.

Jibe at yourself—not at your Audience. Emotionally, your listener is a Very Important Person!

5. Include every listener when you speak.

Catch *every listener's* eyes—even those on the fringe of the group. Don't overlook *anyone!*

Let your listeners *know* that you know they're important.

The instant your conversation begins to lag, finish *your* sentence with a question. Let someone else "carry the ball"; emotionally, the changeover is visual, mutual, and refreshing.

Use your listener's name—especially when other people are

around. People are always pleased to hear their names favorably mentioned. If you do not remember the name, use "You." "How are YOU?" "Nice to see YOU!"

Include *every listener* when you speak. This is good etiquette and better Emotional Appeal!

6. Don't underestimate your listeners' intelligence.

When your words, actions, story, or vocabulary do not cause the reaction you seek, why explain?

Sense of humor and area of interest are deeply individualized. Four people may "listen" to your joke. One laughs heartily; the second chuckles lightly; the third forces a courteous grin; the fourth grunts and remains as Preoccupied as when you started.

Most of the time people don't seem to understand because they have not been made interested enough to listen.

A science teacher was said to have complained to his department head about John, a student in one of his classes.

"Whenever I try to cover a subject, John is always the first to ask a question or interrupt. Isn't there some way to squelch him?"

"Please don't try to," smiled the department head. "John may be the only one in the class who is really listening!"

Use visual words and actions; seek these ingredients in the stories you select and the way you communicate your ideas.

Self-Preservation, in Emotional Appeal Technique, includes the fact that people will do things the easiest, most enjoyable way possible. Since it's easier to watch than to listen and more pleasurable for others to see than to hear, dramatize your words with visual effects.

Double and triple the attention and interest of your listener with the ever-activating Romance Appeal of the New Experience and the Recognition Appeal of Questions.

When your communication fails, blame yourself—not your reader, viewer or listener. A listener is usually as smart as a speaker—sometimes much smarter.

Don't underestimate the intelligence of your listener. "Reach him" with the *right* Emotional Appeal!

7. Appreciate others.

Why neglect the compliment that people deserve? Why not say "Thank you" more often?

La Rochefoucald once said: "We sometimes fancy that we hate flattery; in reality, we only hate the *manner* of flattering."

Be sincere. You'll be amazed at the responsiveness and kindness that others will give you for a few words of appreciation!

Hope is the last thing that dies in a person. Often, it is merely the hope for a kind word or two of appreciation or reassurance.

Appreciate others . . . and notice how much more they will appreciate *you!*

8. Don't "pick" on a previously-proved "sore spot."

An individual's opinion about "right" or "wrong" is a foundation of his emotional makeup.

If your attitudes have rubbed a person the wrong way once— expect them to cause trouble again!

Take care! This is a danger signal in such day-in, day-out relationships as wife-husband, nurse-patient, supervisor-employee, parent-child, salesman-customer. It has disrupted intimacies, respect, friendships, social and family relationships.

Remember the husband who felt that his wife's Irish stew wasn't ". . . as good as my mother used to make?" Recall Vincent, the six-foot supervisor who repeatedly "picked on" one of his office staff by calling him "Shrimp" . . . "Inch-worm" . . . "Knee-High" and such?

Take heed! The "sore spot" may be your clue to a person's *big* Emotional Appeal—the "listening factor" that "reaches him" and makes you better-liked and more persuasive!

Cultivate this Recommendation.

To improve your powers of Personality and Persuasion, *don't "pick" on a previously-proved "sore spot"* in a person. To do so is to play with emotional dynamite!

9. Listen more attentively.

By doing so, you achieve three rewarding objectives:
  a. You give the speaker Recognition.
  b. You gain knowledge.
  c. You help uncover the *big* Emotional Appeal that will make the speaker listen to you!

"Listen" with your eyes. Look *deeply*. Mirror your *interest*— not the far-away look of Preoccupation.

Your speaker is speaking because he *wants* you to listen.

Listen more attentively—and the speaker will pay more attention to *you*.

10. Smile more.

Want to make swift emotional contact? Smile!

A smile is a splendid silent compliment . . . a welcome without words . . . an attitude in action.

A smile argues without offending. Accompanied by a handshake or a pat on the shoulder, a smile can express more than words alone and stimulate a much-desired emotional reaction in the person with whom you communicate.

Smile more. Although a smile contains priceless Emotional Appeal, it is a gift you can well afford to give freely!

11. Relax emotionally.

Good health, good health habits, and good medical care are an inseparable trio. Without proper relaxation, however, good health is rarely retained.

Relaxation is an emotional attitude. Because there are individual differences in emotional and physical needs and reactions, relaxation means many things to many people.

Want to fall asleep more easily and amend insomnia? Seeking *relief* from tensions? Care to *feel* better and be a better parent, friend, or lover? Need the advantage of *improved* job, family, and personal relationships?

R-E-L-A-X!

Millions say or feel: "How wonderful it would be to relax—but how can I? It takes too long!"

Yes, it *is* necessary to *prepare* yourself to relax. It is simple and easy, though, when you use Emotional Appeal for *self-communication*.

This Technique for Relaxation was created and developed at the Emotional Appeal Institute. It is an Emotional Appeal *communication* Technique that requires a little practice . . . develops creative imagination . . . and is surprisingly effective.

To successfully relax, we must successfully communicate with ourselves—break our own Preoccupation—and control our most activating emotions!

Here's how:

a. Clearly understand the Preoccupation-breaking, Preoccupation-holding Fatal Four Emotional Appeals of Self-Preservation, Money, Romance, and Recognition. Know the scope of each. These are carefully described and exemplified throughout this book.

b. Identify your own *big* Emotional Appeal and your *second* most important one.

c. Concentrate your attention on *any* aspects of the remaining two Emotional Appeals.

For example, if Recognition and Romance most rapidly awaken response in you, they are your two dominating Emotional Appeals. Take your mind *off* these Preoccupation-holders, and concentrate *on* the remaining two—Money, and Self-Preservation.

Imagine finding money or a valuable object like a diamond or watch under unexpected circumstances, winning money or a big prize in a sweepstakes or contest, gaining a reward, planning a way to save or "stretch" a small amount of money. Think perhaps, of eating a food you enjoy, doing a disliked chore an easier way with a new method or apparatus, sleeping in a hammock under swaying palm trees—or other situations related to the Self-Preservation Emotional Appeal.

Like Emotional Appeal Technique, relaxation is a good health habit. Unfortunately, however, most people who have the best conditions for relaxation find it difficult to relax! Why?

Because *a Preoccupied mind cannot relax!*

Break your own Preoccupation and relax whenever you wish by concentrating on your *least* activating "listening factors" among the Fatal Four—the two that are *least* likely to awaken response in you.

Notice how soon you will de-concentrate your concentration! Since you have *less* Preoccupation-holding interest in your two *lesser* Emotional Appeals, it will not take very long for them to *leave your mind.*

R-e-l-a-x you will, into sleep, exercise, work, or play.

Proper relaxation is a daily essential.

Use the Emotional Appeal Technique for Relaxation at least ten minutes each day or before retiring. Certainly you can find ten minutes—even at the end of your lunch time—to help yourself towards better sleep, appearance, health, and outlook!

R-e-l-a-x *emotionally.* You will relieve nervous tension and revitalize your Emotional Appeal!

12. Emphasize your Emotional Appeal more than your appearance.

Appearance is important only as it relates to your own and your listeners' or viewers' emotional needs.

Choice of wearing apparel, hair styling, or ornamentation may pass unnoticed, cause offense, stimulate gossip or inspire a compliment—according to the emotional individuality of an observer. Not everyone reacts the same way, not even when we watch TV.

On screen, a famous female singer smiles at us and awaits her cue to sing—but thousands of viewers make *their* comments part of *her* communication with remarks like: "Look at her hair-do!" Or, "She's much too fat to wear such a low-cut dress!"

The singer, mind you, hasn't even started to sing! Or, has she?

In the eyes of others, we are all performers who compete for attention, response and remembrance. If we do not blend our appearance into our "acts," we become *distractions*—not attractions!

Whatever you say or do, relate your appearance to your listener's emotional needs before relating it to your own!

Bolster it by embodying the *right* Emotional Appeal. Don't try to overshadow others with words, actions, *or* appearances; you'll only put *yourself* in the dark!

Appearance is important—but not nearly so important as your Emotional Appeal.

Emotional Appeal is your ability to control the awakening of response—the ability to get others to *want* to listen—your key to Personality, Persuasion, and Better Outlook. Appearance may be a prideful direction, but it can also be a short route to a catcall or a compliment.

If you have an obvious physical defect, your use of Emotional Appeal Technique will be extra-advantageous. When you can identify the emotional urges that others will most quickly respond to, you can focus attention *on their own inner feelings* and *off* your defect. Experience with thousands of physically handicapped people has evidenced this time and again.

Lee, a student of Chinese origin, had a most unusual speech defect. Despite years of attempted correction, he continued to stammer in sing-song!

When he spoke, his face contorted, his words spluttered, his actions splashed and his fingertips pitted his fingernails into his palms. Minutes seemed to poise hesitantly on an impatient precipice before the subject of a four-word sentence caught up with his verb!

The first time Lee spoke in class, his actions and sounds were so upsetting that his listeners writhed in tense discomfort. When he finished speaking, there was an audible "Glad that's over" reverberation of relief.

Instead of taking his seat, however, Lee hurried to the blackboard and picked up a piece of chalk. While we watched intently, he wrote: "*I hope that my stammering will not make you think less of me. My father and two brothers are ashamed because I stammer. Please—don't you be ashamed of me too!*"

Instantly, twenty-eight listeners changed their minds about Lee and opened their hearts! He had emotionally transferred attention off himself and on to his listeners' inner feelings.

Suddenly, they *liked* him!

Lee sat down, little realizing that he had revealed the *big* motivating Emotional Appeal that could end his stammering.

A week later, the class met again. Each student, including Lee, had a speaking assignment. Before Lee's turn came, I grabbed his elbow.

"See that empty seat in the third row? That's *my* seat. When you speak, look at me. Pretend that I am your father and that the other students are your brothers. *We're either going to be ashamed to hear you—or happy to have you in our family.* Now, stop the stammering and speak to us!"

Lee's eyes popped. For a moment, he stared after me while I hastened to my seat. Then he squared his shoulders, marched to the front of the class, pursed his lips determinedly, and clearly spoke his Preoccupation-breaking first sentence.

He did not stammer—and has never stammered since!

The *right* Emotional Appeal—Recognition—had entered his mind and changed it. And Lee had told us how to "reach" him by writing: "My father and two brothers are ashamed because I stammer. Please—don't you be ashamed of me too!"

We were not "ashamed" of Lee; we were proud. And Lee was proud of his accomplishment!

Watch for the "listening factors" in your listeners. They will help you direct and emphasize your Emotional Appeal far *more* than your appearance.

A person who is *not* good-looking to himself can become very good-looking to others by adding well-aimed Emotional Appeal to his words and actions!

But good looks, without better Emotional Appeal, may *hinder* you more than you may imagine.

Dark-haired, twenty-eight-year-old Jean, a student at the Emotional Appeal Institute, was one of the most beautiful women who had ever come to my attention.

Her sparkling eyes were dewy, deep grey; her teeth were bright-white, lustrous, and perfectly formed; her figure was as excitingly contoured as her face was lovely; her mouth was a tantalizing cupid's-bow when she listened and a tempting invitation when she smiled. Her voice? Well-modulated and delicately ingrained with rippling warmth.

And Jean was unhappy!

"I've been whistled at and proposed to by strangers, talked about by women, offered jobs by executives who have been willing to by-pass my work experience and references, and dated by men whose reason was to have friends see me in their company," she lamented. "Girl acquaintances have always been jealous and stand-offish and I have only one friend—a spinster who is nearly old enough to be my mother!"

Jean sighed. "I'd like to fall in love and get married—but this seems impossible too. My beauty makes me either untouchable or too-touchable to men. Both ways, there is a barrier. Can you help me?"

Love is communication; so is Emotional Appeal.

Real love arrives and remains only when people can repeatedly "reach" one another with the *right* Emotional Appeal in words and actions.

Beautiful Jean was a woman whose appearance was *too good*— and whose Emotional Appeal *wasn't good enough.*

She learned to emphasize the motivating factors of communication *more* than appearance. Use of Emotional Appeal Technique sparked her initiative and creative imagination and aimed her words and actions at the Fatal Four Preoccupation-holders of the people with whom she came in contact!

By controlling *your* Emotional Appeal, you can *gain* attention —or turn attention away from yourself and back to the inner feelings of your listener. No matter how you appear, you can be liked or loved by those to whom you say "Hello" for the first time . . . or for the fifty-thousandth.

In your communication, concentrate upon your Emotional Appeal *more* than your appearance. You will assure a better-looking, better-liked, and more persuasive *you!*

These Twelve Ways are not "sometime" Rules; they are Recommendations for Successful Daily Communication. Like other phases of Emotional Appeal Technique, they were formulated after thousands of face-to-face reactions, word-and-action studies, classroom projects, personal observations, and consultations with students, educators, lecture audiences, and clients.

Here they are again:

1. *Ask questions.*
2. *Tell people what they want to hear.*
3. *Remove the "I" pronoun wherever possible.*
4. *Jibe at yourself*—not *at your audience.*
5. *Include* every *listener when you speak.*
6. *Never underestimate your listener's intelligence.*
7. *Appreciate others.*
8. *Don't "pick" on a previously-proved "sore-spot."*
9. *Listen more attentively.*
10. *Smile more.*
11. *Relax* emotionally.
12. *Emphasize your Emotional Appeal* more *than appearance.*

Put these Twelve Recommendations to work for you. They will rapidly improve your Initiative, Outlook, Personality and Persuasion.

With Emotional Appeal Technique, you will better understand *yourself* . . . uncover and blend into the *feelings* of your listeners . . . particularize your communication and gain greater *control* over the *emotional reactions* to your words and actions.

The Technique is yours to use . . . even to help others "see things your way."

Since communication problems will constantly arise in your personal, marriage, family, social, and occupational relationships, it is suggested that you re-read this book and retain it as a revitalizing reference for whatever situation the future may bring.

Today and in all your tomorrows, the difference between *trying* to communicate and communicating *successfully* . . . is the *right* Emotional Appeal in your words and actions.

Why?

Because Y-O-U *and* your Emotional Appeal possess the ability to motivate and make others *want* to listen!